GUIDE TO EASIER LIVING

One-room apartment furnished entirely with inexpensive and practical *Easier Living* group of products designed by Russel Wright. Draperies (22), floor tile (22), and seat covers in dining corner are of vinyl. Carpet in seating section has "spots" designed-in; daybed, with bedding compartment, and lounging chairs have slip-cover upholstery for ease of cleaning. Coffee table has a top of scratch-, stain-, and burn-proof porcelain; all wood is finished to withstand water and alcohol marks. (*Numerals refer to listing of manufacturers, Appendix B, page 194. Photo courtesy of McCall's.*)

Easier Living: A living room with asphalt-tile floor, well-defined conversation and dining areas, tight-seat upholstery, contour plywood chairs, simple drapes, simple lighting equipment—all of which make for ease in housekeeping and a warm and friendly appearance, in a medium-priced home. (Idea House II, designed for the Walker Art Center, Minneapolis, by William Friedman and Hilde Reiss. Photo courtesy of McCall's.)

Mary and Russel Wright's

GUIDE TO

EASIER LIVING

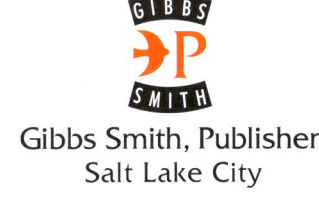

Gibbs Smith, Publisher
Salt Lake City

First Edition
07 06 05 04 03   5 4 3 2 1

Text and illustrations © 2003 by Russel Wright Studios

All rights reserved. No part of this book may be reproduced by any means whatsoever without written permission from the publisher, except brief portions quoted for purpose of review.

Published by
Gibbs Smith, Publisher
P.O. Box 667
Layton, Utah 84041

Orders: (1-800) 748-5439
www.gibbs-smith.com

Edited by Suzanne Gibbs Taylor
Designed and produced by Kurt Wahlner
Printed and bound in Korea

Library of Congress Cataloging-in-Publication Data

Wright, Mary (Mary Einstein)
    Guide to easier living / Mary and Russel Wright. — 1st ed.
        p. cm.
    Originally published; Mary and Russel Wright's Guide to easier living. New York : Simon and Schuster, 1950.
    ISBN: 1-58685-210-8
    1. Interior Decorating. 2. Housekeeping. I. Wright, Russel, 1904-1976. II. Wright, Mary (Mary Einstein). Mary and Russel Wright's Guide to easier living. III. Title.

NK2110.W68 2003
747—dc21   2002033916

INTRODUCTION

Russel and Mary Wright lived in that passionate time when the "modernist utopia" was a distant but reachable reality. It was indeed a marvelous dream, bringing the American spirit to a beautiful new dimension. Unfortunately the dream was shattered—before it could reach a conclusion—by the emerging forces of egocentrism, which for the last thirty years have brought us any form of revivalism to feed the greed and complacencies of a generation.

The Wrights' times were full of ideals and beliefs of a better world where one could work to share a dream. Russel Wright's life was dedicated to creating a new lifestyle in every detail—from the spoon to the house, from the private to the social world—to make a beautiful, easier way of living.

This book, half a century later, has all of its original vitality and is still a perfect guide to modern living. It was written as an alternative to the formal obsolete mannerisms left over from the Victorian era. Today, its sober elegance and real values appeal to a new generation that refuses to comply with the gross vulgarity and phony styles portrayed by the media. It is refreshing and appropriate to republish this guide to a clean, beautiful, and serene modern life because it bridges the gap from utopia to today.

It worked for me then—and still does today.

Massimo Vignelli, spring 2003

FOREWORD

My parents, Mary and Russel Wright, first published *Guide to Easier Living* in 1950. Together, as prominent and successful designers, they pioneered the development of products that were aimed at easier and more informal ways of living, such as furniture, flatware, glassware, rugs, lamps, and even jukeboxes. But more importantly, they were known for their tabletop designs—the most famous being American Modern, which is the best-selling dinnerware in American history.

It was apparent Americans were borrowing heavily from European styles, not realizing that our own designs were both noteworthy and interesting. It also became evident that Americans were moving into an era where servants were no longer "the norm." My parents' intention was to furnish good American design for everyone. The *Guide to Easier Living* was a result of their longstanding dissatisfaction with the drudgework necessary to run a household. (In fact, they estimated that routine household tasks take up to more than eighty hours per week!) My parents' aim was to "increase the enjoyment and satisfaction of life in your home by drastically reducing the time and labor required in running a home." The book was instantly a success.

Russel and Mary tell us the entire fiction of "gracious living" is a cruel charade imposed upon us by a set of standards we should have discarded long ago. This advice seems as timely and useful now as it was in 1950. Our lives and households today still face complicated challenges. In many instances, we have expanded and accepted the new roles and definitions of the word "homemaker," but we will always have homes. Even though our attitudes are less restricting and more open to compromise, the workload of keeping house still remains daunting. We all attempt to make household chores as painless as possible, and although our homes are large, our standards for what we can accomplish still seem to get higher and higher. Experimentation abounds, but *Easier Living*'s sense of organization and workable suggestions are very helpful.

It is with great pleasure that I have taken part in the re-release of *Guide to Easier Living*. With its unfaltering tips for family and household organization, everyone who has worked on this project believes this book will once again stand on its own. My parents' advice is timeless, their sense of prioritization of everyday life is appropriate, and their impeccable timing is still applicable today. With cell phones, computers, and other modern-day conveniences, we seem to be constantly on call and always in demand. For these reasons, organization becomes a necessity and prioritization a must. Without such things, we might never have a free moment or a stress-free environment.

Rather than update this historic piece, we felt that we would leave the reader with the opportunity to apply these timeless principles to his or her daily modern lives. It does indeed seem easier to follow a well-chartered course and then apply these principles to your own needs. Improvisation and good humor seem to be the key ingredients in putting together an informal, comfortable, well-designed, and, last, but not least, organized living space for you and your family.

As Russel and Mary would say, "Don't look back, but as exponents of the new etiquette, help to create it!"

Ann Wright, spring 2003

GUIDE TO EASIER LIVING

Acknowledgments

We wish to acknowledge the very great help we have had from Orrin Keepnews, our patient and capable editor, and Ruth Goode, and to thank them both for all of their writing and re-writing.

A prodigious amount of work in every phase of the book was contributed by our untiring office associates, Frances Johnson and Edwin Fitzwater.

We also wish to acknowledge with thanks the co-operation and assistance given us by magazine editors Mary Davis Gillies, Elinor Hillyer, Elizabeth Ramsay, Demetria Taylor, Charlotte Adams, Lee Chapman, Lazette Van Houten, and Eleanor Cook; by Mary Koll Heiner of Cornell University, and Professor M. E. Mundel of Purdue University; by Bernard E. Brennan of Macy's; and by our friends, Kate and Ted Hecht, Anne and Guido Barbieri, Petra Cabot, Dionne Beattie, Charlotte DeVrees, Barbara Blake, Celia Hecht, Niña Covency, Pat Troy, Jane Siepmann, and Sparkle Furness.

We are indebted to the talented James Kingsland for all of the drawings, executed under our direction—and to Carol and Joseph Roberto for the planning of the closets.

Dedication

We dedicate this book to: Dorcas Hollingsworth, who for years served our household with great artistry, and whom we miss very much. On the other hand, if she hadn't left us, we would never have written this book. . . . And to: the whole present generation, who will never have a Dorcas Hollingsworth.

I   **Home, Sweet Home, 1**

II **Room to Relax, 11**

>Planning the Living Room, 12; Floors and Walls, 16; Lighting, 19; Furnishing the Living Room, 20; More-than-one Living Room, 24; Fireplaces, 27.

III **The Vanishing Dining Room, 28**

>Planning the Dining Area, 29; Floors, Walls, and Windows, 32; Furniture, 33; Lighting, 33; Table Service, 34; The Dining-Kitchen, 37; Breakfast in a Hurry, 45; Now You See It, Now You Don't!, 47.

IV **Private Lives, 50**

>Planning the Bedroom, 51; Floors, Walls, and Windows, 52; Lighting, 52; Furnishing the Master Bedroom, 53; What, No Victorian?, 67, Bathrooms, 68; The Child's Room, 70.

V   **All Around the House, 82**

>Entrances, 82; Stairs, 90; Hallways, 93; Doors, 93; Windows, 95; Window Screens, 98; Window Coverings, 99.

VI **Outdoor Living, 106**

>Planning, 106; Outdoor Furniture, 108; Outdoor Dining, 114.

VII The Housewife-Engineer, 124

>Time-and-Motion Studies, 125; Work Simplification, 126; Division of Labor, 135; Scheduling, 137; Household Tasks, 141; Things Professionals Can Do Better, 154; Housekeeping Standards, 155; Tricks of the Trade, 155.

VIII Today's Servants, 159

>Individual Help and Professional Services, 159; The Maid—and How to Get Along with Her, 160; The Maid Plus Auxiliary Help, 161; The Invisible Servant, 162.

IX The New Hospitality, 164

>The New Etiquette, 166; Meals for Small Groups, 168; Meals for Larger Groups, 176; Refreshments, 183; House Guests, 187; What About Looks—and Taste?, 188.

Appendix A, 191

>Cleaning Routines, 191; Sample Division of Labor, 192; Equipment List for Entertaining, 193.

Appendix B, 194

>List of Manufacturers and Distributors of New Products and Materials.

Charts

Wall Materials and Coverings, 116
Table-top Materials and Coverings, 118
Floor Materials and Coverings, 120
Casters and Slides (Furniture), 200

CHAPTER 1

HOME, SWEET HOME

BE IT EVER SO HUMBLE, the words of the song tell us, there's no place like home. But the American home today, it must be admitted, is far from living up to that comforting lyric.

Do our homes really express the ideals of democracy and individualism we all profess? Do they provide a place where we can relax together, where a spirit of family living can thrive? Are they efficient, capable of being kept in order without an unduly heavy expenditure of time and energy?

The answer to any such questions, in all too many cases, must be a sorrowful No.

In this increasingly mechanized civilization, our homes are the one remaining place for personal expression, the place where we could really be ourselves. But in actuality they are more often than not undistinguished and without individuality, monuments to meaningless conformity.

As most of us live today, routine care and maintenance of the home demands an exhausting amount of labor. According to a survey conducted by Bryn Mawr College, a rural housewife spends an average of almost 61 hours a week at her household tasks, and a big city housewife about 80 hours!

All too often, comfort, ease, and spontaneity are all sacrificed to an unrealistic dream that makes home life formal and unsatisfying. Far from drawing families together, our homes send adolescent children to the juke joints for their fun, lead husbands to prefer a movie or the local bar for their after-work relaxation, make entertaining friends an ordeal of drudgery. We face today an increasing amount of juvenile delinquency, and an annual divorce toll that approaches 25 per cent of the marriage rate—a clear statistical indication that there are serious lacks in American family life. There are in our times a multitude of complex motives for adolescents getting into trouble, or marriages breaking up, but it is not too far-fetched to say that our homes and the way we live in them must be listed among the important causes.

If the American home is inadequate, it is our belief that this inadequacy must be attributed primarily to a continued adherence to an ill-fitting and outmoded cultural pattern.

Apparently impelled by feelings of inferiority, Americans have until comparatively recently begged or borrowed much of their culture from abroad. Thus the stilted ritual of the English manor house—where life was rigidly formal and a staff of servants waited on master and mistress hand and foot—became the standard of "gracious living" for the American home. But a hard-working democracy was poor soil for this aristocratic way of life. Except for a small minority of families, the American version of such feudal luxury was never more than a patched hand-me-down.

Nevertheless, this tradition is still very much with us. Bequeathed to us by our grandmothers, nurtured by our mothers, and subtly preached by that able evangelist Emily Post, the Dear Old Dream dominates writing and merchandising concerned with the home, haunts domestic architecture across the country, and tyrannically rules American family life.

Perhaps the Old Dream suited our grandmothers. But today an industrial democracy is swallowing up the remnants of the feudal past. A broader base of education, and drastic changes in our entire social and economic outlook, should make it obvious that a pattern of home life based on aristocratic snobbery is not only absurd, impossible, but actually something to be ashamed of.

Our way of life has changed sharply even from that of the preceding generation. Wives are now more likely to have business careers of their own, to have other interests besides management of the home. The home itself is smaller; rooms must serve more than one purpose. And with most of those who might once have made up a "servant class" now engaged in a variety of other occupations, we must manage these homes with part-time help or no help at all—instead of with the retainers on which the aristocratic life depends.

Yet the Old Dream has saddled us with fussy homes, with a code of snobbish manners in a time of social change, with a dictatorship of etiquette that stifles individuality. We don't dare break the rules, however idiotic they may be, for fear someone will think us "uncultured." We shape our home lives as if they were exhibits in a national competition designed to make our neighbors feel that we are better than they are.

All over America we build and furnish our homes, and live in them, as though there were retinues of servants to do the work, even though the majority of American families have never been able to afford domestic help. We set a superfluously ornate table for company at dinner and play at being lord and lady of the manor —even though we must double as cook, butler, waitress, scullery maid, and footman.

All this brings about a basic conflict. Certainly more than a few of today's many frustrations and guilt complexes, as well as family failures, have their roots in the struggle to fit our twentieth-century selves into an eighteenth-century corset. The Dear Old Dream is deeply imbedded in the minds of both the American husband and the American wife. It is true that each can often perceive the irrationality of the other's attitude toward the home, but they can rarely see the motes in their own eyes.

From childhood, men are taught to be unsympathetic toward housework, ignorant of its problems and techniques, and contemptuous of it as "woman's work." Few men have the courage to be caught with a broom in their hands. But the weekly working hours of the man have generally been reduced to 40, while, as Bryn Mawr's report of the housewife's 60-to-80-hour week shows, despite modern labor-saving appliances, "woman's work is never done." Any wife would appear completely justified in resenting the masculine hands-off attitude.

And if a man does at last become aware of the monstrous daily routine of keeping a house in order (a job to which his thoughtlessness contributes no little), he is likely merely to suggest another mechanical device, a collection of appliances, a push-button fantasy.

The Dear Old Dream has set up other impractical attitudes in the woman of the house. The home is traditionally woman's responsibility; the rearing of children who will mind their manners and abide by conventional rules is her task; and she is expected to keep a home that will compete favorably with those of her neighbors. The legend also makes the home her only proper means of expression, her absolute domain; it encourages her to plan, furnish, and decorate without regard for—often in direct conflict with—the needs of her husband and children. Hence the pressures that make scolds out of so many women, who are constantly after their families to keep coke bottles off the coffee table, feet off the sofa.

Tradition dictates that the housewife must be a fluffball of femininity, resistant to all masculine attempts at budgeting and planning or to any scientific suggestions for simplifying her work. It also encourages her to fill her house with all kinds of impractical sillinesses: a woman must be impulsive and romantic about her home, even at the price of an aching back.

Lastly, the aristocratic tradition has implanted in both men and women one attitude in common: the thoroughly unrealistic attitude that housework is menial, low-class, degrading.

Manufacturers and retailers of furniture and home furnishings, national magazines, the women's pages of the newspapers (with a few notable exceptions), have long done much—whether consciously or not—to preserve these attitudes. The Old Dream House, or some facet of it, is still repeated in millions of full-color magazine pages monthly, on millions of newspaper pages daily. Tempting in its romantic nostalgia, it subtly implies that a woman whose living room is not modeled after Mount Vernon is really no lady. Even when they coax us to buy something "modern" this year, the style monitors generally mean something that merely looks different, but is not better suited to our way of life. The industry spends uncounted amounts of money and talent in selling us a "new look" each year—Chinese Modern today and French Provincial tomorrow.

The entire fiction of "gracious living" is a cruel charade, imposed on us by a set of standards we should have discarded long ago. We are victimized by the illusion of generations who had the kind of servants we do not have, afraid to change anything in the interest of comfort, work-saving, or better family living, hearing inside our very walls the scornful whisper that we can't afford, or don't know how, or haven't the taste to do things "properly." The Dear Old Dream dictatorship is a stifling influence in American life.

So there is a need for a new pattern, one more suitable to the world of today, a new kind of home and a new way of living in it. What will it be like? This book will attempt to point the way.

We believe the new American home will be a much simpler one to live in. Its size and its furnishings will be determined by the family's needs, not by the arbitrary dictates of fashion. Living in it will be based on an informal and improvised design, rather than on a formal, traditional pattern. Its etiquette will derive from modern democratic ideals.

A new way of living, informal, relaxed, and actually more gracious than any strained imitation of another day could be, is in fact growing up, despite the etiquette despots and the die-hards. There is evidence all around that the hard shell of snobbish convention is cracking. Casual clothes invade many precincts once sacred to formal attire. The relaxed cocktail party or barbecue is a far more popular way of entertaining friends these days than the stiff dinner or the formal tea party.

The truth is that the American woman of today does not live in the elegance that the books of etiquette prescribe or the advertising industry would have us believe. She cuts corners and makes compromises in order to get her work done, but she does so as though it were a secret vice. She apologizes for the cooking pot brought to the table to double as a serving dish. She gives an outdoor barbecue in an easy, informal style, but does not dare to entertain indoors with the same casualness.

The whole home furnishings industry shares her state of embarrassment. Manufacturers seem uncertain whether to cling to the old way or plunge into the new. But those who serve the American home—the manufacturers who produce for it, the retailers who distribute the products, the press that educates us to their use—can profit as much from selling *service* as from selling *style*. The appliance industry is shining proof of this.

The kitchen is the one place in the home where the fact that the American woman does her own housework has been honestly faced. In the kitchen the combined genius of architects, engineers, designers, home economists, and manufacturers has dramatically lightened women's work and has provided one of the great technological contributions to home life in centuries—an American achievement as typical, and as impressive, as American skyscrapers, highways, and jazz.

The kitchen still continues to be scrutinized by experts with a zeal for even greater improvement. The appliance industry sponsors home economics research in the universities and maintains laboratories of its own, which have helped it to produce miracles of work-saving profitably, from the pin-up can opener to the deep-freeze. They are now developing an electronic range that can bake a potato in 45 seconds.

Let other industries turn such scrutiny and energy on the rest of the home. In this most clothes-conscious nation, furniture manufacturers could focus attention on the still unsolved problem of clothes storage. Let experts make a study of home recreation habits and how best to provide for them. Let the makers of floor coverings subsidize a research project aimed at reducing the drudgery of cleaning the floor. Let chemists evolve better disposable dishes, soap manufacturers underwrite research in the cleaning of woodwork, utensil manufacturers produce pots that their customers will not be ashamed to bring to the table.

But it will not be until homemakers show definite indications of adopting a new ideal for their homes that the producers and distributors can be expected to meet such demands.

A new pattern is not evolved overnight. Meanwhile, this transition period is difficult for all of us. We cannot relinquish all at once attitudes deeply rooted in us from childhood. But for the sake of human economy and a fuller, richer home life, we must consciously strive to free ourselves from the outmoded Old Dream.

The American man has learned to push a baby carriage with pride, and to listen to the child psychologists on his important role as a father. He will also learn that it is not beneath his dignity to push a vacuum cleaner. More important, he must learn, with his increasing free time, to find more and more self-expression in the home. As the assembly line encroaches more and more on our working life, crowding out individual creative expression, the need for a home in which we can realize ourselves as individuals becomes increasingly urgent.

The American wife must come to recognize this need, and she must also realize that a good home is no longer a one-woman operation. Indeed, the participation of the whole family is very much needed; unless she wants to remain a drudge, the American woman will have to make room for her husband and children in the planning and running of the home. (Even if he only washes the dishes, let him wash them in his own way!)

Part of this new attitude is the realization that while housework is unavoidable, it need not be old-fashioned drudgery. What is the validity of the aristocratic notion that housework is, in itself, degrading? Why should we consider housework in our own homes as "beneath" us? After all, it is our own dishes we are washing, our own beds we are making. This is all part of the natural process of our lives; surely it is better that we, rather than outsiders, should do work that is so personal.

Once we have learned to arrange our homes and our work realistically, housework can be fairly painless. Under certain conditions it can even be relaxing and pleasurable; when the work becomes part of family life, getting it done *together* can be as productive of family growth and understanding as playing together.

The housewife must scrutinize her scale of values and ask herself which means more to the family: a delicate cream-colored carpet or a pet puppy; keeping up with Mrs. Jones or a livable home. If after thinking it over she still wants the cream-colored carpet—or a Regency living room or shelves of Dresden figurines—let her at least also face the fact that this means more work, and balance that kind of pleasure against the labor it entails.

We feel certain that once she has realized the total absurdity of the Old Dream, the American woman will choose the more practical approach, the less romantic and less laborious path. Many women already accept this idea in principle. They see the compelling good sense as well as the deeper values of shaping the home realistically, not to impress the neighbors or to live up to a tradition, but to serve their families and themselves. Putting the principle into practice, however, is quite another matter.

What will such a home look like? With so much concentration on the useful and the laborsaving, won't warmth and beauty be left out? Will life in this home sacrifice all grace and charm? In giving up the Dream Home of the past may we not be giving up the "finer things of life," the niceties that were always supposed to indicate "breeding" and "culture"?

Beauty and grace are not easy to talk about, except for poets. Few of us feel secure before such words as "taste," "design," "harmony." This is one more reason why the conventional styles maintain an iron grip on us. How much easier to follow a well-charted course than to adventure into the unknown with only your own judgment as a guide!

But there is more than one kind of beauty, charm, or grace. Standards are constantly changing: the lush curves of a woman who was beautiful to Rubens would not be beautiful to us, and the gingerbread architecture adored by our grandmothers is not our idea of a beautiful house. The beauty of an eighteenth-century drawing room was a perfect expression of its time, but it is not a perfect expression of ours.

The beauty of the Old Dream Home is based on formal design, and on the romantic associations derived from shapes and materials of the past. Another kind of beauty is to be found in informal design, and this kind is the apt expression of our own times. We too can create beauty, but in new shapes and materials, without nostalgic associations but with something added that the old forms do not have—the excitement of newness and the reality of belonging to us, our own creation out of our own way of life.

Of course not everything that is new will automatically be beautiful, or even pleasing. We are entering a period of experimentation, and much that is offered is certain to be found wanting, and be discarded by popular taste. But if we keep our minds unfettered by tradition, a new standard is bound to develop that is both practical and good-looking—the best expressions of our own era will inevitably come to be what we can truly consider "beautiful."

This new beauty is already developing. There is no need to venture out into totally uncharted seas. There are whole groups of people in America who have broken away from convention to make their own setting for living, and we can learn from them.

For example, there are the many artists whose studios are part of their homes. They manage to work, raise children, and entertain their friends—more often than not in close quarters and without servants. Their way of life is, by choice, informal. From them we can learn freedom from pretension.

There are the Californians, who are exerting a real influence on us in many ways. They seem to follow primarily an impulse toward light, space, and color, expressing a willingness to disregard tradition and try anything new. From them we can learn improvisation.

And there are the devotees of modern design, who, with more culture than cash, often manage to convert a tenement flat into a jewel of functional organization. From them we can learn how an informal home can be as meticulously perfect as a formal one.

Good informal living substitutes a little headwork for a lot of legwork. It doesn't need wealth, but it does take thought, some ingenuity and resourcefulness, and more than a little loving care to create a home that is really your own.

You will live in your home, and you must weigh the value of the things that go into it. You alone can estimate labor in proportion to happiness and comfort. Eliminate trimmings that give little return for your care, and concentrate on those things which have real value for you. Buy slowly; know what you're buying and for what purpose.

With this approach you look for furnishings that are practical as well as appealing. You think of the floor not just as a base for the handsomest rug you can afford, but possibly as a space to clear for dancing, and certainly as a surface to be taken care of. You hunt for a type of flooring that is not only durable and easy to clean, but also good-looking in a particular room.

Copying your living room from a magazine may seem easier, just as it seems easier to remember how Mother used to serve dinner or to look up the "right" way in the etiquette book. But it is not easier in the long run; a way of living borrowed from anyone else, from Mrs. Jones or Emily Post or your mother, can't fit your family. The more imitation, the more discontent, frustration, and discord.

A home carefully planned around the requirements of your own family will provide much richer satisfactions. Imitation of other people's ways holds pale pleasure at best beside that of creating one's own. You will find that you have your own way of cooking, your own way of housekeeping, that you can develop your own brand of entertaining. In evolving the family pattern together, you and your family may well find new understanding, perhaps even some undiscovered talent.

Once you've shaken free of traditionalism, don't, for heaven's sake, go looking for a new type of Dream House, or for a new Emily Post to put yourself in bondage to. Don't swallow anyone's ideas whole, not even the ones in this volume.

This book is not intended to lay down a new set of rules. It is a tour through the house, room by room, function by function; it is an examination of floors and walls and furniture, of housekeeping and entertaining your guests. It offers a host of workable ideas, suggestions, and concrete information tested in the laboratory or in our everyday life. Certainly, some of it will not fit your situation; even what you reject, however, may stimulate your imagination toward something that will suit you—and your improvisations may be as good as ours, or better than ours. We hope you will steel yourself against traditionalism for its own sake, and use this book as a guide toward your own best plan for a home and a way of living in it.

We believe that the new way will be a better one, because it is more honest and better attuned with our time. We believe it will bring values to home life that far outweigh the disappearing values of the past. Whatever mysterious pleasure a man has derived from wearing a tuxedo is well compensated by the comfort of a sports jacket. A weekend in the home of good friends may even be more enjoyable if you make beds and help with meals: briefly you are sharing in their lives. A father who remembers to buy ice cream for dessert on his way home, and takes time to play with the children after dinner, has probably achieved a complete break from the worries of his day's work, and certainly gains a closer sense of identification with his family.

In short, we believe that a formal dinner served on bone china by lackeys, with antique crystal and old lace and candlelight, isn't in the same league with the relaxation and friendly warmth, the comfort and gaiety, and the much better digestion of a meal free of servants and strain, served at the kitchen table.

CHAPTER II

ROOM TO RELAX

The LIVING ROOM, where leisure hours are spent, should be the most satisfactory room in the home. Instead it is the most frequent cause of cross words. Daughter leaves her shoes under the sofa, son brings milk and crackers in with his math book, and the man of the house is caught putting his feet on the coffee table. A gathering of teen-agers makes a shambles of the room. Even a quiet adult evening may leave its cigarette burns and moisture rings. Most living rooms today just can't take being lived in.

Our demands on the living room are quite extensive and varied. Consider this not extreme, probably not even complete list of leisure-hour living-room activities:

For the Family	With Others
after-dinner sitting	cards or more active games
reading, including Sunday papers	dancing, and square dancing
knitting, sewing, dress-fitting	business, committee meetings
radio, phonograph listening	refreshments
television, home movies	formal and informal parties
letter writing, accounts	of all sizes
children's homework	overnight guests
father's homework	dining
hobbies	
family discussions	

Then consider that we also attempt to make this room serve as the family's show place—a room that must always be formally correct and beautiful, always kept immaculate in case guests drop in unexpectedly, and always intended to make the world think we have a bit more culture, more expensive tastes, and a larger income than we actually do have.

The Victorian parlor was a room devoted exclusively to receiving, entertaining, and impressing guests—but unlike so many Victorian homes, most of us haven't enough space to permit a whole series of specialized living rooms. Yet housewives continue to hang onto the parlor idea, making their single living room impractically "impressive": deep-pile carpets, dust-catching over-decorated furniture, intricately carved chairs, fragile coffee tables and consoles—old-fashioned in spirit, no matter how it may be "modernized" with reflector lamps, Venetian blinds, and other such anachronisms. The largest share of the average family's furnishing and decorating budget is spent on the living room; the most persistent and exhausting housewifely attention is devoted to it; nevertheless the average living room fails to serve adequately what should be its most important function—being the family's room for relaxation.

The only conclusion possible is that the housewife must abandon the Victorian ideal—unless she is prepared to sacrifice the family's relaxation, and also to subject herself to extensive and unnecessary housekeeping labor.

Of course we want our living room to be attractive as well as comfortable. A room that is well planned, and properly equipped, to serve its purposes will meet both these requirements—and also keep its good looks while being used.

The Japanese living room is a model of planning: a bare room, into which you bring, from closets in the walls, the seats for people to sit on, the books for them to read, the paintings for them to enjoy. Though we are never likely to live like the Japanese, actually the idea makes sense for a room that must serve so many uses: uncluttered space, a few comfortable and easily moved seats, and the rest stored away in the walls to be brought out as needed.

Planning the Living Room

1. There are two basic steps in planning your living room—or any room:

   a. Decide what the uses of the room are to be.

Some kinds of work usually done during evening leisure hours may, particularly in a large family, overburden the living room, and are better done in other parts of the house if that is possible.

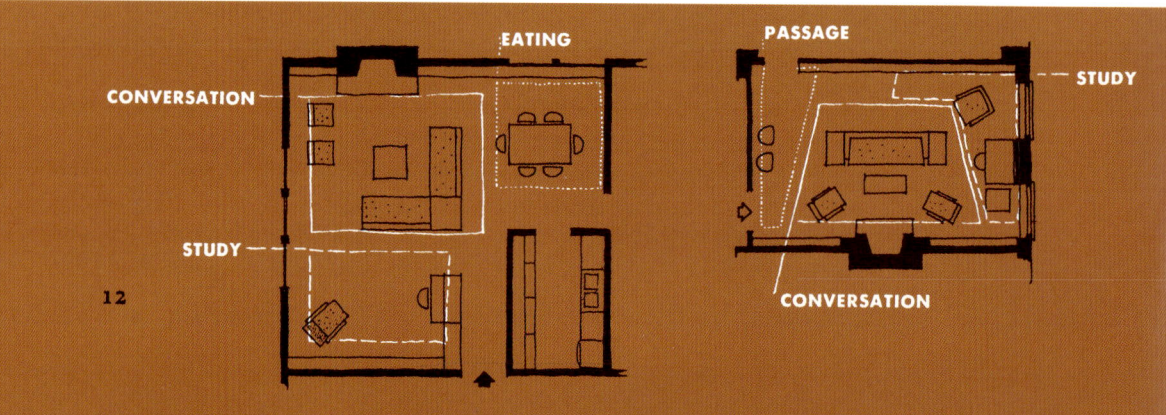

Dressmaking can have a compact corner in the bedroom or laundry or kitchen, wherever there is space. A desk in the children's room is usually possible for homework, and in the master bedroom for letter writing; household accounts can be pigeonholed with menu-making in the kitchen. So, for the most part, we recommend removing from the living room all work—even leisure-hour work—and keeping it a room for recreation. Even so, we've left plenty of work for the living room to do!

    b. Divide the space according to the furniture required for each activity.

This makes several rooms out of one. Use the furniture itself—the back of a sofa, a low bookcase, a desk, a library table—as the line of demarcation between the subsidiary living rooms. And in arranging them leave passageways, so that you don't have to track through one section to get to another. In this way steps and labor can often be saved in the use of the room and its care, and you gain comfort and convenience. If you spend an evening at canasta in the game corner, the rest of the room won't require an entire going-over the next morning.

Possible Groupings

A conversation group, sofa and chairs arranged around the fireplace, if you have one.

A music corner, radio-phonograph-television with record storage handy, and the seating so arranged that you can watch television or home movies with a minimum of chair-shifting.

A reading corner, away from the music and the talk, so the reader can be undisturbed: chair, good light, table or shelf for smoking things, book shelves and magazines.

A game corner, with chairs there or nearby, a permanent table or space to set a game up, good light, surface for smoking things. (If Father likes to work on his stamp albums or Mother on her darning with the family around, then this is the place for it.)

A dining area, one in the living room is often desirable; it saves an extra room and the care of it.

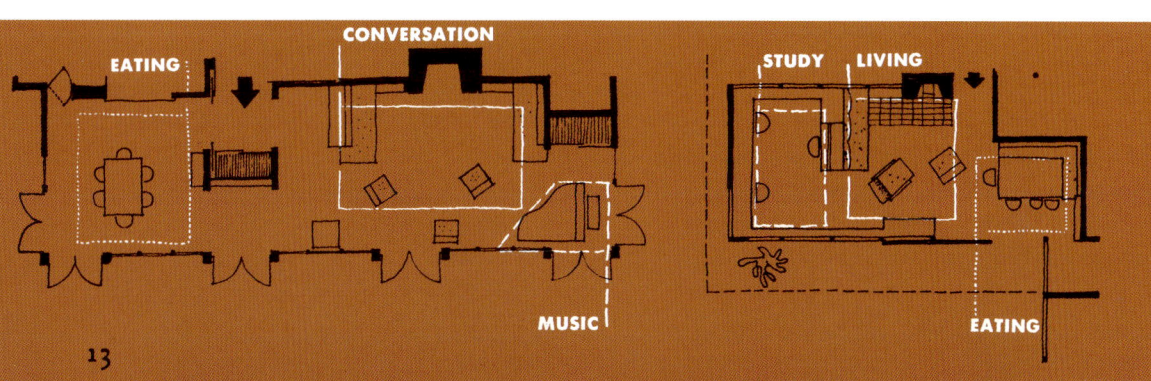

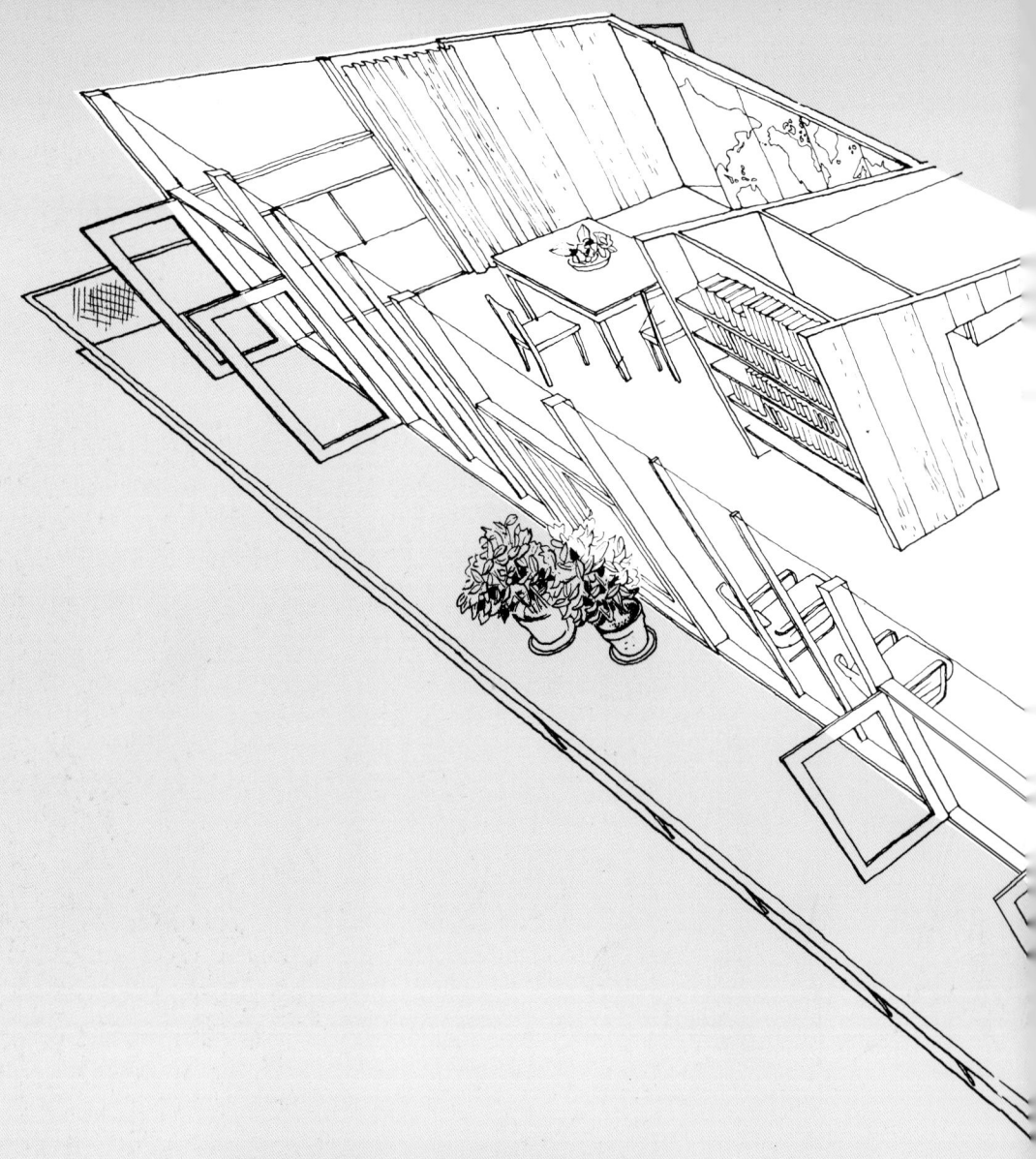

The most satisfactory living-dining room we know of, in a house in Berkeley, California, designed by architect Harwell Hamilton Harris. This room is a masterpiece of planning, with well-defined areas for entrance, conversation, music, and dining. Passage between areas is planned to avoid tracking through or disturbing them.

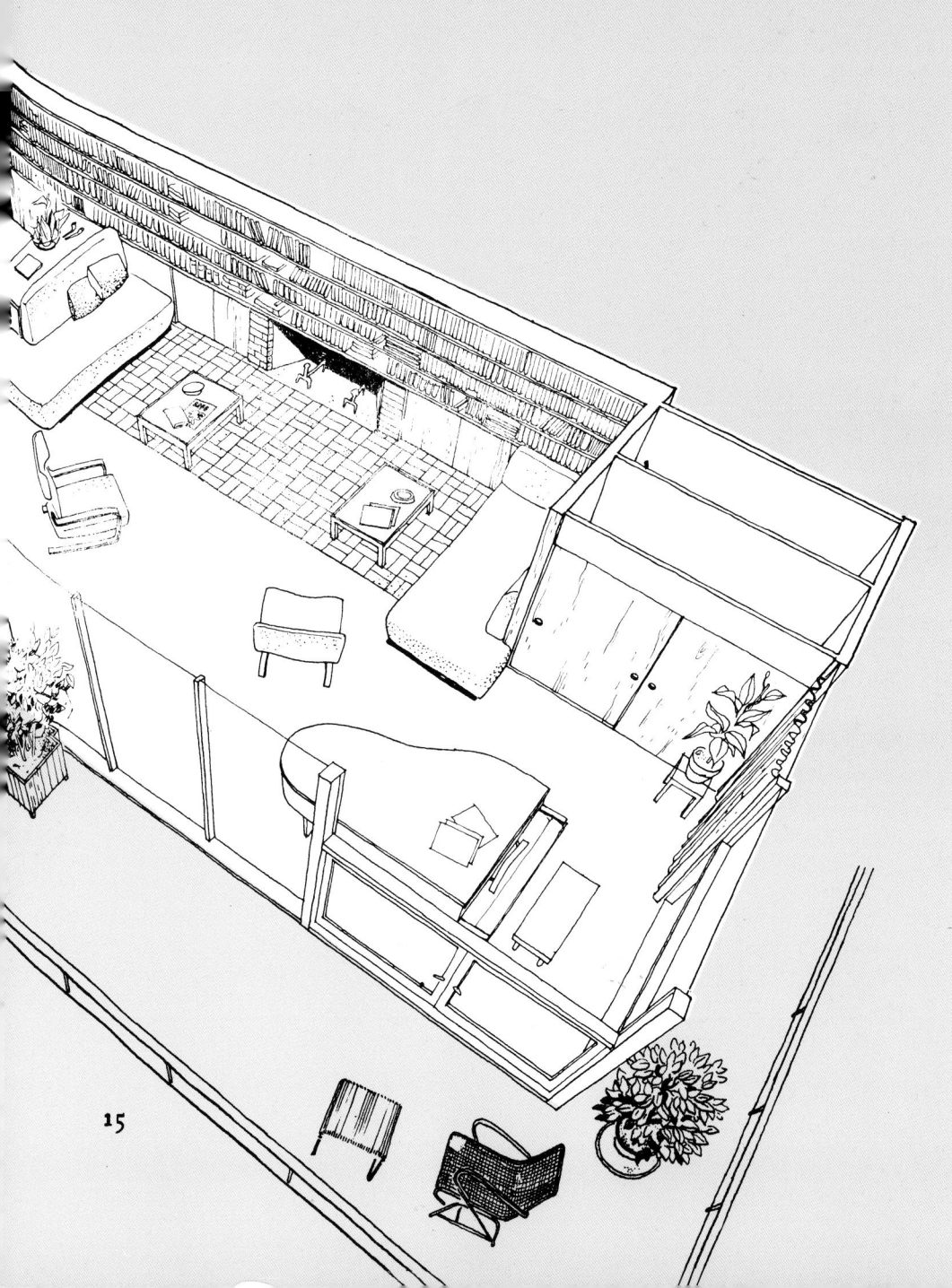

15

Living Room Needs

A floor that can be easily cleared for active recreation or a large party.
Furniture that is sturdy as well as comfortable, and easily moved.
Ready access to the kitchen for refreshments.

Storage for games, smoking accessories, books and magazines, records, movie equipment, folding chairs and tables.
Areas where direct lighting is preferable, as well as suitable; agreeable lighting throughout.

Those who are building or remodeling should also consider the placing of the living room in relation to exposure, privacy from the street, and access to the outdoors.

Floors and Walls

2. Ideally, the floor should be bare, with throw rugs in the seating areas. Large rugs and carpeting demand too much care, are too easily damaged, and make conversion of the room for dancing and parties a strenuous or impossible job.

Hardwood, the most familiar floor material, is good in the living room, but requires more maintenance than these newer ones:

New Floor Materials

Latex-bonded terrazzo (1)*: small chips of marble or glass in a matrix of latex (neoprene rubber), resilient, most durable, least maintenance.
Magnesite (3): magnesium oxychloride mixed with particles of hardwood, with a smooth surface, lightly mottled, which takes waxing but doesn't require it; comes in *any color*, resilient, very durable; the material used in subway car flooring.
The new plastic tile flooring (4, 22), which requires no waxing (in a mottled color).
See Floor Chart for comparison of wear and maintenance of these and other materials.

To keep throw rugs from slipping, there are several standard devices (5) available.

Wall Storage: Particularly for the small-apartment dweller, invariably cramped for storage space, walls can serve an added function. Most of us have learned to keep books and records on built-in shelves. But we continue to use, for storage, end tables and consoles, secretary desks, large cabinets, and other bulky articles of furniture that actually have comparatively little storage space. These all add to the labor of dusting and furniture-shifting, and become loaded with accessories that must constantly be rear-

*This is the first of more than a hundred reference numbers to be found throughout the book. The numbers are keyed to Appendix B, which begins on page 194. It is a listing (with addresses) of manufacturers or distributors of the many new and comparatively hard-to-find products and materials we describe and recommend in these chapters.

ranged, and offer constant danger of breakage. A great number of items—anything from linens to bridge tables—can and should be moved into the walls.

Living-room furniture usually represents the largest single portion of a family's furniture investment. Elimination of the more useless of these is likely to just about offset the cost of installing wall storage; and the saving in room space and in housework is enormous.

Types of Wall Storage

Carpenter-built into the wall according to your specifications, with hinged or sliding doors for access. This is the most satisfactory, also the most expensive. Not necessarily permanent; an architect can design it to be removable.

Factory-made wall storage units (6), fastened in place, from floor to ceiling. Not necessarily less expensive than the car-

Factory-made wall storage unit (6) can look like a built-in, made-to-order job. Remarkably complete and compact, it eliminates need for such articles of furniture as bookcases, desk, radio, music cabinet, china and linen cabinets—thus saving space and housework.

penter-built; they can be removed when moving.

Homemade adjustable shelves; least expensive, but don't scorn them—they can be good looking. The smallest headache to an amateur carpenter is this method:

Put up store display keyhole brackets (7), from floor to ceiling, or bricks or cinder blocks. Buy shelving cut to length. Hang a blind of wood or bamboo slats or plastic-coated material, or a draw curtain of practical fabric harmonious with the room, or one that draws aside on tracks.

Consider Also These Work-savers

House books in glass-front shelves (8)—bought or built-in—and records in closed cabinets. The glass not only keeps books and shelves clean, but keeps the books in better condition.

Put sculpture, bric-a-brac and other decorative objects in a glass case set into the wall, or built out into the room, or under a glass table top; light them to show them off. But watch out for lighting too dramatic for an informal room.

Put compartmented trays (such as are used for table silver) of plastic or wood in drawers, to organize their contents.

Wall Finishes: With so many washable and waterproof ones available, there is no excuse for impractical wall coverings. Even a favorite wallpaper can usually be made washable with a coating of transparent lacquer (9)—but not lithographed papers, which are special, expensive types. See Wall Chart for maintenance ratings.

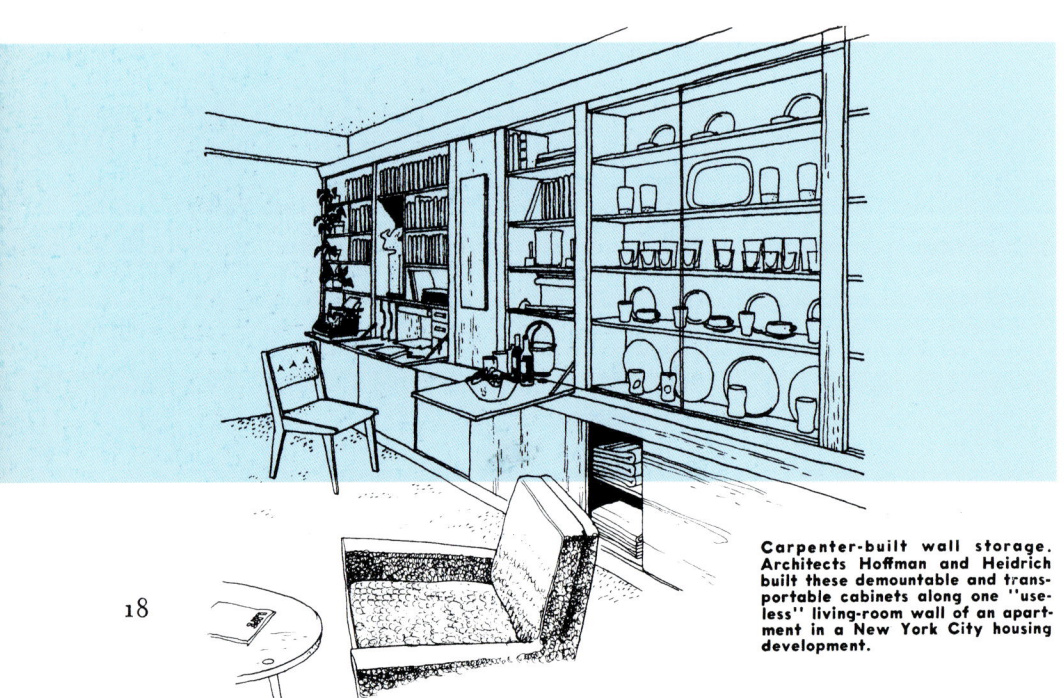

Carpenter-built wall storage. Architects Hoffman and Heidrich built these demountable and transportable cabinets along one "useless" living-room wall of an apartment in a New York City housing development.

Lighting

3. In our opinion, whatever decorative value portable table lamps and floor lamps may have cannot compensate for their capacity for creating housework and mischief. They fall or get knocked down, are unrivaled dust-catchers, and not only a nuisance but a hazard at cleaning time. Their wires snarl the furniture and trip the feet, their reflector globes are moth cemeteries and spider havens, their bases are soon scuffed; their shades soil, tear, and are always being tilted by someone who really needs light. Their spotty lighting, with sharp contrasts between bright and dark, is actually bad for the eyes. In general, we recommend built-in lighting.

For General Illumination, agreeable for talk, music, parties:

Light reflected against the ceiling, or against the wall if it illuminates a large surface; that is, cove or panel lighting.

Light from simple, flat ceiling fixtures of the diffuse direct type.

A rheostat, a special type of switch for dimming, can be put on light circuits for varied degrees of light. Keep appliances such as radios and clocks on a separate circuit, however.

For Lighting Specific Areas use built-in devices:

A tubular light on the desk, over or inside the record cabinet, on the bookshelves, along the wall behind the sofa.

Pinpoint spots (15) in the ceiling, directed where needed.

Inexpensive, homemade storage wall. Wooden shelves placed on bricks or cinder blocks; can be concealed by a draw curtain.

For Lamps, If You Must Have Them	Simple design; a column or shank without ornament, easy to clean with a few up-and-down strokes. Stability; a wide enough, heavy enough base. Chromium, or aluminum, brass, or copper with transparent lacquer *baked* on to prevent tarnish (unbaked lacquer has a much shorter life). To lacquer lamps you already own, clean first with carbon tetrachloride (cleaning fluid) or lacquer thinner, and brush on a clear lacquer recommended on the can for metal or spray on a plastic finish sold for tarnish prevention (16). A reflector or a shade of simple shape and scrubbable material. On a floor lamp, legs, not a solid base—easier to sweep under, and saving the base from kicks and scuffs. If one is used for reading, be sure it can be adjusted, or is tall enough and with a shade wide enough to throw light where it is wanted. Many decorative table lamps make reading difficult.
For the Lamp Cord Hazard	Have many wall outlets, or a continuous strip of them (17). Tack lamp cords against the baseboard, or where this is not possible, secure cord with small, inconspicuous hooks (like cup hooks) on the baseboard. An inexpensive patented gadget (18), which works like a fisherman's reel, can be attached under some lamps to hold the cord taut.
Furnishing the Living Room	**4.** True comfort here means that you can put a drink down anywhere without hunting for a coaster, a foot down anywhere—even on the furniture—without feeling guilty. A cigarette fallen from an ashtray should not ruin a table, a rug, or a friendship. Admonitions never yet saved a chair arm from cracking or a table from being marred. How much better to have furniture that can take it! Science and designing have provided such furnishings, much of it still high-priced, but rapidly becoming more reasonable. Our own living room has been so furnished for years; the saving in repairs, replacements, maintenance, and domestic tranquillity has been worth many times the original cost. **Upholstered Furniture:** Caring for the conventional kind is one of the housewife's worst problems. Almost every day she plumps

cushions, brushes fabric, dusts arms and legs. Periodically she vacuum-cleans or washes, polishes the wood, removes spots, puts slip covers on or takes them off. She must move heavy pieces to clean underneath. And many of them aren't even comfortable.

There is on the market a new type of upholstered furniture (19), which we think is the answer to many of these problems. The upholstery can be slipped off the furniture for dry cleaning or washing, and easily put back in place. Also, for more comfort and durability, and less care:

"Tight" seats, eliminating loose cushions, are easier to care for and sometimes even more comfortable than some overstuffed types.

Contour design (molded plywood is one type), simplifies cleaning. Seating of this type, if well designed, is comfortable enough for use as side chairs and desk chairs, though not for lounging.

But where you do have conventional furniture, in general we consider upholstery in a really practical fabric much less trouble than the additional use of slip covers, which are more difficult to brush or vacuum, and require constant adjusting and handling—which means more frequent washing or cleaning. But of course long-wearing upholstery costs a good deal more.

Choice of fabric is the key to work-saving, and it involves both the type of material selected and its weave, construction, and finish.

Durability: This is one important consideration, and it is largely a matter of weave. Chairs and sofas are subject to much wear and tear, so don't try to economize with sleazy, thin, or loosely woven fabrics; select tightly woven, heavy, abuse-proof material. Also be sure the colors are guaranteed "fast"—if this isn't stated on the label, consult the DuPont booklet, *Testing for Colorfastness in the Home* (20). Slip-cover fabric should be washable, and upholstery fabric safe in the cleaner's hands. All materials should be amenable to home spot-and-stain removal. Water-repellent fabrics are recommended, too; these are not generally designed specifically

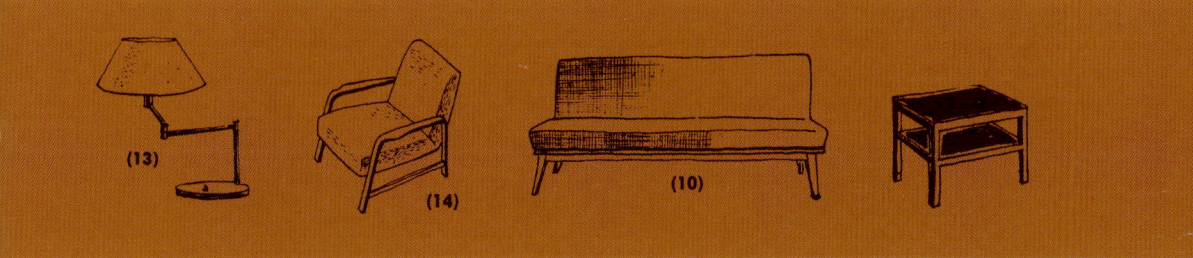

for indoor upholstery, but water-repellent rain wear and outdoor upholstery materials can be adapted for such use.

"Soilability": This is by far the most important factor. One approach to this problem is *camouflage*, achieved by choosing variegated colors in the weave or by printed patterns, avoiding plain, solid colors. But the basic solution is *selection of the proper type of material*. The very new woven plastics (now used as automobile upholstery) can create the illusion of wool or cotton fabric, with much less dust-catching and spotting. As yet, they are available only in Saran (21), but more attractive variations, combining Saran with other yarns, will probably soon be obtainable.

Plastic-coated fabrics (22) are excellent, too; and another new development is plastic film, in textures that are a direct imitation of fabric (23). These are more comfortable than smooth, nonporous plastic materials, but take longer to clean—a scrubbing brush must be used to remove dirt from the depressions in them. Other plastics, imitation leather, and leather can all be wiped off quickly with a sponge and a mild detergent. Plastic webbing is another possibility. Its two advantages are that it's easily cleaned with a sponge or cloth, and that single strips can be replaced individually, without going to the expense of a complete upholstery job.

The most common upholstery and slip-cover materials are of woven cotton, which we have found the most easily soiled yarn—unless it's processed with a water-repellent finish (24). Fabrics containing rayon, wool, and mohair yarns—alone or combined with cotton—are somewhat less impractical, being more dirt-resistant and easier to spot-clean and vacuum.

Nubby, highly textured and pile fabrics (if they're strong, tightly woven, and in good camouflage colors or pattern) can be considered practical only if you have a vacuum cleaner to suck out the dirt; they catch and hold much more dirt than flat-woven fabrics.

Furniture Frames

Solid wood is better than veneered, though it adds weight compared with aluminum. Medium-colored woods like cherry, walnut, gum, need less care than blond; get natural finish, not stained or bleached.

Lacquered aluminum is easily cared for until the lacquer wears off in spots, causing grayish discoloration; you must remove old lacquer, repolish, and relacquer. Anodized aluminum is expensive, but will last for years and never rust. Lighter, easier to move than heavy wood frames.

Chromium-plated steel stays shiny for years, is easily cleaned, but eventually rusts, and the piece must be taken apart for replating. A coat of clear lacquer (9) will make it last longer before rusting.

Unless you happen to think them worth the great amount of extra work and caring for they involve, *avoid*: deeply carved wooden chairs—dust collects in the cracks—and sled legs (horizontal bars at floor level, often found on chairs of modern design)—they are clumsy and scuff very easily.

The usual furniture-top factory finish of rubbed lacquer is ruined by a drop of water. We suggest:

Table Surfaces; Furniture Tops

Ordinary plate glass, cut to size by your local glazier, to cover; better but more expensive is tempered glass (25), which will not break.

Spar varnish (26) or marble floor varnish (26); withstand alcohol and water, though not lighted cigarettes.

Cigarette-proof thermosetting panels — Formica (27), and Micarta (28) are brand names —can be applied to your table top by a cabinetmaker in his shop. Veneered Micarta — called "true wood" — is available in walnut, mahogany, Prima Vera, korina, and oak.

A table top made entirely of glass toughened by new processes (25) is handsome and practical, resisting almost any damage. Disadvantage is its weight.

Hard marble, slate, tile, have the same pros and cons as glass.

Porcelain-enameled steel, laminated on pressed fiber panels (29) can be bought and applied to the top of your table.

Metals show scratches, and some metals tarnish. Not recommended.

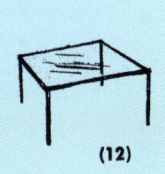

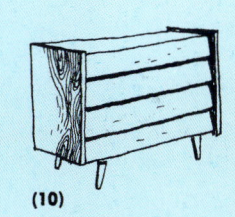

(12)   (11)   (10)

23

The Table-top Chart rates these and other materials and finishes. But if you find a material with a permanent finish too expensive, at least provide lots of ashtrays for your tables, deep enough to prevent spill-over and burning, and a full supply of coasters, too.

Casters, rollers, domes: Put them on all possible articles of furniture, even including wall pieces, for maximum movability. Furniture can then be easily shifted for cleanup and at parties. Saves not only backaches, but wear and tear on floor coverings as well. (Caster brakes are available, to keep furniture stationary.)

Much of the work of lugging chairs for television-viewing can be avoided if you use either the new swiveling television type, or chairs with large casters on the bottom. We know one household where secondhand swiveling office chairs were upholstered attractively for this purpose.

More-Than-One Living Room

5. Up to now we have been discussing the single all-purpose living room. But even with the best of planning, the living room is often overburdened. So, where space and budget permit, auxiliary living areas often spring up: a daytime living room and playroom for a mother and children in a sunny modern laundry; a leisure area in the bedroom; hobby rooms of all sorts in attics, basements, garages, or any unused space.

If two living areas are possible, here is one way to divide their functions:

A Quiet (Old Folks at Home) Room, where such sedentary pleasures as books, music, conversation, and bridge may be peacefully enjoyed. Less space than one all-purpose living room, and no need to clear the floor; here, if anywhere, wall-to-wall carpeting.

An Active Room. In planning this, think of a gymnasium: lightweight furniture, and a minimum of it, or folding furniture which can even be hung on the wall; wall storage where everything, even the ping-pong table, can be put away. A superhard, supersmooth floor: a bowling-alley floor, which is hardwood with an almost indestructible varnish (30); or terrazzo or magnesite (see the Floor Chart).

Some of the best subsidiary living areas are *outdoors*, on porch, terrace, or lawn. This is a story by itself, which you'll find in Chapter VI.

A "Quiet Room." With brick floor, rug in the seating area only, knee-high Bermuda fireplace to avoid stooping, this is planned and furnished for passive uses.

An "Active Room." For as many of the more strenuous leisure activities as the family desires—a room that can have real warmth and life. There's a gymnasium in the corner of this room, and provision for ping-pong, shuffleboard, photography, carpentry, pattern-making, painting; plus a lounging and drinking area.

Fireplaces

6. Fireplaces make work, but most people find that the pleasure they give outweighs the nuisance. Decrease the labor involved by measures like these:

Close off the flue when the fireplace is not in use. You'll want a damper you can easily reach: an extension on the inside damper handle, or a crank on the outside, a patented device that can be built in (more expensive).

Instead of a separate fire screen, have a mesh curtain that draws across the opening (31), another patented device.

Bring in the fuel in a solid-bottom or lined carrier, of ample size and with a cover.

Have the woodbox big enough to cut down refilling trips.

Have the woodbox open from the front rather than the top, for easier access to the wood, for cleaning, and so you won't have to remove vases, ashtrays, books, each time you open it.

Make sure the fireplace is built to draw. This is pure engineering; have a contractor with a reputation for successful jobs. There are also prefabricated metal linings for fireplaces (32) with directions for their installation, which are built to give proper draft plus heat circulation.

Lay a masonry hearth the full width of the fireplace and at least 2 feet into the room.

Frame the fireplace in a fireproof and easy-to-scrub wall area at least 1 foot wide on each side and 30 inches above. Glazed tile or glass is good; unglazed brick and cement are too porous.

Build in a fire screen like a double-hung window, which will slide up into the front wall of the chimney. This must be custom-built.

Have a trapdoor in the fireplace floor to drop ashes into a container in the basement. Fireplace builders know how to do this.

Build the woodbox into the wall with an opening to the outdoors through which the box can be filled; thus fuel isn't carried through the house.

Cut down on kneeling and stooping with a fireplace built knee-high—this is called a Bermuda fireplace.

A fireplace is a pretty dead symbol of warmth and hospitality if it isn't used and enjoyed. Avoid the foolish tendency to make it nothing more than a permanent exhibit—surrounded by such impractical paraphernalia as petit-point fire screens and over-decorated, polished-brass hardware.

CHAPTER III

THE VANISHING DINING ROOM

WE DEPLORE the passing of the American farm kitchen, with its massive dining table in the center. This is not mere sentimentality. That big table was the logical place for the family to dine. The hot biscuits were really hot out of the oven, the second helpings kept warm on the back of the stove, and Mother did not waste a step in setting, serving, or clearing.

Today, we do seem to be coming around again to the conclusion that a room used only for dining is a waste of space, steps, and labor. The dining room is already becoming extinct. You are not surprised at its absence in a modern city apartment or a new house. It has been replaced by a number of arrangements—by a dining area in the living room, or perhaps by a dining foyer, or by a dining alcove in the kitchen or separated from it only by a pass-through counter.

Thoughtful architects are murmuring against the "efficiency-size" kitchen in which there is no room for a table. The American family for which they design a home today is usually one in which the woman does her own work, and where is the efficiency of a kitchen that isolates her from the family group and costs her many wasted steps daily in the serving of meals? We actually conceive of the kitchen not only as the place to dine, but as the center of family living.

If you live in an old house and are cursed, as you think, with a big kitchen, or if you are rebuilding or remodeling and in danger of shrinking your kitchen to a size that forever exiles the dinner table, consider the case for the Dining-Kitchen in a later section of this chapter.

But wherever your dining area may be, there are basic ways to plan, furnish, and use it which can cut the work pertaining to meals to a minimum and increase their enjoyment proportionately.

Planning the Dining Area

1. We are solely concerned here with ease in setting, serving, and clearing away meals. If your dining area is not in the kitchen, but adjoins it, you can save much time by altering the wall or partition that separates the two areas. (Since this wall is very seldom a bearing wall, or one that actually supports the ceiling, parts of it can usually be cut away, and without much expense. But consult a builder first.)

Open-Wall Ideas

Have a counter that opens through the wall or across the partition. Pass the dinnerware through in serving, back for washing. Have the counter stainproof and heat-resistant (see Table-top Chart).

Flanking the counter, and above and below it, have shelves that open through into both kitchen and the dining area, and drawers that slide in both directions. Keep silver, everyday china and glasses, serving

Save time by using a double-door refrigerator (34) opening in both kitchen and dining area, and a pass-through opening to the sink center.

29

dishes, platters, and trays here, so that pieces can be returned to their places after washing, and removed on the dining-area side when they're to be used at table. Store trays vertically, file-cabinet style; platters the same way or on thin shelves, not stacked.

Store linens in cupboards below the counter and shelves. (See suggestions for kitchen storage, Chapter VII, pages 127-129.)

Place the refrigerator in the partition, with doors opening both front and back. This can be custom-made for you, at a price, by a restaurant supply house or a commercial refrigeration equipment company, which can be found in most large cities.

Below the pass-through counter have double doors — like the lower half of Dutch doors (these can be either sliding or hinged). Then a dining table, on casters, can be set in the kitchen, *passed through* for dining, and back for clearing.

Pass-through partition between kitchen and dining area. This can also be used as a bar for breakfast, snacks, children's meals; for serving at cocktail parties and buffet meals *(Idea House II, Walker Art Center)*.

If your dining area cannot be placed in the kitchen or next to it, you can still use a counter arrangement for serving. This can be either a shelf built onto the wall or a piece of furniture—a bookcase or a buffet; you can also use a cart or large trays. Table linens can be stored in this dining area, but it wastes time to keep china, silver, and glassware elsewhere than in the kitchen.

Floors, Walls, and Windows

2. For a space where chairs are forever being moved and traffic is heavy, where crumbs must fall and food may spatter, easy cleaning is as important as good looks.

A rug or carpet on the floor here is really absurd. A smooth surface, easily washed, stain-resistant, and needing little care is what you want.

Floor

Terrazzo (1), cement or rubber bonded, meets all these specifications and is very durable.
Fieldstone, glazed brick, and ceramic tile are long-wearing but, with rougher surface and masonry joints, less easy to clean.
Linoleum, asphalt tile (if of the greaseproof type), in mottled and medium-dark colors, are clean and resilient to walk on, but need more scrubbing and must be waxed. Have them laid with cove corners and curved baseboard to eliminate the crack between floor edge and wall.
Plastic floor tile; seldom has to be waxed (22).
Cork makes a handsome, nearly noiseless floor, especially good in a living-room dining area, but has some maintenance as well as pretty high initial cost. Not recommended for kitchens.
Hardwood, the most familiar material, is good if it has a resistant finish like spar varnish, not a polished wax finish, which even water spots. Also not suited for kitchens.
See the Floor Chart for comparisons of these and other floors.

Walls should be really washable, and resistant to food spatters, grease stains, and furniture scuffing.

Walls

High-gloss enamel paints of either alkyd resin (26) or oil base are the only easily washable paints. Diluting or dulling them reduces their washability. Flat paints of all kinds are altogether impractical.
Plastic and coated wallpapers are washable; there are many on the market.
Plywood paneling, very handsome, is coming within reach of a modest budget.
More information on these and other wall coverings in the Wall Chart.

If privacy is needed or the room is too sunny, we suggest for your windows:

Windows

Roller blinds in translucent or plastic-coated fabrics.
Bamboo or wood shades or drapes.
Draperies, or glass curtains of plastic film or coated fabrics that are easily washed down.

Look for pleasing colors on the dark rather than the light side, or allover patterns.
For other window coverings and for efficient drapery hardware, see Chapter V, pages 99, 103.

Furniture

3. Furniture takes more punishment in the dining area than anywhere else in the house, and should be sturdy.

Get a table that stands firm and steady without cross-bracing, which the family feet would inevitably scuff. Put the right casters on it to make it easily movable for cleaning (see the Caster Chart for the kind that suit your floor) and caster brakes on two diagonally opposite legs to hold it still while in use.

A table top that is stainproof and heat-resistant really saves work. It eliminates table linens; but if you are addicted to these, it still cuts down most of the table-polishing. Hard marble or tempered glass are very practical surfaces.

Table Tops

Phenolic thermosetting laminated plastic — forget that jawbreaker and ask for Formica (27), Micarta (28), Textolite, SatUSPly. The first three come in both cigarette-proof and standard form, the former more expensive. Cigarettes will burn the standard form but the mark is not apt to show on medium or dark colors.
See Table-top Chart for others.

Seats should be robust ones with strong joints and plenty of bracing, but lightweight. You should be able to lift and move a dining chair with one hand. For this reason benches are not recommended unless they are built in.

Seats

Aluminum chairs can be sturdy though feather-light. But avoid sled legs on metal chairs—they scuff too easily.
Upholstery is not essential to comfort and good looks; careful proportioning and contour modeling make some unupholstered chairs handsomer, and equally comfortable.
If you must have them upholstered, use stain-resistant fabric that can be scrubbed, like supported plastic (23); plastic-coated (22); or plastic-woven (21) fabrics.

Lighting

4. This should be from directly above the table. Side lights are more work to care for and indirect lighting is wasted: all you need during meals is to spotlight the table.

A flush ceiling fixture or one set against the ceiling exposes the least surface to dust.
A hanging fixture should not be merely decorative, but also easy to clean and to refill, so

hang it low, or have it on a cord for easy raising and lowering. A pinhole spotlight (15), set in the ceiling, for the living-dining room; no fixture visible to

call attention to the dining area when it is not in use, and perfect lighting when it is. A construction job and more expensive.

Table Service

5. Here is where the work budget can really be slashed. Serving a meal occurs roughly a thousand times a year in the American home. For one sample meal served in the conventional way—a family dinner for four—we counted the number of separate pieces carried to the table: there were 82.

The menu was soup, roast, mashed potatoes, one vegetable, gravy, salad, gingerbread with whipped cream; there were no guests, no cocktails or wine. Here is the list, and beside it our Family Cafeteria Dinner setting, which slices the number of pieces by more than half. Our meal differs from the conventional one in menu as well: by using a casserole dish (ideal as a one-dish main course for both family and company dinners) plus salad, with fruit for dessert, several additional pieces of tableware are eliminated.

Family Cafeteria setting. The meal is arranged in a T-shape, on a spar-varnished table top. Across the bar of the T: cutlery, plates, rolls, butter, water pitcher and glasses, so that each diner can help himself as he moves along before taking his seat at the table. The leg of the T contains the one-dish main course (in the piece in which it was prepared), salad bowl, dessert (in its dish), and serving utensils— 35 pieces instead of the 82 of the traditional setting.

Table Settings

Conventional Setting	Family Cafeteria Setting
1 tablecloth	—
4 fabric napkins	4 paper napkins
4 dinner plates	4 dinner plates
4 soup plates	—
4 salad plates	1 wooden salad bowl
4 bread-and-butter-plates	1 butter dish
4 dessert plates	4 dessert bowls
4 water glasses	4 water glasses
4 cups	4 coffee mugs
4 saucers	—
4 knives	1 cutlery tray (holding 4 knives, 4 forks, 4 spoons)
4 forks	
4 salad forks	1 scissor salad server
4 soupspoons	—
4 dessertspoons	—
4 butter spreaders	1 butter knife
4 teaspoons	—
1 meat platter	—
2 vegetable serving dishes	1 casserole
1 gravy boat	—
1 dessert serving bowl	1 dessert serving bowl
2-piece carving set	—
1 gravy ladle	—
3 serving spoons	3 serving pieces
1 salt	1 salt-and-pepper set
1 pepper	—
1 sugar bowl	1 sugar bowl
1 cream pitcher	1 cream pitcher
1 bread basket	1 bread basket
1 water pitcher	1 water pitcher
	1 coffee maker (and server)
Total: 82	**Total: 36**

The simplified menu, and also the use of stove-to-table and refrigerator-to-table utensils (so that food can be served in the same container in which it was prepared), results in additional laborsaving: you are spared the bother of handling and cleaning many pots, pans, and other kitchen utensils for the meal. Kitchen preparation of the conventional meal called for use of all of these: roaster, pan, rack, and cover; 2 saucepans and their covers; a soup pot with cover; 4 kitchen spoons; 3 mixing bowls; measuring cup; cake pan; colander; egg beater; kitchen knife; masher; and coffeepot—23 additional pieces to be washed. The cafeteria meal called for only 2 kitchen spoons and a kitchen knife, making a total of

105 items to be washed after the conventional meal, 39 after ours.

Since man has outgrown the cozy custom of dipping into the common bowl with his fingers, there is an irreducible hygienic minimum of tableware. But it is convention that piles on the extras. There is no good reason why salad can't be eaten with the dinner fork, and on the dinner plate. And why not put the bread and butter on the dinner plate too, and spread the butter on the bread with the dinner knife? Therefore we've made the following list:

Radical Time Savers

No cloth or mats (see Table-top Chart for stainproof types).
Paper plates and cups as well as napkins. Plastic-coated plates and cups (33) on which you can cut your roast beef and pour your gravy, and a paper cup that doesn't gratuitously flavor your coffee (33), have recently been developed.
Stainless steel flatware, smooth-handled for easier washing.
One fork, one knife, one spoon per diner.
No butter plates or butter knives; no salad plates or salad forks.
One-dish meals.
Stove-to-table cooking utensils and refrigerator-to-table ware: good-looking pots and dishes, to be used also for serving.
And let each member of the family set and clear his own place, with dishes in stacks, silver and napkins in holders, cafeteria-style.

You won't accept all these timesavers, nor will you use them for every meal. Until manufacturers perfect disposable plates and cups that have *all* the virtues of china and glass, you'll reserve many of these short cuts for the occasional picniclike cold supper when the menu is right for them and the mood is casual.

But perhaps you can use more short cuts than you think. See Chapter IX for table settings that involve the least equipment and fewest trips for fetching and carrying, as well as simplified menus.

Table linens are a convention, not a necessity, for either appearance or cleanliness, on a good table top. Stove-to-table and refrigerator-to-table ware is no wishful dream; a careful choice of inexpensive cooking pots and refrigerator dishes can look quite presentable on the table, and more expensive ones expressly designed for such use are as good-looking as many conventional serving dishes. Casserole dishes that come to the table are surely no novelty; or you can use large platters with gravy wells to serve an entire main course at one time. In any case, choosing dishes of simple shape and design, rather than ornate ones, will mean less time and work in dishwashing. Also avoid fragile, thin-walled ware.

Because our first list is frankly too radical for daily use, here is a second one:

Conservative Time Savers

Table covers or place mats that can be wiped off, such as printed or covered cork, pandanus leaf, Chinese matting, split bamboo, plastic, plastic film, or coated fabric.

Table covers and napkins of material you wash but don't iron, such as seersucker, loosely woven or machine-knitted fabrics.

No saucers; mugs for coffee and tea.

A cart, or large light trays, to cut down trips to and from the table. (You can buy carts with electrically heated tops to keep food warm.)

A two-tier or three-tier serving table or a counter within reach, so you can clear between courses without getting up.

Melamine plastic, or very durable heavyweight (vitrified) china of simple shape, which can be washed quickly and safely.

Plastic tumblers, for speedier dishwashing. Those of nylon or polyethlene are the best. Unbreakable glass is not yet on the market, but Libbey-Owens tumblers with beaded edges take a lot of rough wear. Any glass with a drinking edge that turns in slightly will stand more abuse than those with flaring edges. Smooth, simple-shaped tumblers of any kind take less care and time than stemware or footed goblets.

A Lazy Susan holding all serving dishes in middle of table within everyone's reach.

The Dining-Kitchen

6. A kitchen in which the family can eat its meals sweeps aside most of the work problems of the dining area. It may surprise you, if you have never seen it done, but you *can* eat pleasantly in the kitchen without the sight of kitchen clutter and the laboratory look of kitchen equipment. According to home economics testing, there are three efficient kitchen plans:

The U-shape, with sink in the center, range and refrigerator one on each side of the U.

The L-shape, with either range or refrigerator on the same wall as the sink, the other on the side wall; again the sink is between the other two.

The strip kitchen, with the equipment on two facing walls, sink on one, range and refrigerator on the other.

Depending on the shape of the room and the plan, your dining table may be placed: 1—at one side or corner of a wide kitchen; 2—at one end of a narrow kitchen; 3—in the center.

The first two are in effect dining alcoves and can be treated as separate from the kitchen. You can in fact separate them by an open, latticelike partition, by glass, a drape, or a bamboo or wood shade. Or use a partition about 36 inches high that contains storage for tableware.

The third plan, with the dining table set in the middle of the kitchen, is the most effective work-saver. It is also in line with our concept of the kitchen as a room for family living.

Into this kitchen bring pleasing colors such as would be considered for any other room, the grain of natural wood, patterned wallpapers, and the like. Fussy furnishings, such as frilly curtains, should be rejected, but in general the kitchen should be treated as a room, not as a laboratory.

Kitchen-dining with the table in a corner. The kitchen does not need to have a utilitarian look; it can, if you like, be cozy and early-American.

Kitchen-dining can be in the corner of a wide kitchen, given an alcove effect by a storage partition.

Dining-Kitchen Colors

Refrigerator (35) and gas range (36) can be ordered in various colors. Cabinets and shelves can also be had in color (37), or they can be painted.

The average refrigerator can be painted (but not the range, which has a porcelain finish). First wash the surface with soap and water, steel-wool it to give it a "tooth," wipe it down with cleaning fluid, then paint with alkyd enamel (26).

Do the whole kitchen in natural wood, plain or knotty pine, or natural chestnut. Build in your sink with the same wood, and paint refrigerator. The Wall Chart lists washable and stain-resistant finishes for wood.

For the walls, use wood paneling, or a bright-patterned wallpaper. For stain-resistant and thoroughly washable papers see the Wall Chart.

Wall spaces above work counters and range, trouble centers for stains, can be covered with wooden slabs with hooks to hang utensils used at that place. See the Table-top Chart for the hardest finishes.

Kitchen-dining at one end of a long room; the antiseptic look is avoided here by natural wood walls and cabinets, and a fieldstone floor.

Dining-Kitchen Furniture

A sofa if you can possibly fit it in, roomy, sturdy, and covered with washable—i.e., plastic—fabric. Here the children can climb and bounce, Father stretches out with the evening paper before dinner, and Mother takes her ease during a free hour.

An easy chair instead of a sofa, or in addition, if your kitchen is that big. How about a rocking chair? Kitchen planners have come around to Grandmother's faith in it as the most relaxing chair to sit in.

A desk or its built-in equivalent, with telephone, writing materials, cookbooks. Kitchen planners prescribe this as a Planning Center; we would expand it to hold not only cookbooks but leisure reading, knitting bag, sewing basket; also household accounts, and engagement and address books.

A posture chair, or a posture stool (38).

A family bulletin board for messages, reminders.

A radio (but *not* television; that's too much distraction).

One hurdle remains: What to do about kitchen clutter. The sight of bowls and utensils with which the dinner was prepared is not an attractive setting for eating. But it is not inevitable.

Avoid Kitchen Clutter

Clean up and put away as you go along.

Use stove-to-table ware and re-refrigerator-to-table ware to cut down on the number of pots and dishes used.

Spotlight the table when dining at night, throwing the rest of the room into shadow.

Hang a roller shade or a wood-slat or bamboo blind, to pull down over the work counter—of fire-retarded material, or sprayed with fireproofing.

Hang a blind vertically and pull it across the part of the kitchen you want to hide. It runs on tracks screwed to the ceiling; to cover one wall, use a pull cord. If there are two walls, have two blinds, each running on a straight track, meeting at the refrigerator, so you can get at it during dinner without pulling the whole blind back. Fireproof these, too.

This last is borrowed from the theatre. You make the kitchen disappear, and provide a whole new setting for dinner, new color scheme, new textures, just by pulling a fire-retarded drape.

Two ways to conceal kitchen litter: spotlight the dining table . . .

. . . Hang a wood or bamboo drape on a ceiling track.

Here is a dining-kitchen where we have dined well, and enjoyed ourselves, too. With young children, and no help, this housewife made a virtue of necessity by transforming her large kitchen into a room for family living, dining, entertaining—with ideal working conditions for herself.

Her sink window has a view of Storm King Mountain and the Hudson River; a sliding window in the wall above her work counter (at left) looks into the nursery—which later can become an adult playroom, with counter and window for a refreshment bar. The sofa is plastic-covered. The colors are pink, green, and yellow; the ceiling is wallpapered with huge pink flowers, the refrigerator is green, and the sink is boxed in to match the cupboards.

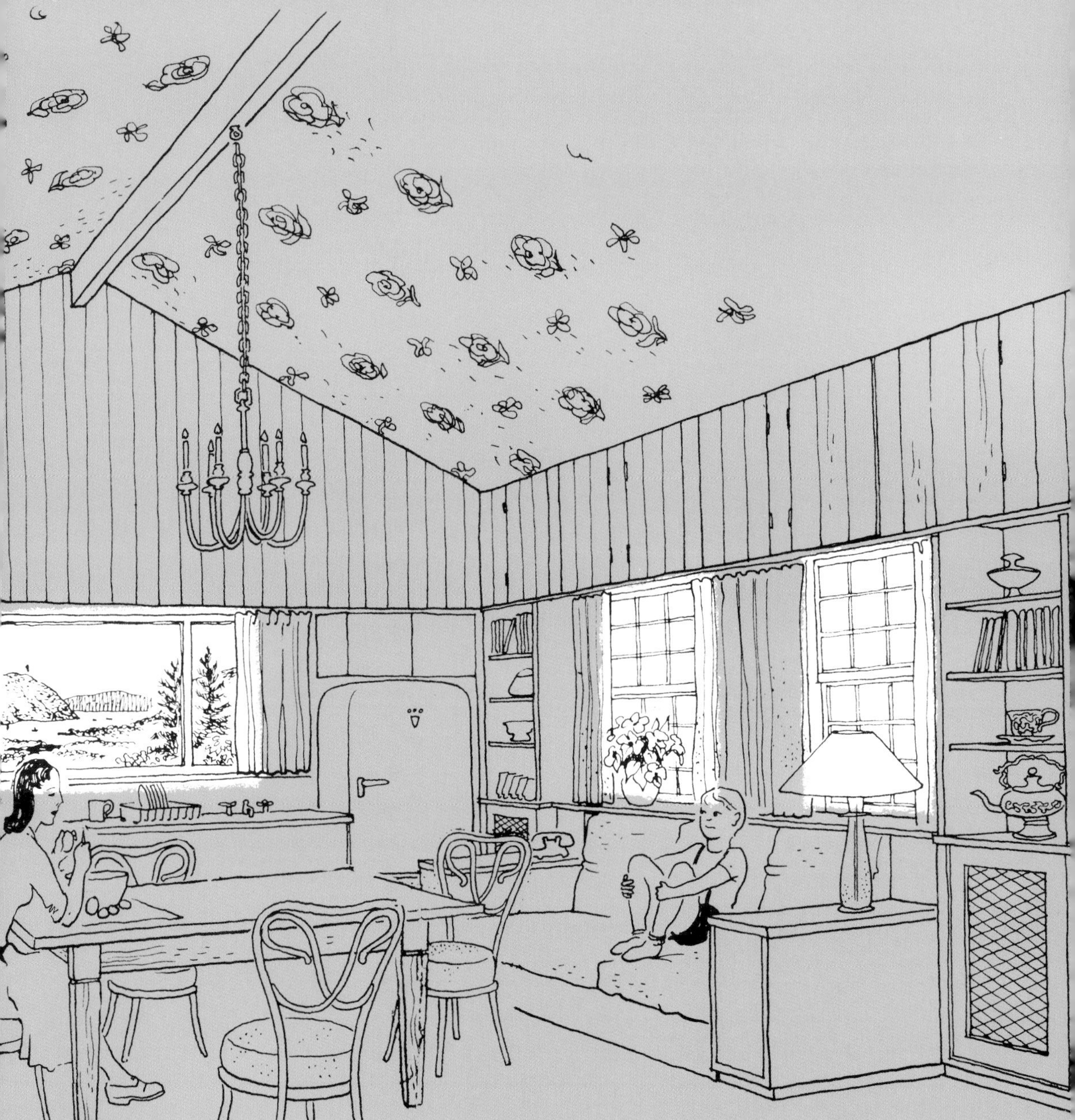

Even if you consider your kitchen too small to make use of the majority of our suggestions, here are some aids in making room for occasional kitchen dining:

Build a drop-leaf shelf that can be pulled up for occasional eating in the kitchen.

A kitchen cabinet is available that contains a pull-out table (39).

An 18-inch shelf built around a corner storage cabinet can seat four for a small kitchen meal.

Breakfast in a Hurry

7. Even if lack of space, or deep-seated personal preference, keeps you from using the kitchen as your room for dinner, the weekday breakfast demands the speed and efficiency of kitchen-dining.

With the husband, and in many cases the working wife, rushing to the office, and the children usually on the verge of being late for school, co-operation (note the illustration) and preplanning are essential.

Set the table, or set out a buffet on the kitchen counter, with everything except perishables, the night before while cleaning up after dinner.

On the table or counter are: dishes, silver, napkins, glasses for juice, mugs for coffee; toaster, coffee-maker; jam pots, breakfast cereals in their original containers.

In the refrigerator (together at the front — not behind last night's roast) are: juice, in a tightly sealed container to preserve the vitamins; a dish with bread and butter already on it; cream, water, and milk in pitchers; eggs in a bowl, ready for cooking, etc.

Keep coffeepot, coffee, and measuring spoon together, near the range if you use a French drip pot (to be filled from the kettle), near the sink if you start with cold water.

The table can be arranged the night before for a hurry-up weekday breakfast for four: one prepares and serves the eggs; another takes care of the toast; a third does all the pouring—juice and coffee; the fourth is in charge of cereal, napkins, silverware.

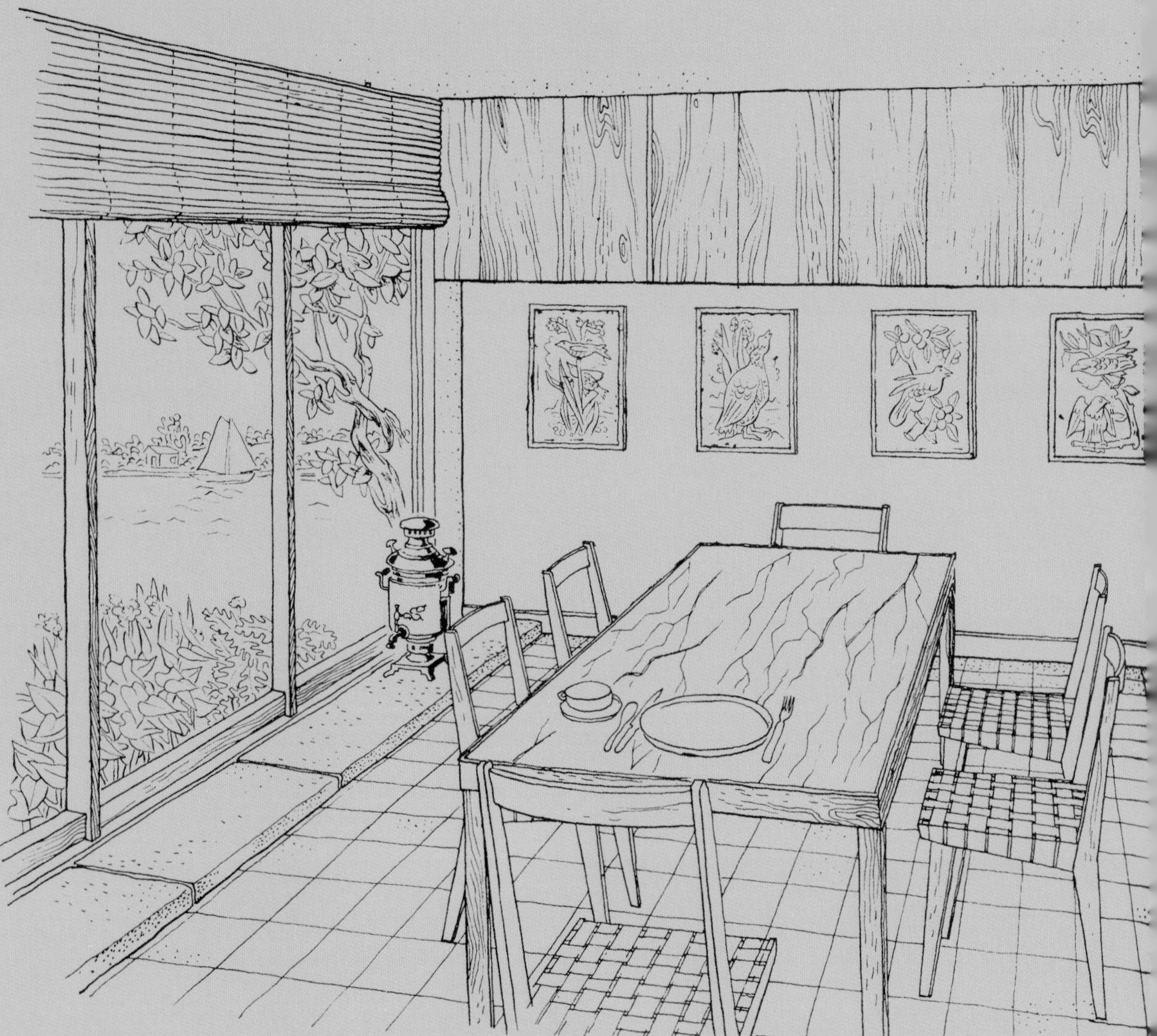

Now you see it, now you don't!

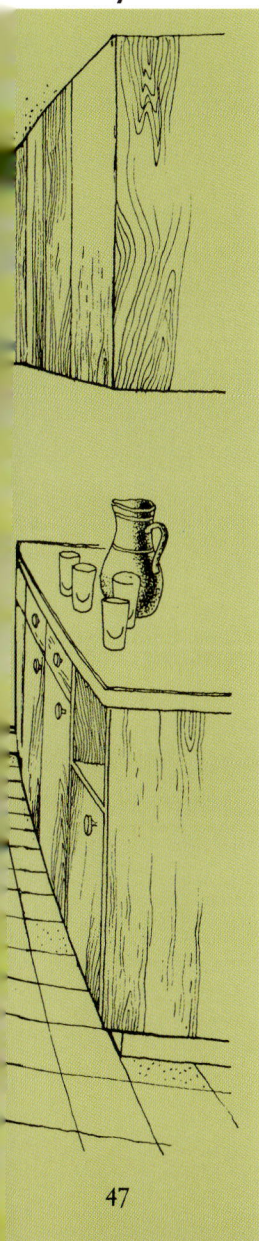

8. To a reader accustomed to a room devoted only to dining, with fixed and formal furniture, we may seem to have done frightening and unstabilizing things. The dining area we have described may be in the living room, in the kitchen, in an alcove—it may even turn up on your porch. It may have no permanent existence, disappearing from the living room after mealtime, or perhaps causing the kitchen to vanish and taking over its place temporarily.

If, in addition, the reader has been in the habit of setting the table according to immutable laws of etiquette, it may even seem not quite respectable to have a table without linens and bread-and-butter plates, with only three pieces of silver for each person, with serving dishes that come off the stove or out of the refrigerator.

We realize that all these short cuts may sound extreme—and we know that they can look slipshod and tawdry, too. But we also know that they can look and be charming, smart, and even beautiful. It's all in the way you do it. What is needed is planning and headwork at the start, to select and assemble everything with care. Find the proper color of paper napkin, the perfect wall color, truly good-looking cooking-and-serving dishes.

Our main thesis here is that formality is *not* necessary for beauty. It shows not less, but more, respect for the good things of life to plan an easier, smoother-running meal in a setting that suits its purpose—and to have more time in which to enjoy the meal and its setting.

We look forward to the day when living room, dining room, and kitchen will break through the walls that arbitrarily divide them, and become simply friendly areas of one large, gracious, and beautiful room. We think that day is not too far away.

The dining room can be made hospitable and handsome without benefit of rugs, drapes, linens, upholstery, or Duncan Phyfe—by careful selection of colors, materials, and furnishings. This room has wood cabinets, chairs with plastic strap seats, a wood blind, a marble-top table, ceramic tile floor and painted wall, and a color scheme of brown, green, and wood-colors.

48

The all-in-one-room, permitting the easiest servantless living and the best kind of family life. The plan is adaptable to many types of houses, and to apartment as well. (This design was executed in a space 16 by 28 feet.)
Kitchen area (upper left): refrigerator, stove, sink and storage cabinets, can be bought in colors (35, 36, 37). Note the glass pass-through shelves to the right of the dishwasher, and the window in front of the sink—for serving to the outdoor table.

The table in the adjoining dining area has a marble top and legs on casters. This also serves as an "old-folks" corner, with sofa, desk, and bookshelves, and thus merges into the living area, where wall storage is behind sliding wood doors. A firewood closet (left of fireplace), can be filled from outdoors. Note small rotating chairs for television, sofa on rollers, marble-top coffee table. Curtains are of vinolyte and seersucker.

49

CHAPTER IV

PRIVATE LIVES

THERE ARE three times as many bedrooms in America as there are kitchens. It is the room in which we spend a good third of our lives. Not only do we sleep there; we also dress and undress, read, sew, write letters, keep accounts, work at our hobbies, convalesce, and relax. Young children play in their bedrooms; older ones study and share confidences with best friends there. It is the most *personal* room in the house, the room in which we live our private lives.

Yet it is the room which we have taken the least trouble to fit even to its basic functions of sleeping, dressing, and storage of clothes.

To the housewife it is easily the biggest headache—more accurately, backache—of all. As she stops in the doorway each morning, toting her dustcloth, carpet sweeper, and mop, consider the scene that confronts her:

Gone is the sweet and charming picture of the night before: the draped and ruffled bed, the delicate night table, the sleek chests and bureaus, the skirted dressing table, all in the mellow glow of dainty, silk-shaded lamps. In the cold light of morning, where is the pretty illusion now? Bedcovers cascade to the floor, and lamp shades hang askew; the housewife must stumble over assorted shoes, slippers, and oddments of clothing that litter the carpet. Drawers and closets are open-mouthed, mute witness of the frantic hunt just made within their disordered depths. The elegant dressing table lewdly bares its skinny legs, and lint is a dingy film over everything.

From coast to coast, in rich homes and poor, the American bedroom at 8 A.M. looks the same . . . like an Okie camp. Think of the millions of hours it takes to put all these rooms in order again before each nightfall.

It is true that architects, designers, engineers, manufacturers, have given the bedroom a poor deal. If they spent a fraction of the energy, imagination, and science on it that they have lavished on the kitchen, or the bathroom, what a transformation we should see! But we needn't wait for them to discover the bedroom. There's plenty we can do by ourselves.

Planning the Bedroom

1. Unless we are building or remodeling, we must generally take the master bedroom where we find it, but in an apartment or a house where there are two or more additional rooms to assign, consider the needs of the occupant. An adult or an older child may like the privacy of a room apart from the others. An infant or a young child who requires attention at night should be near the mother's room, and also, if possible, away from the living room, to sleep undisturbed by evening entertaining.

A great work-saver would be a daytime sickroom adjoining the kitchen, especially for childhood illnesses, a continuous marathon for a mother while they last. The so-called maid's room, now rarely occupied by a maid, is usually well situated for this purpose. A sewing room, a playroom or a guest room while the family health is good, could be planned for easy conversion in time of illness.

Remember the steps in planning as we followed them in the living room: a. Decide the uses of the room. b. Divide the space according to these uses, keeping the different areas distinct by grouping the furniture.

Ideally, the bedroom for adults should be divided into three areas: sleeping, dressing and clothes storage, and leisure. Where space is limited, it is better to put a hobby elsewhere in the house than to cramp the dressing and storage space.

In the sleeping area, placing the bed with head only against the wall is most convenient for bedmaking. Provide enough space for a *large* bedside table, too. For the dressing and clothes-storage area you need a substantial unbroken space for the occupant—who literally needs elbowroom. Try to place this area near the bath. Best of all, of course, is a separate dressing room. You may find a way to approximate such a luxury:

A dressing space in the bedroom, away from the beds, across which a drape or screen can be drawn.
A corridor outside the bedroom, near the bathroom.
A closet built into the wall that separates bedroom and bath, opening into both rooms, so each can be used for dressing; with bathroom available for dressing, less bedroom space is needed. A solution for two people in a cramped room.

The leisure area, designed to take some of the burden from an overworked living room, should be a clearly separated corner to take care of such activities as writing, keeping accounts, and doing night work from the office; for sewing, light hobbies like stamp collecting or drawing; or as a game area.

Floors, Walls, and Windows

2. If you will remember the daily labor of putting this intensively used room to rights, you will make housekeeping, not fussy decorating, your first consideration.

Under the bed, in the dressing area, and certainly in the leisure area, a smooth bare floor for easy cleaning is best, like linoleum or cork (40)—see the Floor Chart. For a warm, agreeable place to rest bare feet beside the bed and in the dressing area:

Scatter rugs that can be picked up for cleaning or laundering. There are standard devices to make them non-skid (5).

A cotton rug, or a runner of carpeting to the bathroom.

Radiant heating in the floor, which can then be of linoleum, asphalt tile, or rubber tile, without any rug or strip. This, of course, is an expensive project.

Walls—especially behind the head of the bed if there is no headboard—should be thoroughly washable and dark, or covered in a washable material, to avoid head marks. Look at the Wall Chart.

Windows in the bedroom demand covering for privacy and light control, but of a kind that won't rattle in the breeze from the open window, and easy to clean. Suggestions:

Plasticized roller blinds, installed at the sill and drawn upward, or double-hung. See Chapter V, page 99.

Draw curtains of washable material that doesn't need ironing, in a dark color. A separate plastic lining gives some protection against rain and soil from the window.

All-plastic curtains, for the same reasons.

Lighting

3. General illumination is necessary, and a flush ceiling fixture will give it. One light should be turned on by a wall switch at the door so that you won't stumble through the dark to the bed light. Floor and table lamps anywhere in the bedroom are worse than a housekeeping problem; near the bed, which is constantly shifted about in housecleaning, they may be an actual hazard. For intensive lighting where it is needed, there are many safe built-in devices.

The Bedside Light should be simple, adjustable, and securely anchored.

You can fasten it directly to the bed, or to the wall at the back or side of the bed, preferably *not* on the bedside table itself. But if it must be on the table, be sure it is secure, and not in a position where a careless motion of your arm, or shifting of the table, would easily topple it.

Another suggestion is to put pinhole spotlights (15) in the ceiling, a construction job and therefore more expensive, but good when two occupy the room and like to read at night—possibly at different times. Or put a light along the full width of the headboard, on the wall behind it.

Light in the Dressing Area should be placed so as to illuminate the entire area, since dressing involves moving about. Most practical is light from the ceiling, or from high on the wall. Or you may want a light fastened to the sides of a mirror. Good lighting inside a closet, or directly outside, is helpful; also paint the closet a bright white for improved visibility.

Light in the Leisure Area: General illumination can come from overhead, but for close work it is better to have it either built into the desk; fastened to the bookshelves or to a wall cupboard above a pull-out work table; or as a pinhole spot (15) above the work or game table.

Furnishing the Master Bedroom

4. Our idea of the best, and most easily cared-for bed, using present-day equipment, would include these factors:

It would be *hand-high*, a real laborsaver to the person who must make it and clean under it. There is no sensible reason for the way beds have been settling closer and closer to the floor, but if you insist on a low bed, why not extend the frame all the way down to floor level, so that neither dust nor lost small objects can collect under it?

Casters or rollers—with caster brakes if required—are probably the greatest energy-saving addition to your bed (see Caster Chart).

A padded headboard, attached to bed or wall, pitched at an angle for sitting up or adjustable, means more comfort and eliminates extra pillows. It should be of scrubbable material, or have a washable slip cover.

A foam-rubber mattress (41), which does not need turning; or an older-style mattress, on which straps are a help in turning—

but actually any good-quality mattress should not require to be turned more often than four times a year. Weekly mattress-turning is merely a myth left over from the days of the straw mattress.

Bedding can be cut to a minimum by using new products—and by eliminating the useless, showy items. Our mothers used to make up a bed with some thirteen pieces; these included such items as mattress cover, bed pad, comforter, and bedspread, pillows with an overticking removable for washing, and a bolster. Much of this has gone and more is going.

Modern Bedding

The mattress cover, for keeping dust out of the mattress, has become superfluous with the vacuum cleaner.

The pad is dispensable on a foam-rubber mattress (which is minus buttons).

Blankets and comforters are being replaced by the single electric cover (42).

An attractive quilt, electric or not, large enough to cover bed and pillows, can also do double duty as a bedspread.

Button the top sheet to the quilt and you have only one piece to pull up in the daily bed-straightening.

Sheets with ready-made mitered corners (43) are available, to cut down the smoothing and tucking of the undersheet.

For the weekly stripping and changing of bed linens, you may want some device for hanging the bedclothes out of the way:

Towel bars on the wall or the inside of the closet door, which can also hold clothes when undressing at night. (Leaving the closet door open when bed-making enables you to air closet and bedclothes at the same time.)

A clothesline stretched across the window that can drop to one side under the window curtain or blind when not in use.

Bedside Tables

The standard 18-inch bedside table-top is never large enough to hold the inevitable clock, books, magazines, telephone, radio, writing materials, tissues, and so on. An adequate table should be at least 24 by 24 inches square, 12 inches higher than the top of the mattress, and with two or three shelves or drawers. Suggested:

A carpenter-made job, with the above specifications plus built-in radio and pull-out tray for eating, reading, writing, make-up.

No bedside table at all, but instead a carpenter-made headboard with everything in it: light, recessed shelves, telephone, and pull-out tray.

Less expensive—a practical bedside table made of two coffee tables fastened one on top of the other, or any two small tables with the right-sized tops, their legs cut down to bring the double-decker down to the right height.

Custom-made bedside chest, with many drawers, a pull-out pivoting shelf (for working or eating in bed), and built-in adjustable lamp.

Headboard case. Provides shelves, drop-leaf bedside surface with a cupboard below, and a tubular light over the bed. **Carpenter-built;** check "Do-It-Yourself" shops and furniture stores for similar ready-made headboards.

Home-made bedside table of generous size. Built by cutting down the legs of two lamp tables and stacking them. Has two large shelves and two drawers.

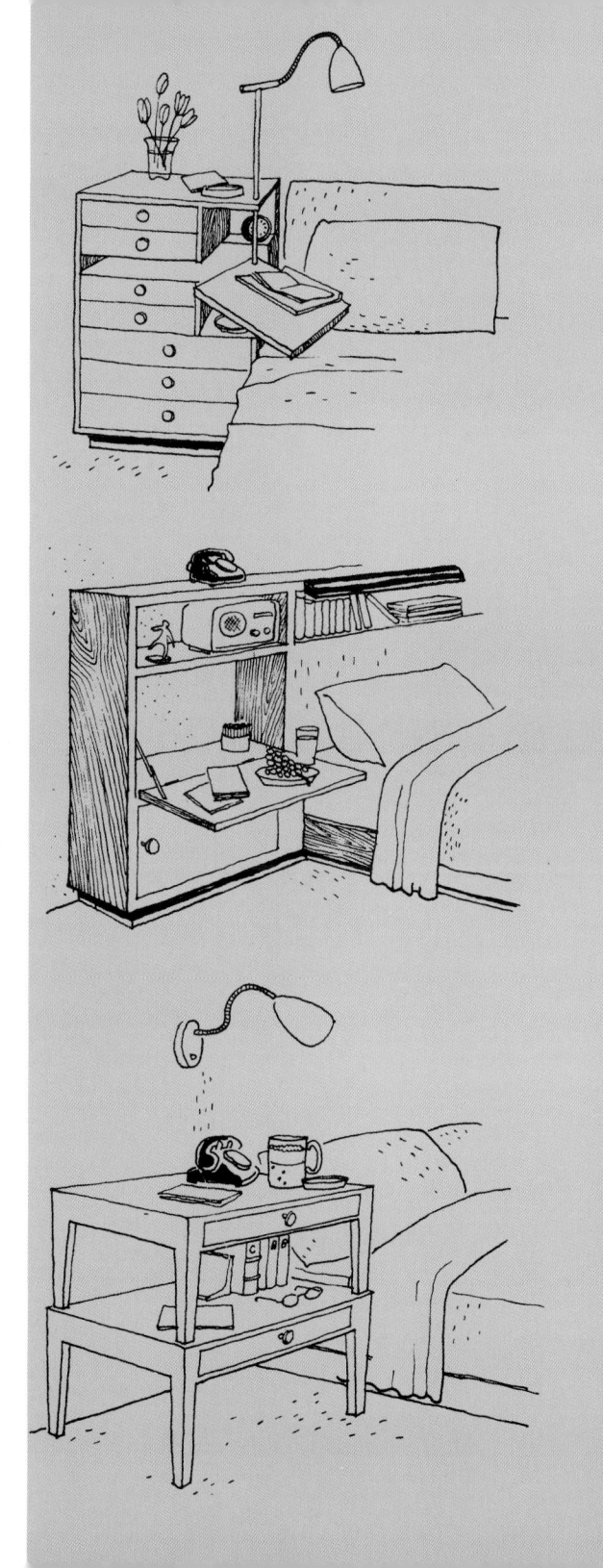

Wall Storage

Storage Pieces—bureaus, highboys, and so on—have undergone little change since the days of the bustle, and are hopelessly unsuited to hold a modern wardrobe in any sort of order. The nuisance of periodically reorganizing their contents, plus the labor of cleaning on top of and around them, indicates the need for built-in-wall storage.

Storage has nothing to do with decoration. It is purely an engineering job, and the best storage engineering is wall storage.

Carpenter-built wall storage is recommended for homeowners; even if you should sell your house someday, you have added an appreciable value to it. But since this is an engineering job, your first step is measurement—to see what clothes you have to provide for. There can be no set rules or average specifications given for a wardrobe closet—your income, your personal tastes, and a variety of other fairly intangible factors must be considered. But at least

Factory-made wall storage comes in sections, which can be combined in many ways to fit individual needs. A more convenient combination than separate chest, bureau and closet.

you can break your clothing list into groups, according to how each item is stored:

Hanging: coats, suits, dresses, skirts, blouses, trousers, slacks.
Drawers: underwear, shirts, scarves, gloves, handkerchiefs.
Shelves: hats, luggage.
Racks: shoes, ties, hats if you have more vertical space than shelf space.

When you have made such a list, you are ready to make your own storage specifications. On the following pages are some sample wall-storage plans.

As an alternative to carpenter-built wall storage, there are factory-made wall units (2). These are recommended for the apartment dweller, since they can be moved.

Chests

Custom-built chests are a second choice to wall storage, and are not much more expensive than high-quality ready-made chests and dressers. You can have the cabinetmaker put in whatever drawer details fit your needs, and also add: legs, of a height to let broom or vacuum cleaner go under, and to give the bottom drawer more usefulness; stainproof, waterproof tops; and such over-all design that they can stand banked together in the room, saving space.

Ready-made chests, including some of the same sort of features as these custom-built jobs, have recently begun to become available, but as yet they are comparatively expensive.

If wall storage or custom-made chests are not for you, improve your present chests with partitions and trays, and improve your existing closet to yield more and better organized space:

Factory-made chests. A new type, carefully planned for *today's* wardrobe (14). Designed by Edward Wormley.

Old-fashioned bureau drawers can be kept more orderly by partitioning. Have plywood cut to size; hold in place with glued strips of square molding.

Sweaters, Handbags

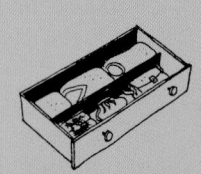

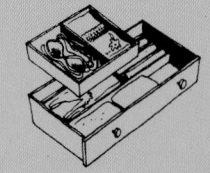

Nightgowns, Slips, Girdles (rolled), Brassieres, Pants

Stockings, Scarves, Gloves, Belts, Ribbons, Bows, Jewelry, Handkerchiefs

Shirts, Sweaters, Scarves

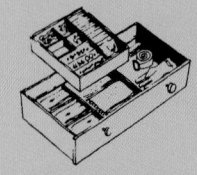

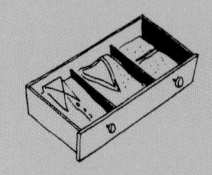

Shirts (filed on layer of corrugated cardboard)

Socks, Gloves, Belts, Suspenders, Handkerchiefs, Jewelry

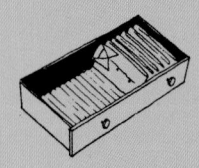

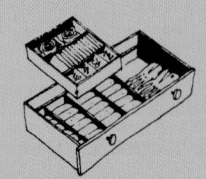

Underwear (rolled), Pajamas

Summer: Shorts, Swimming Trunks

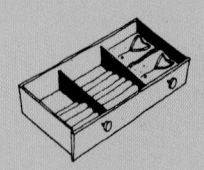

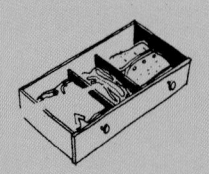

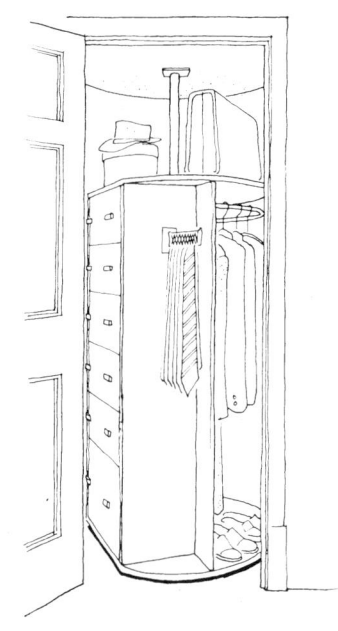

For maximum clothes-storage space in a small closet: The two views indicate how this circular device, known as a "Roto-Closet," rotates on a pipe stem, with access at the closet door, so that almost all the area is utilized. Must be installed by a carpenter.

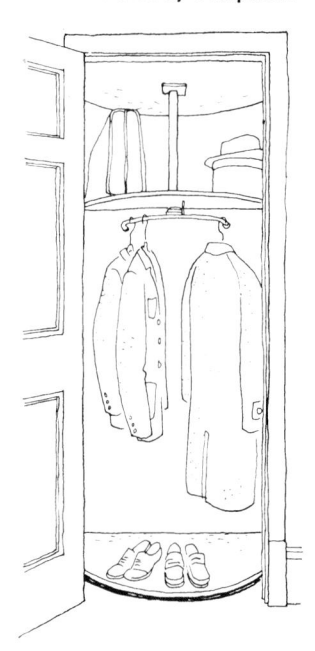

58

Closet Aids

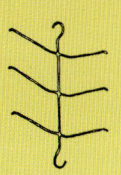

Reversible blouse and skirt hanger (47)

Skirt hanger (46)

Children's closet rod doubles closet hanging space (47)

Coat hanger—for high-up hanging (51)

Pull-out rod for narrow space (7)

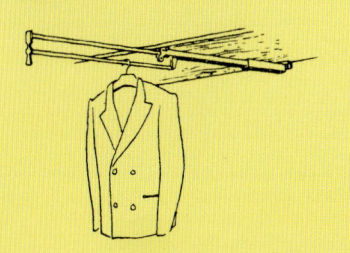

Instead of the customary single bar, 5 feet 6 inches high, subdivide your closet. Use the usual bar only part way across—for overcoats, evening dresses, and other long articles of clothing. For blouses, jackets, suits, use bars at two levels, the upper bar still within reach at 80 inches, the lower above dragging level at 40 inches.

If your closet has enough height, 9 feet or more, hangers are available mounted on 3-foot poles. With these, you can attach hangers to hooks on the closet ceiling, or to a bar or a rod near the ceiling, lowering them off easily when needed.

Use the back of the door and the inside of the closet for additional space—as shown in the illustrations on these pages.

Wire hangers are inexpensive and in common use—but remember that while they may easily hold a woman's blouse, they are likely to lose shape, or even collapse completely, under a man's heavier coat.

Many space-saving devices are available in department and hardware stores; this seems to be a fertile field for mechanical ingenuity.

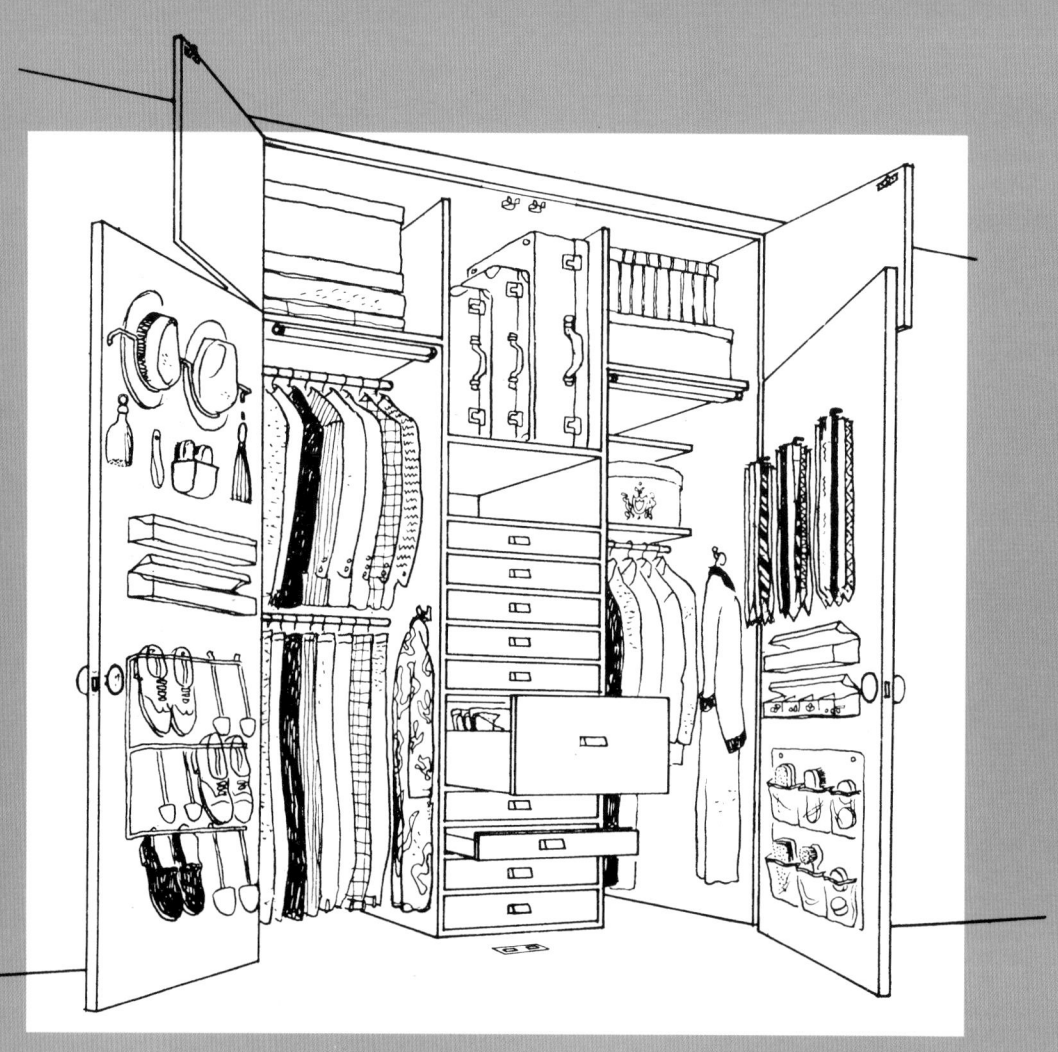

CLOSET FOR A MAN

Good, spacious closets can save much housework. Confining all that pertains to dress in a single well-organized area minimizes litter, and saves daily dusting and arranging of chests and bureaus. Note the lighting, the drawer knobs (143) (that can be marked for identification of their contents), two-tier hanging, transparent bags and boxes, the slanted rack for handbags, hook for hanging current night clothes.

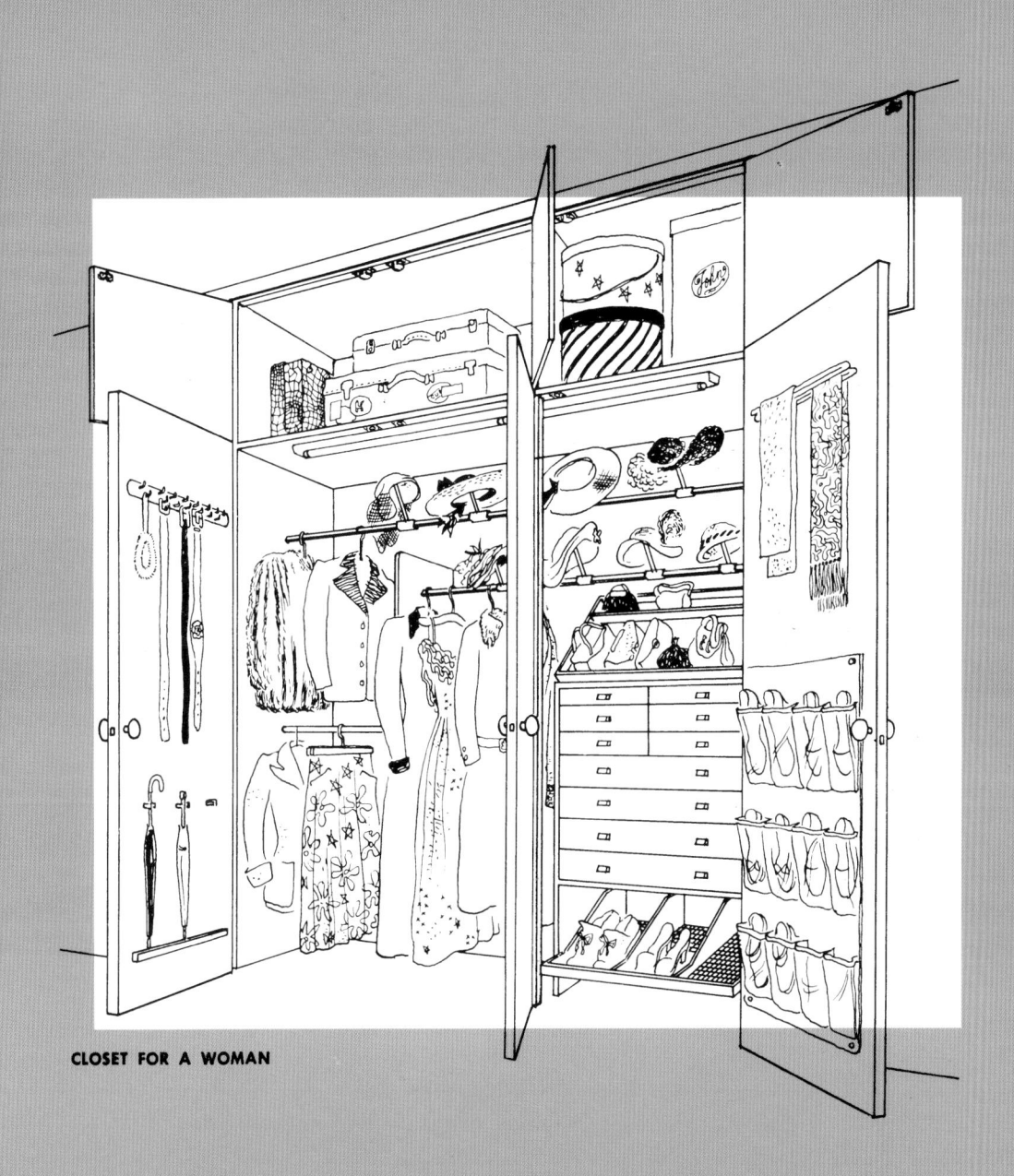

CLOSET FOR A WOMAN

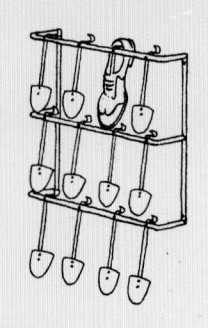

Shoe rack combined with shoe trees (45)

Rack-type shelf for closet door (49)

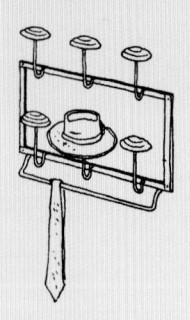

Hatrack plus rod (7)

Folding tie rack (7)

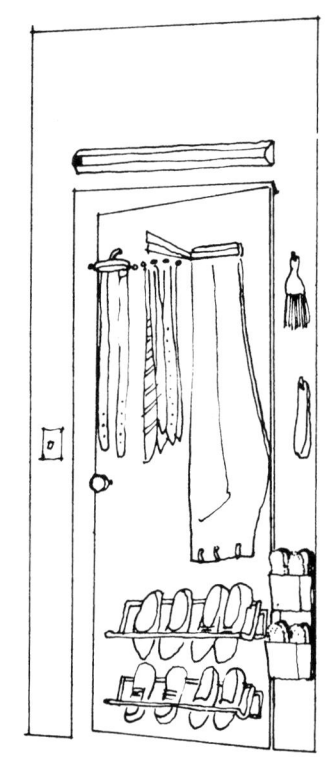

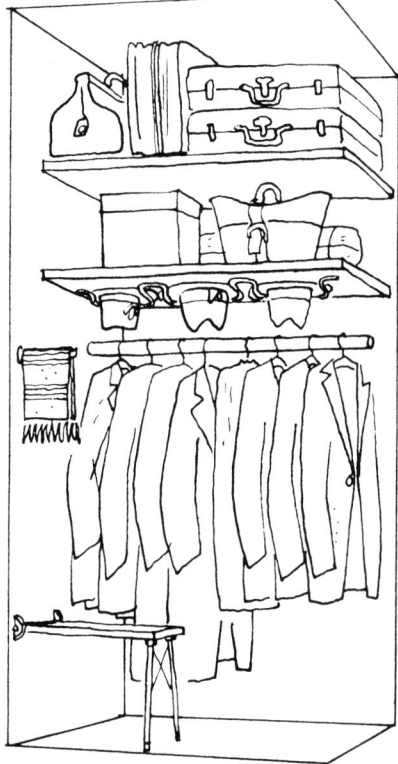

Ordinary 3-foot closet fitted for a man. Note fluorescent light above the inside of door, drop-leaf bench for shoeshining and for reaching luggage, use of the underside of the shelf for hats. (Use of back of door shown on "torn-away" wall at left.)

Cabinet attached to back of door (44)

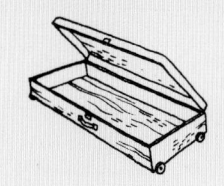

For storage under beds: cedar or aluminum boxes (50)

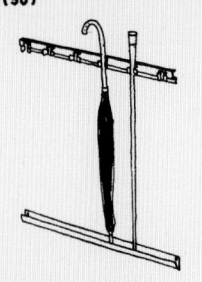

Umbrella holder (7)

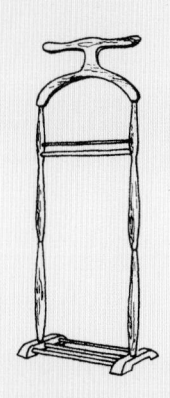

At night, hang clothes on valet stand (51)

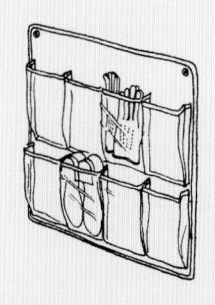

The usual 3-foot-wide closet with a small door can be made more useful by installing some of the excellent hardware now on the market. (Shown with wall torn away at right to indicate fittings on door and surrounding area.)

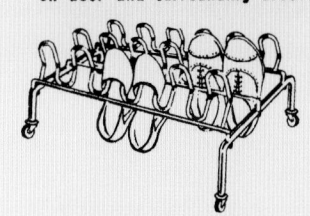

Keep shoes on rack that rolls out of closet (47)

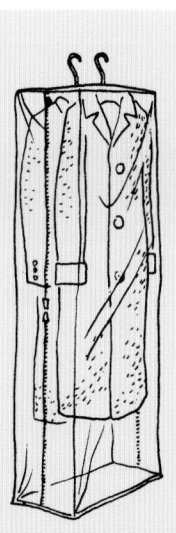

Use vinolyte shoe bag for many things (48)

Transparent vinolyte storage bag (48)

63

Furnishing the Dressing Area: Beside storage facilities, you need these for dressing: a chair or a bench; a full-length mirror or a smaller one, high enough up; a shelf or a drawer for a man's combs and brushes; and provision for hanging clothes as they are shed, such as:

Rungs on the back of the chair;
Bars on the wall or closet door;

A silent valet (51), or an old-fashioned costumer.

The dressing table may be eliminated entirely to save space and housework; many women prefer to comb their hair and make up before the well-lighted bathroom mirror. For this, provide an extra medicine chest deep enough to hold cosmetic jars, or shelves of glass or laminated plastic, or a small chest of drawers.

A woman who uses a dressing table should realize that it is really a workbench, and keep it functional, with no ruffled skirts to gather powder and dust and get caught in the drawers. Here are some desirable features, though no ready-made piece we have seen combines all of them:

Functional Dressing-Tables

Stainproof top: glass; or see the Table-top Chart for other materials and finishes.
A light fixed to the mirror, or a light on each side.
Easily washed interiors of cosmetic drawers; some come with enameled metal lining. You can line yours with plastic cloth or the aluminum foil you use in the kitchen.

A hinged door with shelves attached, which can hold cosmetic bottles—in effect a tray.
Storage space for your accessories: such as a shallow tray-type drawer for jewelry; shallow drawers for gloves, scarves, belts, handkerchiefs; a sectional drawer for stockings; a deep file-cabinet type of drawer for handbags.

Furnishing the Leisure Area: Each leisure-hour activity calls for its own furniture. Save both space and housekeeping with built-in arrangements:

Counters or pull-out slabs for work or writing surfaces.
Wall cupboards for storing tools

and materials.
A bench or stool to slide under counter or into wall cupboard.

To avoid putting away work in progress, hide the whole work area with a screen, or a roller blind, or a draw curtain of fabric, wood, or bamboo.

Whatever seating you have in this area should have simple, lightweight frames, rollers or domes, and tight-seat upholstery, for easy maintenance.

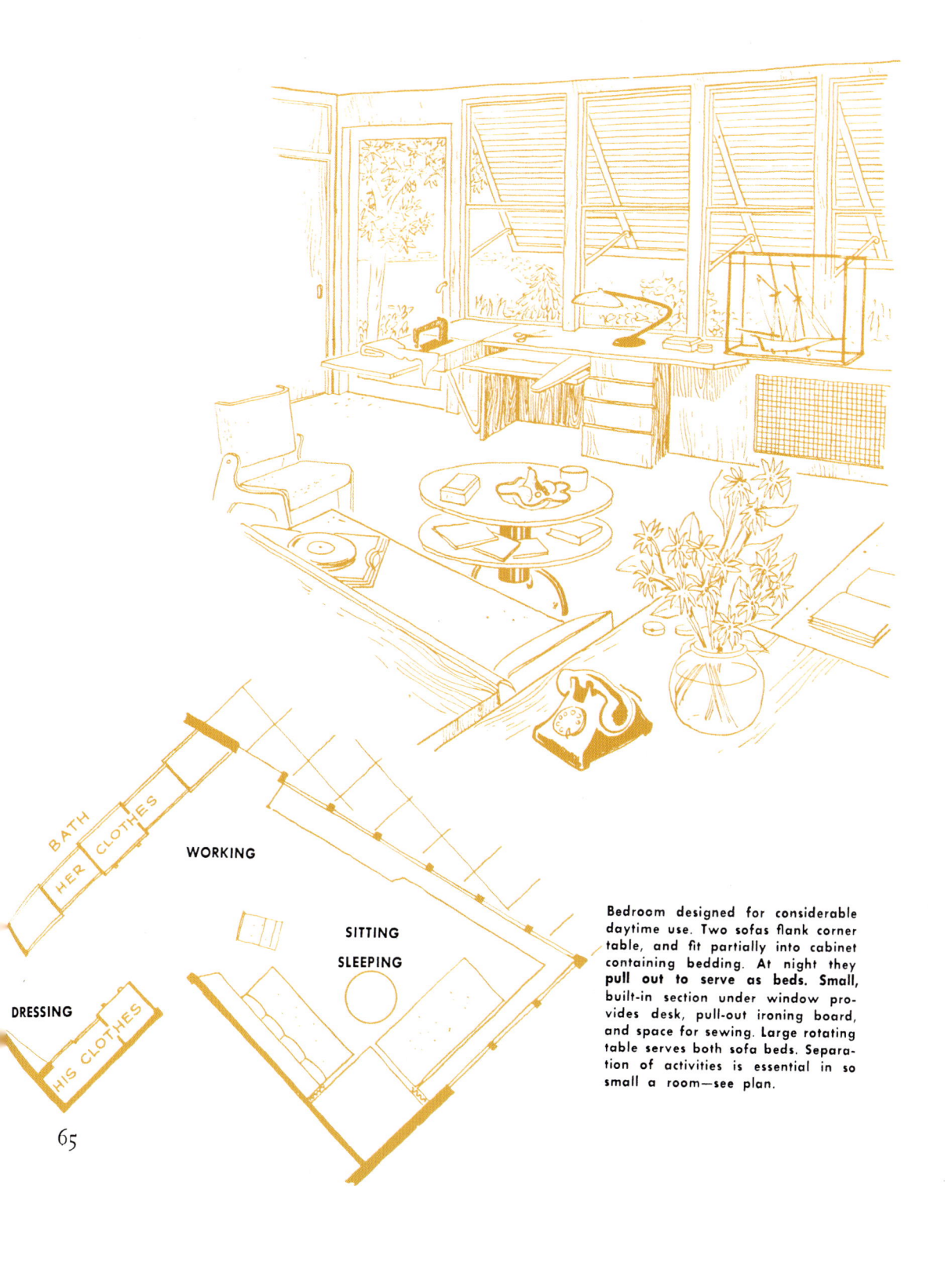

Bedroom designed for considerable daytime use. Two sofas flank corner table, and fit partially into cabinet containing bedding. At night they **pull out to serve as beds.** Small, built-in section under window provides desk, pull-out ironing board, and space for sewing. Large rotating table serves both sofa beds. Separation of activities is essential in so small a room—see plan.

None of the traditional heart-warmers—no canopied bed, delicate night table, fluffy lamps, skirted vanity, drapes, valance, or tie-backs—and yet we consider this classic of modern design by architect Richard Neutra the most beautiful bedroom we have ever seen.

The Bedroom for a Single Adult: This is not actually a separate problem. Basic principles of planning and furnishing are the same here as for the master bedroom, with less space needed for sleeping and dressing-storage areas and more for leisure. This is an extremely personal room; its character is determined by whether its occupant is an elderly relative, a grown son or daughter, or a guest rather than a permanent resident.

What, No Victorian?

5. We can well imagine the headshaking of many readers as they go through these pages—because for many generations the bedroom has been considered the sentimental core of the home, and, through the dictates of fashion and etiquette, has become a veritable Valentine chock-full of all the feminine goodies, the classic models being the Victorian, Colonial, and French bedrooms so popular today. It is for this reason that we pause briefly here to argue and amplify the aesthetics of our case.

If you are so enamored of the charm of other centuries that you can stand the gruesome, tawdry look of such rooms each morning and then do the work of other centuries to restore order—then have such a room. But if you really want to save work, and to have a room that properly fulfills its intended functions, you'll have to give up your dreams of living in another age and enjoy your own twentieth century.

Of course, in a room as personal as a bedroom, the occupants' personality should be expressed. And, if designed and planned properly, the simplified interiors prescribed here can serve as a flattering background to set off dramatically and effectively whatever personal touches you want. Your favorite pictures can be hung on one wall, or your favorite collection (old coins, or shells, for example) kept under glass. New coated fabrics and wall coverings enable you to surround yourself with favorite colors.

Perhaps you will have to change your ideas of charm and beauty. After all, there are lots of different kinds—Georgian and Victorian are only two brand names.

The bedrooms illustrated in this chapter are devoid of traditional furnishings . . . yet they possess qualities of charm, dignity, and a serene kind of beauty that cannot be found in traditional rooms. Learn to enjoy them.

Bathrooms

6. This adjunct of the bedroom is probably the most-used room in the house; its planning and furnishing, therefore, should receive serious consideration—instead of being taken for granted as a standard, unalterable arrangement.

Storage is probably the most neglected item. A recent survey by the Pierce Foundation disclosed that bathrooms contain the least adequate storage space of any part of the home. So if you're planning a new bathroom, or if you're able to remodel, minimize the time and energy consumed in lugging things in and out by a built-in closet large enough to hold all bathroom supplies: toilet paper, soap, and so on; and also provide room here for all necessary cleaning materials and tools. (See Bathroom Cleaning Closet Check List, Appendix A, page 192.)

Fixtures: The standard medicine cabinet is often sadly inadequate, too. Consider installing an oversized one, or having several—perhaps one just for cosmetics, if this serves as a dressing room.

A stall shower will eliminate the water-splashing that's inevitable with a tub shower. If possible, have the floor level of the stall below that of the rest of the room, and have a sliding glass door rather than shower curtains.

A closed-in bathtub, if possible—square ones provide seating space at the corners and are helpful for dressing, washing feet, or bathing young children.

If the bathroom is used by adults only, you can save back-bending by having your washbowl higher than the standard 30 inches—we find 40 inches best for us.

If it's a family bathroom, consider dividing it in three: shower or bathtub compartment, with door; toilet closet, with door; lavatory or washbasin section. Fixtures will cost no more than usual, and the space required need be little more than for the standard arrangement. If this isn't practical, consider having two washbasins, if there is room for them.

Lighting: Have the simplest, most washable fixtures. We prefer the tubular incandescent type, which is so easy to clean, installed either across the top or at the sides of the mirror above the washbasin. The most practical location for the electrical outlet is alongside the basin, on a level with the top. For general lighting: a flush, or diffuse direct, ceiling fixture, so constructed that the glass can easily be removed.

Floor: Most easily cleaned is glazed, vitreous tile in a dark color.

Consider a drain, so it can be hosed, with no wiping necessary.

Walls: In a room exposed to such extreme changes in atmosphere and temperature, these should never be painted; paper or other coverings are apt to peel. Vitreous tile or glass is most practical.

Furnishings: These should be as carefully planned and worked out as in a ship's galley—with nothing superfluous. The fancy curtained, over-decorated bathroom soon becomes a travesty of the rest of the house. Our formula is: light-colored tile and fixtures (they show spots less quickly); dark floor; ceiling, window and trim painted a bright color. Solid colors throughout, with no curtains or decorations.

Work-Saving Bathroom Furnishings

An adequate-sized hamper, preferably the built-in, bin type.

A step-on garbage can; more sanitary than a wastebasket; or, ideal, a rubbish chute.

A towel rack for *each* member of the family (with a name plate over it), long enough to hold the full, unfolded width of the towel, if possible.

A labeled towel rack for guests, and paper guest towels.

A paper-cup dispenser, eliminating washing glasses, and more sanitary.

A paper towel holder, saving laundry, and handy for immediate wiping up of anything spilled.

A holder for facial tissues.

A bath-mat bar—of an adequate size, to discourage leaving the mat on the floor, or over the edge of a just-cleaned bathtub (into which it's apt to shake dust, talcum powder, etc.).

Individual unbreakable containers—a plastic box or bread basket will do—for tooth paste, toothbrush, shaving articles, comb, brush, etc. These prevent clutter, and they're more likely to be used by your family than the medicine cabinet.

Soap dishes (with removable plastic insert for easy cleaning); a cellulose sponge here, too, to encourage cleaning of tub and basin by each user.

Pegs or hooks on the walls, to hold shower caps, back-scrubbers, a young child's seat cover —all paraphernalia that's frequently used and otherwise might clutter the floor, basin, bathtub corners, etc.

If you have small children: a shelf with a raised front edge over the bathtub, for boats, rubber toys, etc.

If you can't avoid doing personal laundry in the bathroom, because of space problems, at least install fold-down metal or plastic drying racks on the wall; or rig up a pull-down ceiling drier over the tub—so you won't have to use towel racks.

For shower curtains, plastic film is the most satisfactory material. It dries quickly, and soap, which is a medium for bacteria-causing mildew, can easily be wiped off it. Fabric-backed plastics tend to peel; water-repellent fabrics catch water and soap in their hems, and mildew.

The Child's Room

7. Planning the Nursery: It should be close to the mother's room, bright and sunny, and big. Often we think of a child's room as small because the child is small, and then wonder where to put bath, scales, high chair, playpen, and accumulating toys. It is important to store all clothing together, and all equipment for feeding and bathing together—each clearly separated from the other. Most important is plenty of clear floor space.

Floor

Linoleum, rubber tile, greaseproof asphalt tile, and latex-bonded terrazzo (1), are desirable floor surfaces, being smooth-surfaced, resilient, and easy to clean (see the Floor Chart for others). Choose mottled rather than plain, dark rather than light, colors.

A permanent rug isn't necessary here. However, when the child is learning to walk, a large short-piled rug, or a washable cotton rug or carpeting, in a fairly dark color, will soften his falls and help him get a grip on the floor.

Walls

For thoroughly washable wall materials, resistant to stains and to scuffing by furniture and toys, consult the Wall Chart. Some on which a child can draw, which quickly wash clean whether he writes with chalk, crayon, pastels, or water paints (encourage crayons and water paints; chalk makes dust), include alkyd-resin-base enamel paint (26), plastic-coated paper or fabric, and the Plus-Lite Board (52), a white blackboard that takes crayon.

Windows

Surely, you want no frilly curtains on the windows here. Your aims are light control and guarding against drafts and sifting dust.

- **R**oller blinds of wood slats (53), or plastic-coated fabric (54), or shades that draw from the sill upward (see Window Coverings, Chapter V, page 99).
- **D**raw curtains, window-sill length, tubbable or plastic material.
- **A** ventilator across the lower part of the window, of aluminum (55), rather than glass for safety reasons; no sharp edges.
- **O**ne-room air-conditioning if the budget can stand it, for cleanliness and work-saving even more than for temperature. (The baby's doctor should be consulted first; he might not approve keeping the nursery much cooler than the rest of the house in hot weather.)

Lighting

Floor and table lamps with their trailing wires are dangerous. Electric outlets should, if possible, be placed high on the wall above a child's reach. Two light fixtures are basic:

- **An** overhead fixture for general illumination, indirect type, of simple design for easy cleaning.
- **A** night light with bulb of low wattage or blue tint, fastened on the wall at adult height, near enough to the crib to throw light there but out of reach of the child when old enough to stand up.

Furniture for the Nursery: The first two years of a child's life are full of strenuous physical experiment: crawling, standing up, walking, climbing. To spare him bumps and frustrations, and his parents anxiety, have all furniture with flush or rounded corners, sturdy, and with nothing loose or hanging or unstable to be pulled down or overturned. Everything from floor to ceiling should be washable. This is an obvious first thought (too often it is also the last). But it does not have to mean a hospital look. There is no good reason for baby furniture to be always anemic white, pink, or blue. You can wash a bright-red chest or crib as clean as a pale one.

Cribs

The frilly bassinet, so soon obsolete, is a waste of money; laundering its trimmings is a waste of labor. Its virtues are its height, and the way you can wheel or carry it around the house. A washbasket with strong handles or mounted on a stand with casters serves as well. But you don't need either, with the right crib.

A wooden crib rather than metal, either in a natural wood finish (see Table-top Chart for the right finish) or painted in hard enamel *without lead*; babies, like puppies, chew.

A crib in which the surface of the bed itself can be raised and lowered, as well as the sides. The high bed is a back-saver during infancy, and can be lowered when the child is standing up so that the sides are high enough for his safety. A less expensive way to raise the bed is to mount an ordinary crib on wooden blocks, removable later.

A crib on wheels with screened top and sides, if there is a terrace or porch where it can be wheeled out for the daily airing. This may replace the big costly perambulator, which is hard to get up and down stairs, takes up space, and is an extra cleaning chore. Later a stroller will serve for walks.

Good rollers or wheels on any type of crib. If you want to move the baby around the house, check the width of your doors before buying a crib with this in mind.

Infant bedding is standard and apparently irreducible. For the useless show pillow, substitute plastic-covered padding now made in bolster-like pieces (56) to fit around all sides of the crib. Crib sheets come with ready-made mitered corners (43) to fit over the mattress, or you can sew corners on.

Storage

We have never seen factory-made storage pieces that really fit a baby's wardrobe. The small drawers in standard nursery chests are too big for orderly arrangement of infant clothes, the big drawers are too small for bulky bed linens. The compartment for hanging clothes is wasted for the first year, when the best-dressed modern baby wears nothing that can't be folded into a drawer. And the small surface area is inadequate counter space. Suggestions:

Infant Clothing Storage

Built-in wall storage with partitioned drawers is efficient, space-saving, and not likely to be more expensive than good baby furniture.

Of the ready-made pieces, a couple of adult-size unit chests with small and large drawers (partition them yourself) are more satisfactory than standard nursery chests. Matching toy shelves can be added later.

If a nursery chest is bought, be sure the hanging compartment has a shelf, or shelves, for blankets, carriage robes, etc., removable later.

For nursery equipment (bath, scales, etc.) use the hanging compartment of a built-in closet, or the normal bedroom closet in the room, or a curtained-off corner of the room for a clutter closet.

A work surface: counter or table of convenient counter height, with shallow drawers like pull-out trays to hold the dozen small items needed in bathing, dressing, feeding, changing; this has yet to be produced commercially—you can perhaps make or improvise one. It will need a waterproof top (see Table-top Chart).

The latest folding bathinette (57) is a godsend for bathing infants. It can hold all the numerous articles that you need for this task, which must be done carefully, efficiently, and quickly. Folded, it can find a place in the smallest room.

With no separate room for the baby, one ingenious father put up shelves between two chests for his son and his paraphernalia.

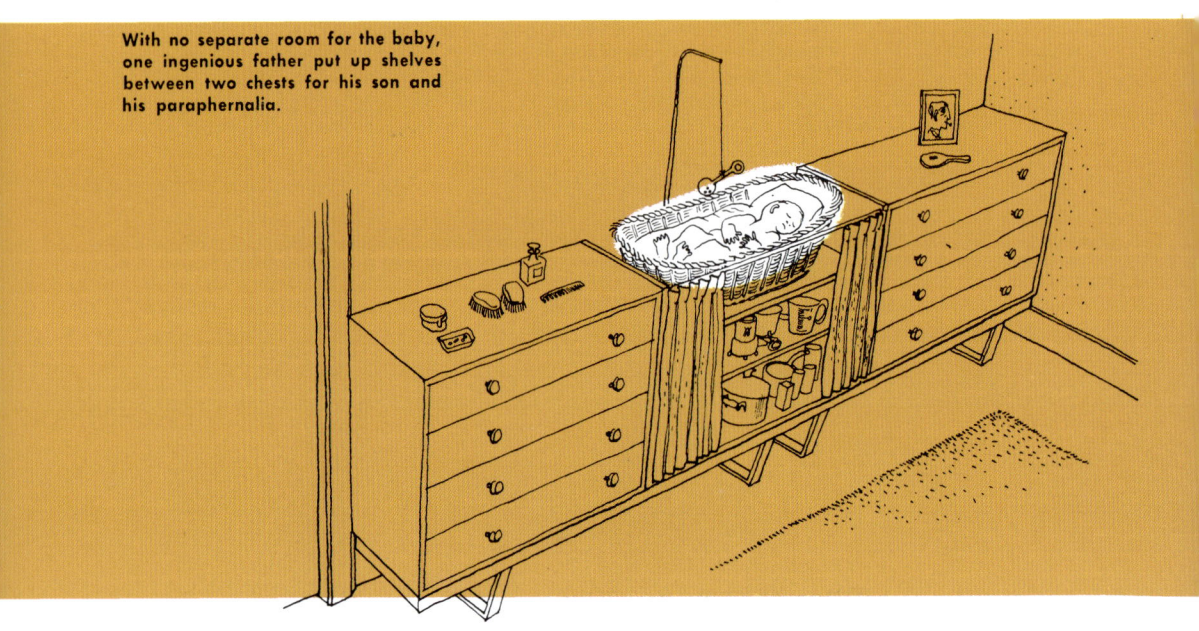

Other Nursery Furniture

A high chair or a chair table.
A playpen: one with a floor of its own, raised a few inches off the floor of the room as a protection against cold and drafts, and on casters. Plastic cover for the pad.
A comfortable low chair or two for adults, upholstered in plastic or plastic-coated fabric.
An adult bed for the mother or the nurse during a child's illness; box spring and mattress on legs only—no hard corners. Cover it with a washable spread.

If space limitations require turning part of the parents' bedroom into a nursery, the leisure area will of course have to be converted. This will mean using only the most essential articles of baby furniture, utilizing leisure-area shelf and storage space for the layette, and above all putting up a screen to shield the baby from the lights that will be on in the room while he is asleep.

Toddler-to-Teen Room: Learning is childhood's work, and young children learn by playing. A good many of the clashes that devour a mother's energy, and frustrate the child's natural drive to learn, can be avoided if the child's play is treated with respect and planned for in his own room.

Toys and Toy Storage

Have a clear floor space, not a passageway, where unfinished construction or other work in progress can be left overnight, or even for days.
Provide adequate storage space *within the child's reach*, so that he can put his own things away. This should be open shelves; it makes cleanup easier, and drawers are difficult for a young child to open. Have some deep shelves, 18 inches high, for larger toys and games.
Have a junk box or corner: one space or container where the child can pile things in any order or none, where he can store odd collections that are precious to him at the moment. Be sure the lid is lightweight and will stay open, if it's a chest; or have it open door-fashion in the front. Collapsible chests of heavy cardboard are good, inexpensive junk boxes.
Provide a sturdy rectangular stool that he can carry or push around to where he needs it. He will be less tempted to climb where he shouldn't and pull things down by accident in an effort to reach them.
Hollow-block furniture (58), very new, can be built—perhaps by the child alone, or with help — into toy shelves, worktables, storage bins, steps for climbing. Construction can be temporary or permanent, and revised with the child's growth. Worktable tops are available for them, with hardy surfaces of inlaid linoleum. A hollow block on casters is a wagon to carry blocks or toys across the room; upside down, it is a sturdy climbing tool; with a square foam-rubber

cushion added it is a comfortable seat.

Attach to the wall a large, soft wallboard, such as Homasote (59)—it saves the walls and can serve as a pin-up board.

Electric train tracks can be fastened to two or more large panels of plywood or pressed wallboard; these can easily be joined together, and after playtime can be detached and stacked against a wall.

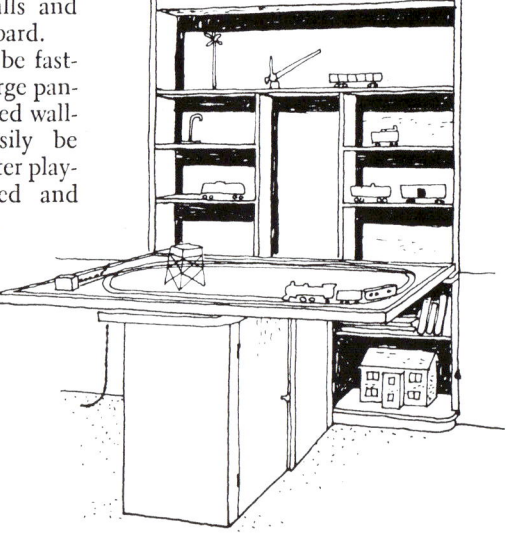

For electric trains, the track is attached to one side of a large panel, which swings up to form the door of a train-and-toy storage cupboard. Designed by Joseph Aronson.

To avoid a lot of nursery pickup: a ping-pong table, or a piece of ¾ plywood, or an old door, or boxes (which can also house toys).

The planned built-in clothes storage of the nursery, or the bank of unit chests, will continue to serve the child as they did the infant. If the child can begin now to learn good habits in caring for his own possessions, it will mean eventual laborsaving for the mother—so be patient during the learning period and provide him with storage he can cope with:

Clothes Storage

Let the bar in the closet be low enough to permit the child to reach it and hang his own clothes himself. A series of sockets at 6-inch intervals upward can be put in now, and the bar raised as he grows.

Drawers in clothes chests should be low and slide easily, should be roomy enough for their contents, and departmentalized to help the child in getting out his own clean things. Paste a cutout on each drawer, representing the clothes within.

Drawers should also be pegged at the inside edges so they don't pull out and dump everything, including the child, on the floor.

The crib is replaced by a 5-foot youth's bed with removable sides. (Resist the temptation to outfit a room used for two children with a cute double-decker bunk; it means most laborious bedmaking.)

When school age arrives, you'll need some new furniture: desk, workbench, bookshelves, a dollhouse for a girl. Select them for sturdy construction and stainproof finish, and begin now to plan in terms of the orderly subdivisions of an adult room.

The Teen-Age Son or Daughter: The room-of-one's-own impulse is powerful from adolescence on—a place for study, for visits from best friends, for radio and phonograph listening without protest from the family—and where the impulse can be successfully met, family harmony is served. The housewife gets her reward, too. A young person in whose room there is a place for everything is likely to put at least some things back in their places.

The same recommendations for sleeping and dressing arrangements, and storage planning, apply here as in the master bedroom. Most important here are the extracurricular uses of the room, an expanded leisure area. To keep this from becoming a major housekeeping headache, it is essential to *departmentalize*, keeping each activity strictly in its own space: dressing, hobbies, study. Use the sturdiest, most practical materials for *all* furnishings—from desk to draperies.

A studio bed for mother to rest on or sleep in on those nights of sickness; marble table top, rocking chair, and closet or chest with lots of small drawers are timesavers when the child is a baby.

76

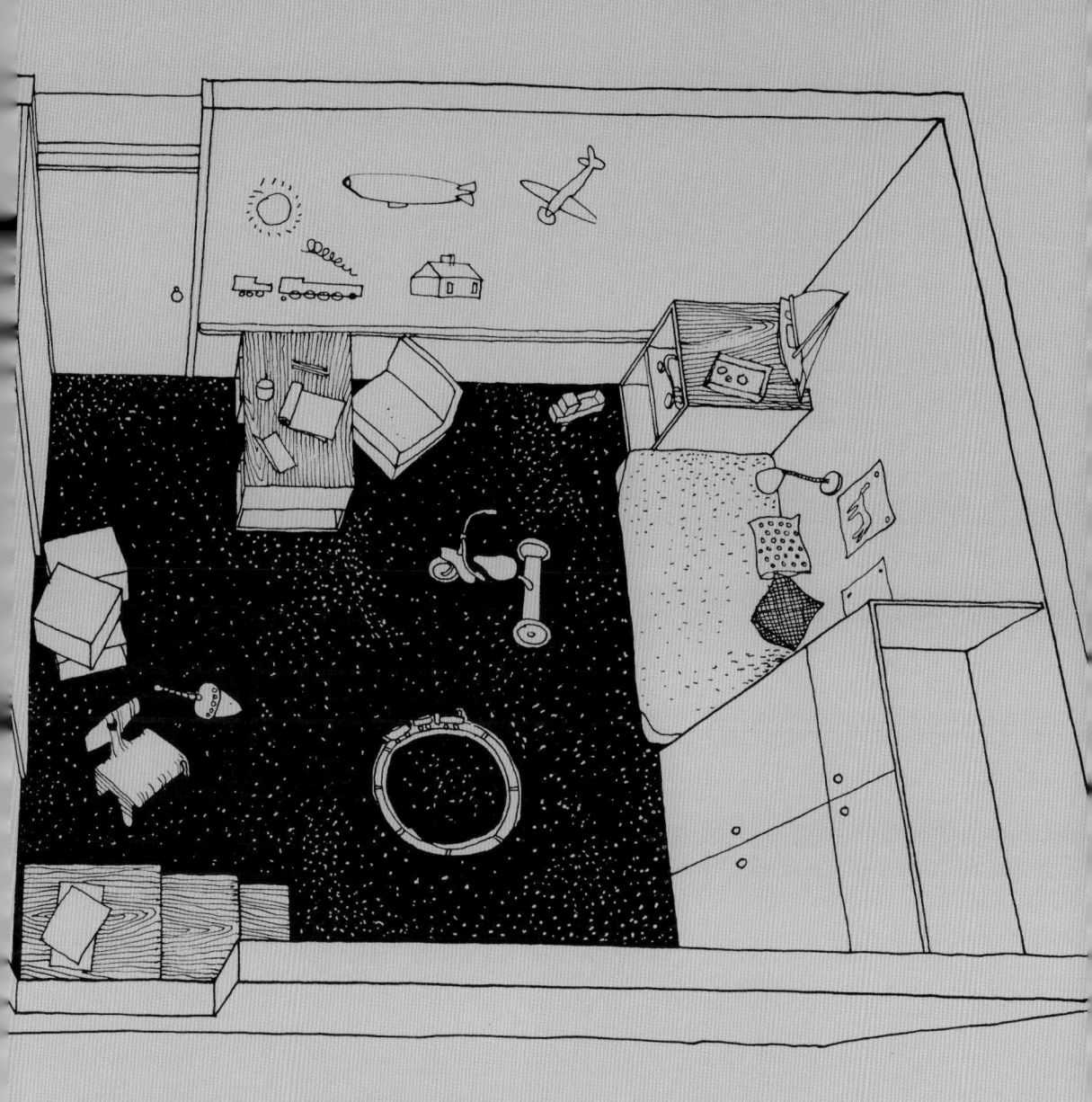

Plan the nursery to grow with the child. Here a large room is divided by a sliding partition into two rooms for two children. Begin with latex-bonded terrazzo on the floor and washable wall covering. In the infants' room, two simple sections of wall storage, rollers on furniture. At the "toddler" stage, a youth bed replaces the crib.

78

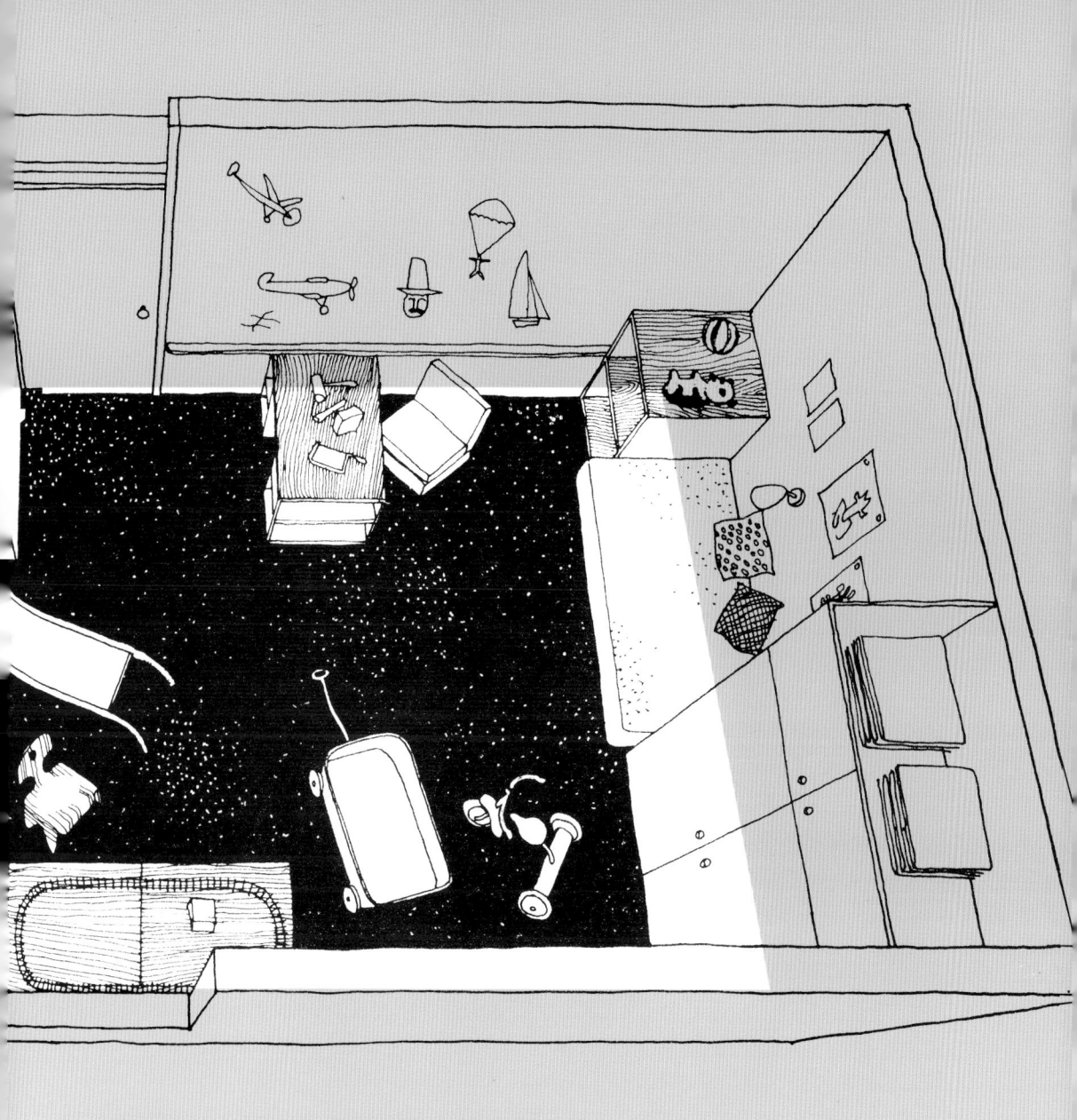

In the second, or "rough-and-tumble" stage, the partition may be rolled back to provide a large play space. Together, the two rooms sketched measure only 25 by 11 feet. Note walls treated to withstand childhood art efforts (52); sturdy, simple, hollow block furniture (58); the swinging wardrobe; the absence of table and floor lamps.

To make housekeeping the teen-age room easier, departmentalize the activities by arrangement. Notice, here, how dressing, sleeping, and study are separated.

In the final stage, the partition is permanently closed; wall storage is completed to include a work section for teen-age boy, a vanity for girl. Colors and added furnishings now indicate individual personality.

CHAPTER V

ALL AROUND THE HOUSE

NOTHING IS MORE EXASPERATING to the housewife who has just finished her labors, who has won the battle against every sign of dust and upheaval within her home, than that awful moment when the outer door is flung open and family or friends carry in mud, dirt, and disorder from the outside. Nothing—unless perhaps it is the perplexing discovery that, in some mysterious way, dust or soot has filtered through the windows to soil or ruin walls and furniture.

So this chapter is largely concerned with the important problem of controlling this dirt and dust that enter by way of doors, windows, and hallways. Also considered, as closely related matters, are the doors and stairways inside the house.

This may seem primarily a chapter for builders and homeowners. But dwellers in apartments and rented houses will find help here too, in the furnishing of a foyer or the improvement of its closet, and the section on window coverings and draperies is for everyone.

Entrances

1. The entrance areas can be effective blockades against outdoor dirt. Modern architects, in rebellion against the clichéd design of old-fashioned entrance halls, have tended to abolish not only the hallway but the foyer as well, and open the front door right into the living room. This carries a good idea too far.

The Front Door and Foyer Area: To do its job properly, this area should make it almost impossible for anyone to come in without

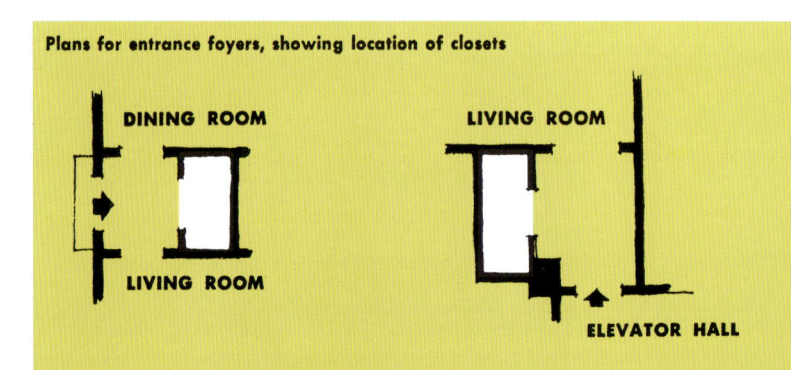

Plans for entrance foyers, showing location of closets

DINING ROOM

LIVING ROOM

LIVING ROOM

ELEVATOR HALL

wiping feet, putting down packages, and putting away coat, hat, scarf, umbrella, rubbers, galoshes, and the like, and conversely should make it easy for them to find their possessions on the way out. It must also be easy to clean and to keep in order. A lavatory here is a good idea, too, for family as well as guests, to avoid tracking outdoor dirt all the way to a bathroom.

Certainly not carpeting, and not even linoleum or asphalt or rubber tile is recommended for the floor here, but a hard surface that can be swept, mopped, or even hosed if you have a drain here.

Floor

Stone, marble, terrazzo (1), ceramic tile, or magnesite (3), of a dark color, mottled.
Cove baseboard and corners in the same material.
A door mat, large enough so that one has to step on it, and of a material that really wipes shoes, preferably sunk flush with the floor just *inside* the door. Foot scrapers are often ignored, rubber and metal mats inefficient. Coco matting is the most aggressive shoe-wiper. It's the one we recommend, although it needs occasional beating and cleaning, and is not especially durable, having to be replaced from time to time.
An outdoor mat may also be of coco matting, though it will not survive many months of exposure. More durable though less efficient, is a metal mat of the chain-link kind, or a deeply embossed rubber mat.
Both an indoor and an outdoor mat will be helpful for most of the year.

Walls

Pick a really washable wall material from the Wall Chart, one which not only is easy to clean but also is rain-resistant. Rounded corners for foyer and closet walls are desirable, but expensive.

Foyer Furniture

Have *no* furniture here, except—
A shelf for putting things down, rather than a table with legs that impede cleaning.
A mirror above this, preferably without a frame to clean.
A bench to sit on for putting on and taking off overshoes, sturdy enough for a young child to stand on for help with a snowsuit.
An umbrella rack with drain.

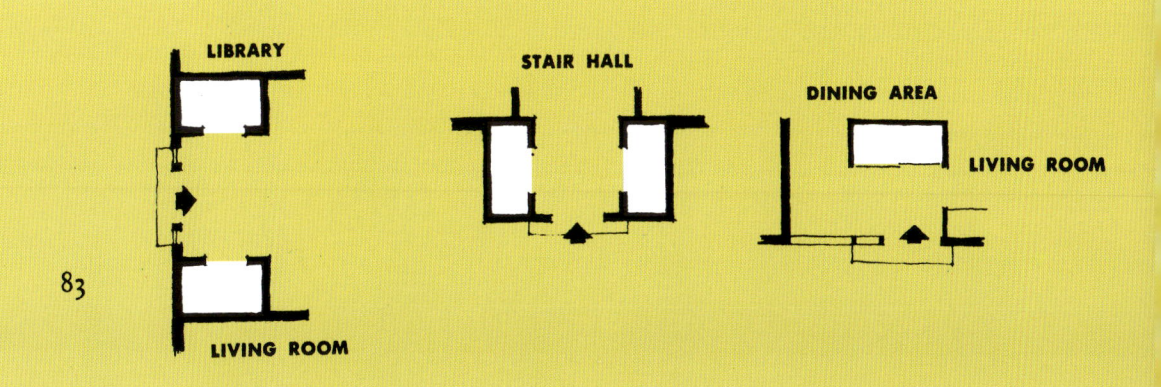

The Entrance Closet is the heart of the foyer. The usual hall closet —too small, too dark, too far from the door, lacking any convenience beyond hooks and a hat shelf—becomes a squirrel's nest of

"Dream" entrance closet. Walk-in closet with two doors for a family living in the country. Tile floor, low rods for childrens' use, name-tagged compartments for gloves and scarves, raised wire shelves for overshoes, shoeshine pullout tray under the sink, a wall for sports equipment, lots of light.

84

tangled clothing and jumbled overshoes, so that the members of the family shy at using it, and scatter wearing apparel all through the house.

The ideal closet is directly opposite the door, and large enough to walk into, even to wheel in the baby buggy or a bicycle. Even if you must make do with an existing closet that is smaller, you can probably make it useful with some of these ideal closet features:

Improving Smaller Closets

Paint it white inside—use alkyd enamel (26), or see the Wall Chart.

Light it below as well as above.

Arrange shelves, rods, and other fixtures within easy reach, no higher than 6 feet, the bottom one no lower than 8 inches from the floor.

For small children, have separate shelves, rod, or hooks within *their* reach.

Label the places where things go, if not for each person, at least for the children.

Have separate bins for each pair of rubbers or galoshes, with bottoms of screening or perforated metal, so that dirt drops through to one place on the floor for easier cleaning, instead of collecting in the bin.

Have a long, shallow, partitioned drawer or shelf for gloves, scarves, earmuffs, hoods, and caps.

Have pegs, high or low, for hanging sports equipment like golf bags, hockey sticks, skates, skis, and a bin or a drawer for balls and baseball gloves. The amount of available space will dictate whether all sports equipment can be stored here, or the children's more plentiful equipment in their rooms, or all of it elsewhere.

A shelf above is a poor solution for hats; hang them in racks on the underside of a shelf (7), or on pegs on a vertical wall, or on the back of the door.

Look into ready-made closet space-savers; some suggestions are made in the preceding chapter, under Clothes Storage.

A closet too shallow to walk into, which is difficult to use because it has a narrow doorway, can be made more practical by tearing down the door and adjoining wall to make the opening extend the entire width of the closet space (provided it is not a bearing wall; that is, one which helps hold up the house). Install sliding doors, or double doors opening out, to cover this entire opening. Or hang a drape or a screen; perhaps a bamboo-slat curtain that is drawn vertically or horizontally, as you prefer.

Even with strictly utilitarian purposes, the entrance can and should express the spirit of the home to which it is the threshold. It can have a pleasant informality, be gay and striking, or be dignified, if you, your architect or designer, select and carefully combine the materials and colors used on floor, walls, doors, and ceiling.

Practical and attractive entrance for a country or suburban home—brick floor with sunken mat, a bench without legs, and lots of closet space directly facing the entrance door.

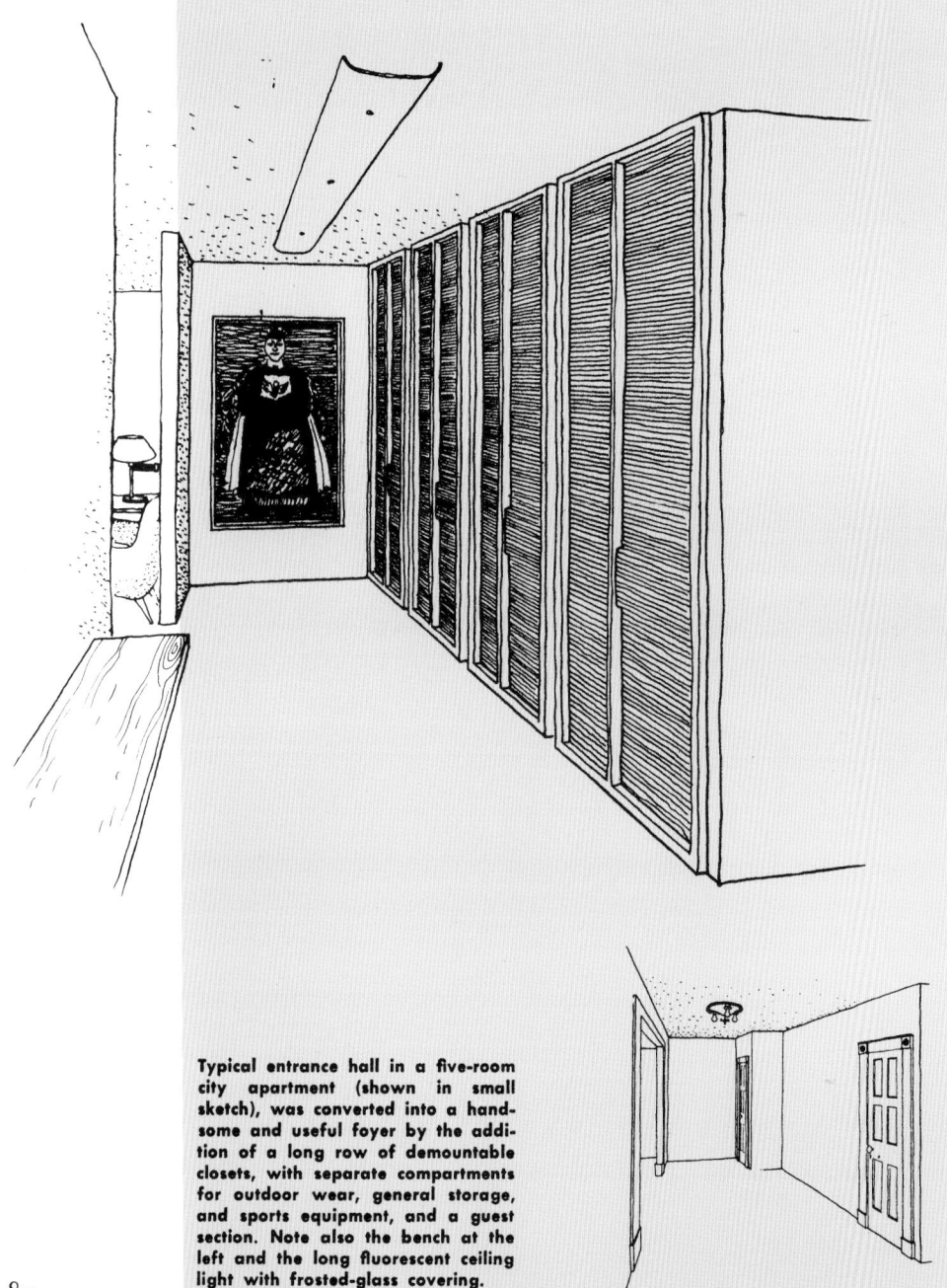

Typical entrance hall in a five-room city apartment (shown in small sketch), was converted into a handsome and useful foyer by the addition of a long row of demountable closets, with separate compartments for outdoor wear, general storage, and sports equipment, and a guest section. Note also the bench at the left and the long fluorescent ceiling light with frosted-glass covering.

87

Other Entrances: Where they exist or can be built, these can take some of the burden from the front door and can make housekeeping easier. They also should have easily scrubbed floors, cove baseboards, washable walls, and door mats of good size. A drain in the floor is often more feasible at other entrances than the front one, and makes it possible to wash down the entrance with a hose.

Back Door 'Shipping and Receiving'

The back door or kitchen door is the delivery entrance, and can be a domestic version of the shipping and receiving department of an office or a factory. Here is where all supplies come in, and many kinds of things go out—garbage, laundry, clothes for the cleaner. It can serve to keep traffic out of the kitchen, and boxes and wrappings out of the rest of the house. Suggestions:

Shelves for dry groceries and certain supplies that do not go into the refrigerator. If the shelves are in the partition between entrance and kitchen, they may also open on the kitchen side. Otherwise, keep immediate supplies in the kitchen, reserves in this entrance pantry.

A shelf or counter for incoming laundry and packages, and outgoing things to be called for. This cuts down interruptions in your work or leisure; you get things ready to go out and put

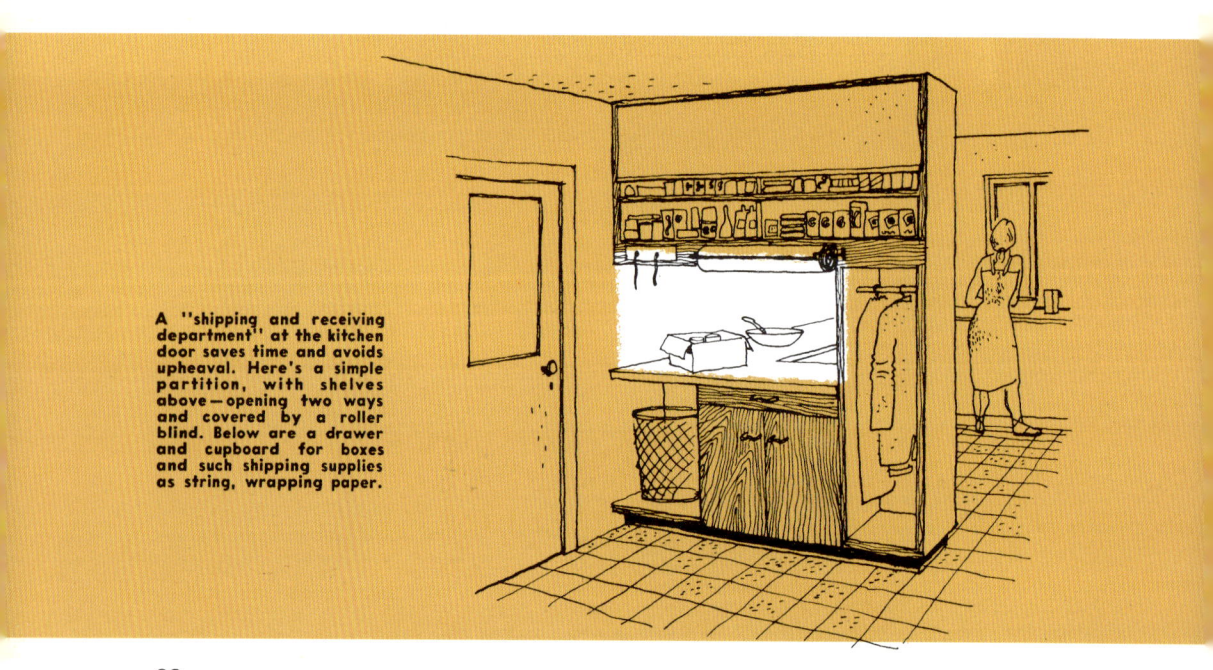

A "shipping and receiving department" at the kitchen door saves time and avoids upheaval. Here's a simple partition, with shelves above—opening two ways and covered by a roller blind. Below are a drawer and cupboard for boxes and such shipping supplies as string, wrapping paper.

88

▌delivered things away at your convenience.
▌Hanging-up places for clothes back from the cleaner, so they won't wrinkle while waiting to be put away.
▌A counter for unwrapping packages and a large wastebasket for wrappings and excelsior. The same counter for wrapping things to go out, with paper, twine, scissors, and wrapping tape at hand. Boxes, bags, and cartons can be stored in a cupboard under the counter.

A side entrance, or garage entrance, can be the garden door, the door the children use, a door for coming in from outdoor work or play. If the garage adjoins the house or is attached to it, it might be used in some of the ways listed below. If there is no side door, perhaps the kitchen doorway can be used for some of them. For several recently built houses, architects have included an attractively designed shed, of inexpensive construction, adjoining the side or main entrance, with provision for several of the following:

Side Door Utility Room

▌Hanging space for work, play, and gardening clothes.
▌Storage space for the baby carriage, bicycles, and play paraphernalia that are easier to cope with here than at the front door.
▌Storage space for small garden

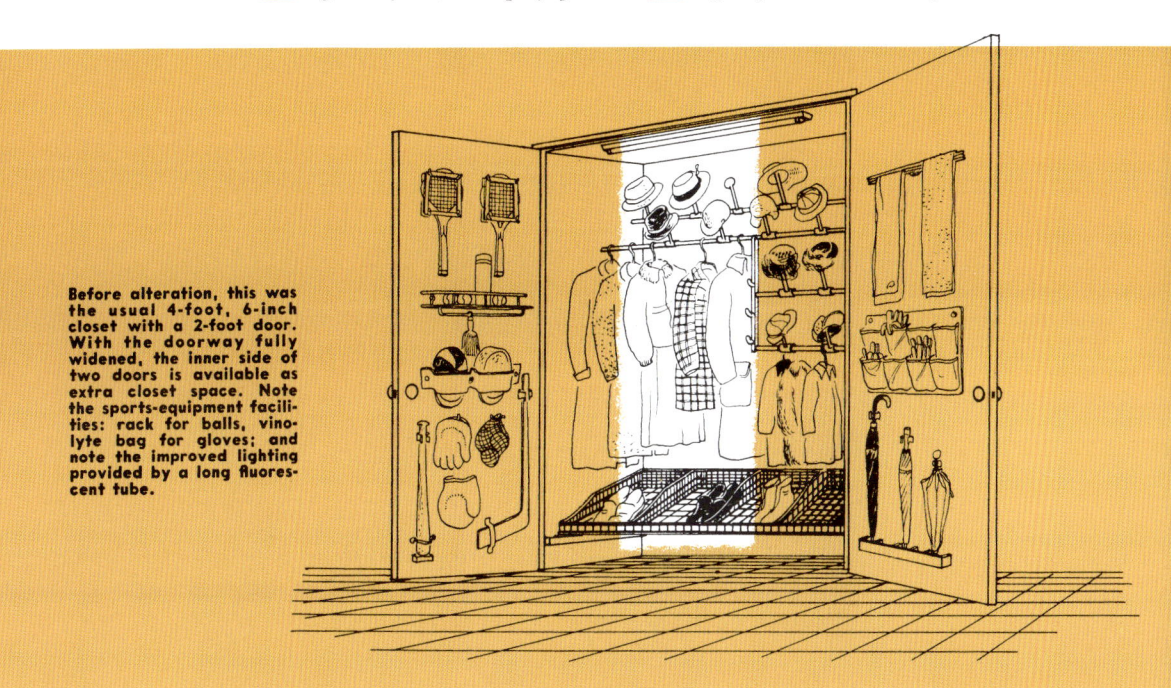

Before alteration, this was the usual 4-foot, 6-inch closet with a 2-foot door. With the doorway fully widened, the inner side of two doors is available as extra closet space. Note the sports-equipment facilities: rack for balls, vinolyte bag for gloves; and note the improved lighting provided by a long fluorescent tube.

89

tools and equipment, perhaps no more than a basket with trowel, claw, flower cutters, for that free hour you might spend in the garden.

A washstand to keep really dirty hand-washing out of the bathroom or the kitchen sink.

A counter for fixing flowers (good even without running water at hand, but better with it), and shelves for flower vases.

A stall shower if space permits; these are of metal, come prefabricated (61), and need only plumbing installation. This is an expensive job, but not prohibitively so.

General Storage: One reason entrance hall closets become such a problem is that they're often used for storing a bewildering variety of items, now that attics and cellars have almost disappeared from our lives. A storage space just for miscellaneous articles—instead of caching them in odd and easily forgotten corners of the house or apartment—can be a great help. Some helpful gadgets are shown in the illustration on next page.

In a small apartment, this type of storage can be at its simplest: shelves on one wall, covered by a drapery, or one whole cabinet.

In a large apartment, one entire closet might be allotted — or even one small room.

In a country house, a section of the cellar or the attic. A friend made a small barn into her general storage area, fitting it with rows of storage shelves like a shipping room.

Stairs

2. Much of the labor of keeping stairs clean disappears with the type of construction described here:

Open risers, like the cellar stairs, can be designed with a light, graceful look, and can be a boon to the housewife, with nothing to scuff and no corners to catch dirt.

The Z-shaped riser, connecting the front edge of the upper step with the back edge of the lower step—a diagonal that escapes scuffing better than the old vertical riser.

A plywood support for the stair rail, built solid, instead of turned balusters, cuts down cleaning, repainting, refinishing. In an old house, all balusters may be enclosed together by an over-all plywood covering, composition board, or lath and plaster.

Balusters placed every 3 feet instead of every 6 inches; this is all the support a stair rail may need, but is not recommended in a house with young children.

Curved baseboards of stairs and landings can be shaped in magnesite (3), or bought readymolded in ceramic tile or plastic tile (22). These materials can be used on treads as well.

Marble or stone is easier to clean and longer-wearing than carpet—and surprisingly quiet.

To eliminate hard-to-clean cor-

90

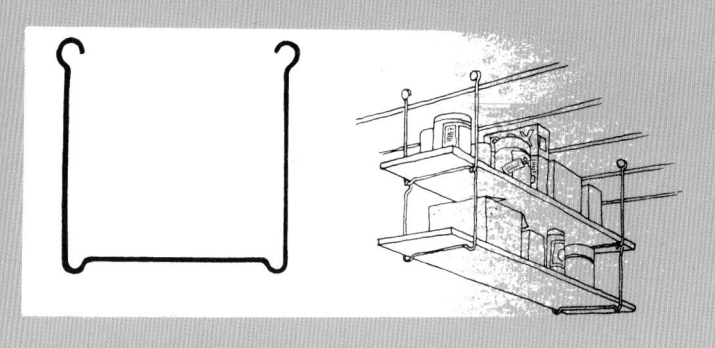

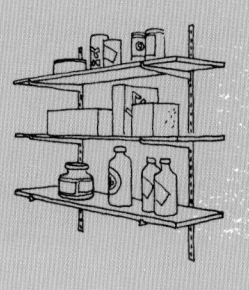

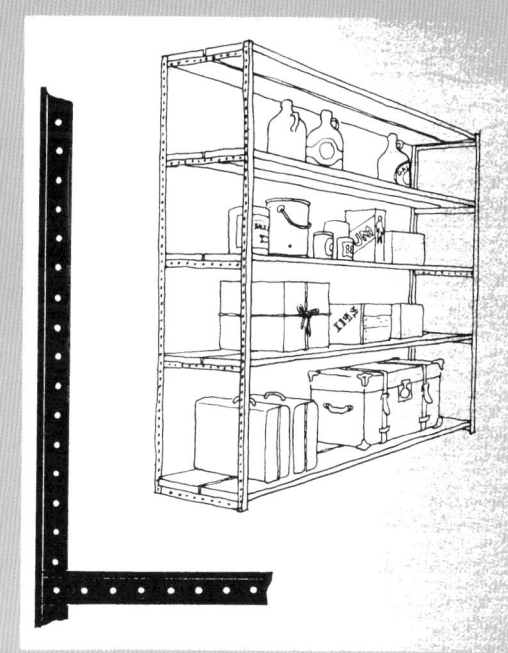

FOR GENERAL STORAGE:

Above. Steel U shelf hangers (62) can be linked together to hold wooden shelves hanging from the rafters in attic or cellar.
Center. Adjustable brackets (63) can be set up, on wall-mounted slotted channels, against walls anywhere in the house. The strong metal brackets fit into the keyholes and can support shelves with any spacing you desire.
Below. To organize unused space in the middle of a spare room, attic or cellar, set up these perforated metal angles (64) as a frame to hold board shelves. (Old doors make excellent wide shelves.)

ners, sheet plastic or rubber can be run up from the underside of the tread nose across the tread, curving up to the riser; but this curve should be reinforced by being backed with metal fillet molding (65).

Terrazzo (1) or magnesite (3) can be cast in any shape desired, to form an integral step-and-riser unit, with coving all around it.

Metal treads are more trouble to clean than any of the others.

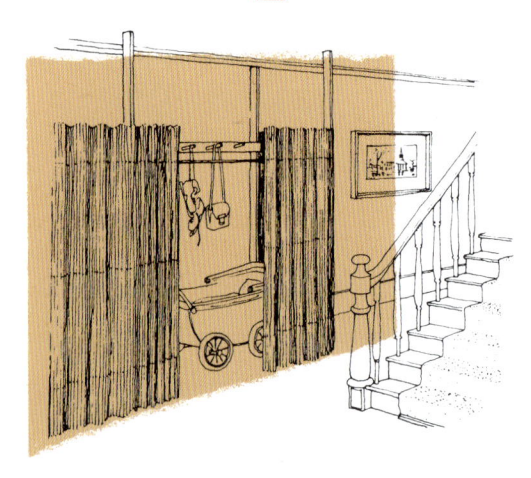

A long hallway, with an inadequate closet under the stairs was altered by marking off a larger "closet" by 2x4 posts—which carried the track (60) for a wood-slat curtain, forming an easily closed paddock for bicycle, baby carriage, and sports equipment. The same idea can be executed with a floor-to-ceiling drape on a pull cord, or with a large roller shade.

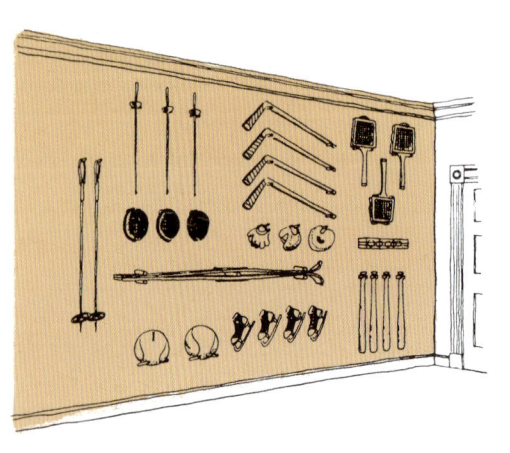

Open risers and closed-in rail save you much work in cleaning the stairs.

If your closets are too small, cover one wall of a hall with a bright-colored, washable covering and arrange such things as sports equipment on the wall like a shop display. Children will like grabbing things on the run, like firemen; and it'll be easier for them to replace equipment here than in a crowded closet.

Walls along the stairway should be dark and washable to cope with inevitable fingermarks (see the Wall Chart). Also provide space here for a cupboard or closet for stair-cleaning tools and supplies; a hand vacuum; twin dusting mitts; waxes; detergents; and a basket to carry both tools and supplies.

Hallways

3. Despite the modern tendency to suppress them, these will never disappear where privacy is needed, as in the bedroom section of the house. To cut cleaning to a minimum, have:

Dark washable walls as on the stairs (see Wall Chart).
Smooth hard floors (see Floor Chart).

No molding along the walls.
Flush doors and doorways without thresholds.
Cove baseboards.

Have no furniture here unless it is useful. Don't decorate hallways in the old-fashioned style of a museum gallery, with chairs, love seats, useless console tables—never to be used but always demanding attention because they are on exhibit. You can make the hall attractive with color and with beautiful materials on the walls and decorate it only with pictures or posters.

Doors

4. Paneled doors, with crevices and moldings to trap dirt, are more trouble to clean than flush doors, and glass is even worse; avoid it unless it's essential for light.

Interior doors with panels, moldings, or glass can be converted to flush, completely smooth doors in one of these ways (not, however, exterior doors):

Cover the entire door face right to the edge with a hard composition board or thin plywood, fastening with finishing nails or screws. (You may have to shift hinges to enable the door to close properly.) Or cover door face short of stop bead, and finish with a quarter round or square molding.
Fill in the panels with plywood, composition board, or similar material, flush with the door surface. Plaster the cracks. Cement on a washable, plastic-coated fabric over the whole, overlapping it on the edges of the door.

Factory-made flush doors are of course available, too, in wood (66) or metal (67). These have flush bucks, leaving only a small border around the opening.

Saddles

Saddles, or thresholds, are a relic of an earlier day, when houses were drafty and heat was precious. They should be eliminated on interior doors to cut out dirt-trapping crevices, to make possible sweeping and vacuum-cleaning through from room to room, and to permit the use of all sorts of wheeled carriers in the house.

But keep the saddle on an exterior doorway to help seal it against dust, drafts, and rain—a metal saddle, interlocking with the lower edge of the door, preferably of aluminum, which needs no polishing and doesn't rust.

Knobs and hinges should clean easily, stay clean, and require no polishing.

Knobs and Hinges

For both interior and exterior doors, chromium-plated or cadmium-plated brass for knobs and hinges. Unplated brass, even when lacquered or oxidized, needs frequent polishing.

For interior doors, knobs of smooth (not fluted) glass, smooth plastic, or old-fashioned porcelain can be used.

Use a one-piece combination knob and lock—one less piece to clean, and it also means less handling (and soiling) of the door itself.

The wooden frame around a door (or window) should be kept simple, to cut down the housekeeping time needed for dusting, washing, repainting, and repair:

To Keep Frames Simple

Strip off some or all of the small molding on the frame, eliminating the little grooves and bevels that catch dust.

It is often possible to strip off the entire frame, leaving the casing of the window or the buck of the door (but first consult a carpenter, or your builder or architect).

Under this frame you will usually find a mess of very rough plastering, holes, or exposed bricks or studs. If you fill this with plaster, shrinkage of the plaster will still leave a crack.

Our suggestion for covering this is shown in the illustration: a strip of wood (½ inch thick by 2½ wide) conceals the crack and is cut to project no farther than the casing or buck.

You can also cover this rough area by covering the entire wall with wallboard, wall covering, or heavy wallpaper extending over the patched area right up to the frame. This can be very attractive; if you are building ask to have the frames made this way.

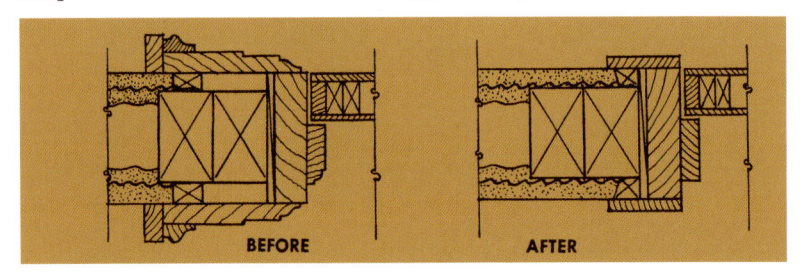

BEFORE   **AFTER**

For finishing wood door and window frames, use spar varnish or enamel with an alkyd resin base (26), paying particular attention to the bottom of the window sash, which most needs weather protection.

Swinging Doors: Opening either way, with pivot hinges allowing them to stand open, these are a work-saver wherever you must go through doors with your hands full. In addition to their obvious value in the kitchen, they are a good idea for the nursery, for a playroom, a sickroom, rooms off a hallway or passage, or in any cramped area where the two-way swing would relieve congestion.

Windows

5. Besides their importance in comfort and heat control, windows are a major housekeeping concern. Poor weather-seal will mean an unremitting battle against dust and soot, soiling, and rain damage. Whether your windows present irksome or minor cleaning problems will depend largely on their design and material.

Window Frames: Metal is better than wood, presenting the slimmest surfaces to clean, no warping, practically no sticking, and with effective weather-stripping built in. Aluminum is better than steel, since it requires no painting and stands up well under most of the weather that might corrode steel. If you prefer wood, get plain frames, order rotproof treatment, and use metal weather-stripping —factory built-in, or applied by a professional.

Resist the temptation to paint window frames white—it's extremely impractical. We have seen very attractive windows with the molding next to the glass painted dark (to camouflage dirt) and the broad surface of the inside frame painted in a light color.

Window Sills can be a lot of trouble, being often exposed to outside dirt and weather. You can have a sill built entirely of marble, but this is expensive. Or cover a wood sill with marble or plate glass cut to size; or strip off all paint and cover with heavy vinolyte film (68) glued on with vinylite cement—this will save much cleaning and repainting.

Window Sashes: Sliding and pivot-swinging sashes are the two basic designs; both types and almost all their variations are available in both wood and metal. Modern home architects have introduced industrial variations—more for artistic than for practical reasons—so if you are building, it is a good idea to know something about the available types of windows, and the advantages and faults of each.

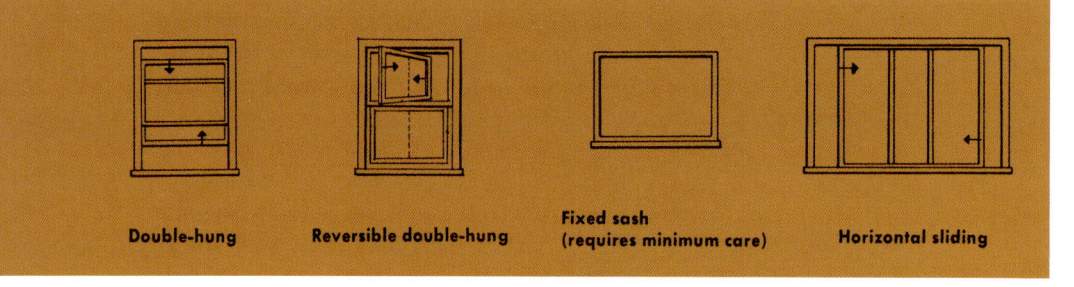

Double-hung — **Reversible double-hung** — **Fixed sash (requires minimum care)** — **Horizontal sliding**

Sliding Sashes

The standard double-hung window is the one you have seen all your life—two sashes sliding up and down past each other.

An aluminum-framed standard double-hung window is unquestionably the most practical. As far as weather-seal, and cutting down the amount of dust entering the room, are concerned, this window is always at least 50 per cent sealed—for even if top and bottom are open, the two sides are always closed. Other advantages are:

Advantages

The simplest frame to clean and maintain (since it is thinner than the wooden double-hung).

The simplest-to-maintain exposed hardware—sash lock and lifts only. The best type of lift bar, continuous for the width of the window, is built in on aluminum double-hung windows, but can be put on others.

The most practical for screening and window-dressing, taking any kind of screen, blind, curtain, or drapery, inside or out.

Disadvantages

In window-washing, the outside being harder to get at than in certain swinging or pivoting windows.

Sticking is a minimal disadvantage with metal frames, and can be lessened in wooden ones with metal liners, or metal weather-stripping.

Sash balances are needed, and these counterbalance weights are sometimes on cords, which often break. Other types, less apt to get out of order, are spring balances (69) and friction guides (70).

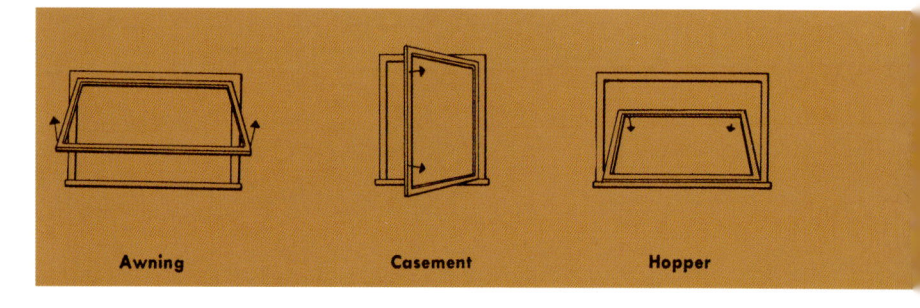

Awning — **Casement** — **Hopper**

96

Other varieties of double-hung windows include:

Horizontal sliding: the sashes open sideways instead of vertically. These sashes can be removed for cleaning both sides (although this is too muscular a job for a housewife to attempt alone), and are available with plastic sills—amazingly little trouble to keep clean.

Reversible double-hung: the sashes still slide up and down past each other, but the entire window in each sash also pivots, opening inward and out like the pivot type. This has all the disadvantages of the pivot-swinging type—discussed just below—notably poor weather-seal.

Pivot-Swinging Sashes

The most common pivot-swinging type is the romantic cottage casement, which swings out. Also available is a type that swings in; other types include awning, hopper, vertical-pivoting, horizontal-pivoting, louver single, double, triple, accordion, etc.

Pivot-swinging types rarely stick, being hinged or pivoted instead of sliding; some are easy to wash both inside and out, and in aluminum their frames offer little cleaning and maintenance trouble.

Disadvantages

Poor weather-seal—like a door, if opened only slightly, the pivot action separates the entire window from its frame and the seal is 100% broken. This lack of partial seal also means more dust entry. Inswinging casements seal poorly at the sill even when tightly closed.

Complicated weather-seal edges are therefore necessary, and these are dirt traps and hard to clean.

Complicated hardware to clean and keep in repair.

Difficult to screen; the outswing must have an inside screen, either hinged to swing in, fixed (with a rotary or lever mechanism through the screen for opening and closing the window), or one of the new types described on p. 98. The whole screen must be shifted for dusting and window-washing.

Difficult or impossible to cover some inswinging types with blinds or curtains.

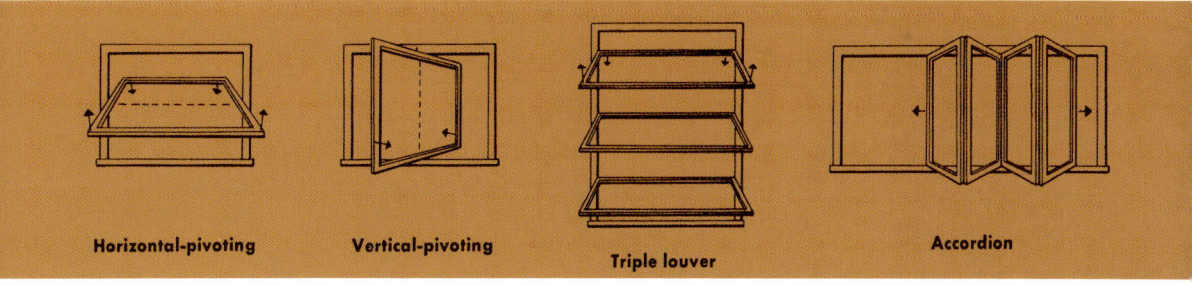

Horizontal-pivoting   **Vertical-pivoting**   **Triple louver**   **Accordion**

Windowpanes: The fewer panes, the less work. Professional window-cleaners take twice as long to wash a multiple-paned window as they do for a single-paned one, and they say that a housewife takes three times as long. The union lets a window-cleaner wash 75 standard-size single-paned windows a day, only 36 multiple-paned. So the cost of hired window-washing is at least twice as much for a multiple-paned window.

Window Screens

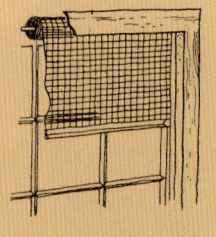

6. Frame screens are the commonest. Metal frames are better than wood, and aluminum is best, because it needs least care. Simple hook-on hardware, and stamped numbers on metal frames or numbered tacks on wood, with corresponding numbers on the windows, help in the annual hanging of screens for summer. Putting frame screens up from inside the house is possible, but requires muscle and reach—a man's job. There is a choice of mesh:

Copper or aluminum screening requires next to no care.

Plastic screening (71), requires no care and will not discolor even in salt air, but it cuts or tears easily.

Very new is screening made of thin horizontal bronze slats (72); it offers the same protection from insects, is easily brushed clean, and has the added virtue of reducing sun heat through its slats (like Venetian blinds).

Two other new screening devices, which may revolutionize screening, are:

The Inside Roll-Up Screen, a permanent installation inside the window, which works like a window shade; it must be rolled up to open, close, or wash the window, but eliminates taking down, winter storing, and rehanging. Cannot be mounted on the outside. A variation of this is mounted on the sash with the end of the screen fixed to the sill: as the sash opens, it unrolls the screen, giving automatic screening.

The Tension Screen, frameless, attached at the top and snapped into catches at the bottom. Tension holds it tight against the sides of the window. It rolls up for storage. Mounted from the outside, it is possible to put it up from the inside—but you must climb on the sill or a stepladder, a dangerous operation at an open window.

Roll-up Screen (125)

Self-winding Roll-up Screen attached to sash (125).

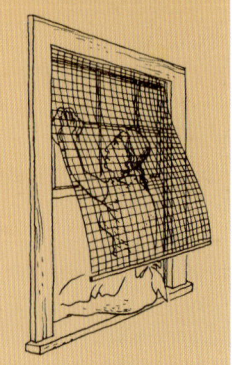

The Tension Screen (72)

Window Coverings

7. If you are really serious about saving work, you will have none of these except where light control and privacy are needed. Shades, blinds, curtains, and draperies present many choices; we look them over from the work-saver angle.

Venetian Blinds: This cliché of early modern architecture seems to have taken over the country, displacing the simple, more practical roller shade. So we feel the need to open this section with the case against the Venetian blind.

It is heavy, awkward, and full of mischief; if made of wood, it gets stuck, hangs askew, rattles in the breeze, and is hard work to clean. (And you'll find the newer vertical type no real improvement over the horizontal-track type.) As many housewives have discovered, the space in between tapes is just about impossible to clean. If you insist on this blind, at least avoid the wooden ones; get plastic (73) or flexible metal with plastic tapes (73), which are much less work to clean. The main justification of the Venetian blind is its control of light, air, and privacy.

Fabric Roller Shades: The plain, old-fashioned window shade, most forthright and practical for privacy and for keeping out light, now comes in a variety of colors and in printed designs. They can be made to order to fit any size of window, even extra large. Cambric and Holland types are not recommended: they rain-spot, are not very washable or long-wearing. Best are these three newer fabrics:

New Shade Fabrics

Plastic-coated shade cloth (74): plastic on loose-woven muslin. It can be washed, scrubbed; very long-wearing; flame-resistant; resists most ordinary stains, grease, oil.

Vinyl film shades (75): available only in limited sizes and colors. They are completely rainproof (like a shower curtain), and completely washable.

Pyroxalin-coated cloth (54): pyroxalin on closely woven muslin. It can be washed, scrubbed.

The usual way of installing shades—at the top, to pull down—is not necessarily the best. You might find these two methods of installation more effective:

Shade Installation

At the sill, to draw upward, the cord drawn through a special pulley at the top of the window. Good in the bedroom, allowing an open upper window, or in a street-floor room for privacy at the bottom and light and air at the top. This minimizes the amount of soot and dirt that collect on the sill.

Double-hung, combining the advantages of top- and bottom-hung; requires two shades, double installation per window.

99

Roller Shades of Other Materials: Shades are also available in these materials, natural, dyed, or painted: beveled wood slats (53), for the most ventilation and privacy; rectangular wood slats (53); small doweling or reed (76); bamboo slats (76).

When covering the window, these give privacy and a certain amount of light and air control, and though not as easy to clean as a fabric shade, they are still easier than the Venetian blind. Hang them like any other window shades, but be sure the roll, which is thicker, can be accommodated. Anchor them at the bottom with side hooks, to prevent rattling.

Drapery Fabrics: Taste is individual, but the problems of wear and maintenance are common to everyone. Of great importance are the invisible chemical finishes that have been perfected in recent years, which render fabrics resistant to practically every household hazard, and make for easier cleaning. Many more finishes are on the horizon. They are often identified by *fact tags*.* These guarantees, which more and more manufacturers are adopting, assure you that the material is "sunfast," "washable," and so on. But remember that most finishes don't last the life of the fabric. Some are removed in the very first laundering or cleaning; some can be reapplied at home or by the cleaner, others can't. Your fact tag will say whether the finish is "durable"—for drapery fabrics this can mean a few years.

Initial know-how saves on future tasks, so whether you buy ready-made curtains and draperies or make them yourself, don't forget that:

Drapery Construction and Design

To drape and hang well, they must have straight, well-finished hems.

Stitching — well secured at the ends — prevents raveling.

Many patterns can be hung upside down at times, to reduce concentration of damage from dirt, fading, and heat. So make identical top and bottom hems.

Headings should be adequate to fit smoothly and easily over the rod.

Draperies that shrink 3 or 4 inches in the first cleaning are a waste of time, money, and fabric. Some manufacturers state shrinkage on the fact tag (1% = ½ inch a yard; 5% means 2 inches). Several mill-applied processes minimize shrinkage. Extra-deep hems are the answer if information isn't on the label.

Something new has been developed for making stationary headings: a buckram hem lining (77) that forms pinch pleats without pins; it saves time in removing and replacing

---

*Some *fact tags* read: Everglaze, Sanforized, Preshrunk, and so on.

draperies, in ironing (once off the rod, the material is flat, eliminating the fuss of pressing pleats), and in sewing (if you make your own you don't have to worry about a "French" heading—just two seams and you're through).

In making your own draw curtains, it saves time to use pin-on hooks in the heading rather than sewn-on hooks.

Avoid using weights; they have to be removed to do a good ironing job. If the fabric is shrinkproof or curtains extra long, you won't need weights.

Linings add to the difficulty of making your own drapes, will often shrink at a different rate from the drapery fabric, and are a cleaning problem. So don't use them unless they're necessary for protection. If they are needed, make them to snap on at top only.

Fading

All drapery colors fade in time, but you can forestall fading, and thus lengthen the life of the drapery, by some precautions:

There are many kinds of dyes, and four enemies of dyed color: light, washing, dry cleaning, air. It's a complicated problem, so before buying consult DuPont's booklet *Buying Fabrics for Colorfastness* (20).

Look for a "colorfast" guarantee on the manufacturer's label. If it's not stated, take a small swatch of fabric home and test it yourself. It's very simple; the DuPont booklet *Testing for Colorfastness in the Home* (20) tells you how.

Rotate curtains from a sunny exposure to a shadier one — or turn them upside down occasionally.

Let draperies cover the window frame, but not the pane during the day—so they're not in direct contact with outdoor light.

Linings keep a lot of the sun's rays away from the fabric.

Plastics are as susceptible to sun as fabric. But if used as lining, they protect fabric from rain, and to some extent from sun.

Acetate rayon dyed blue, or any shade containing blue (green, brown, purple, gray), turns pink or bronze from gases in the air.

Dust

Dust accumulates on any kind of material. However, some show it more than others, and here are some tips on how to cut down on drapery cleaning:

A print or woven pattern is a camouflage for dust.

Black and dark colors show every particle of dust.

Fabrics with a smooth, glossy surface (glazed chintzes, etc.) are easily dusted, and plastics can be dusted or wiped with a damp cloth or suds. But accumulated grime attacks plastics and glazed fabrics too, and can be removed only with vigorous scrubbing.

Textured, nubby, pile, and any loose-weave fabrics are dust pockets, because of weave construction (even when treated with special finishes). If heavy

dust is your problem, avoid:
  brocatelle,
  burlap,
  cotton and theatrical gauze,
  damask,
  cotton, rayon and nylon marquisette,
  cotton nets,
  organdy,
  rep,
  tapestry,
  casement cloth,
  velvet,
  corduroy.

Rain-spotting

Some spotting from rain is inevitable if you leave windows open, but it can be minimized if you:

Line draperies.
Use plastic or glass window ventilators.
Fasten draperies away from windows.
Select colors sufficiently waterfast to prevent running (see DuPont's *Buying Fabrics for Colorfastness*).
Buy fabrics labeled "water-repellent" (24, 78). Some are "durable"; or find a licensed cleaner to apply the finish after each cleaning (79, 80), or try applying a finish at home yourself (80).

Spots

Spots, other than from rain, are usually not much of a problem—draperies are out of range of spilled foods, and so on—but in a house where there are children, or pets, you can expect soiling and spotting, so it's helpful to know that spots can easily be wiped off plastics (woven, coated, or film), and that draperies treated with water-repellent or starchless finishes are less vulnerable to spots (except grease), since the fiber is protected.

Fire

Only expensive glass-fiber draperies are completely fireproof and therefore safe for areas where a fire hazard exists. Fire-retarded finishes are being developed; at least one has been perfected. Where there is a real danger of fire, beware of cotton and theatrical gauze, net, ninon, organdy, marquisette, plastic, and paper (unless labeled "fire resistant"), or any flimsy material.

Moths

Animal-fiber draperies (wool, mohair, horsehair) are meat for moths.

Look for a label stating that the fabric has been mothproofed. Some of these finishes survive dry cleaning (82); others are "permanent," take laundering as well (81).
Some cleaners are licensed by manufacturers to apply mothproofing finishes; a few can be applied at home (82).

Mildew

If you live in a damp area, or a coastal region, look for a fact tag indicating "mildew-resistant" (85). Some such finishes can be applied in the home (84).

102

Loss of Shape

Don't let your draperies be weather barometers—when exposed to excessive heat and humidity, some materials tend to lose shape immediately, have a "morning-after" look.

Plastics (except rayon and nylon) tend to dry out in excessive heat.
Paper draperies will curl up if hung over radiators.
Loosely woven fabrics (and filmy nets) don't hold shape well.
Look for fact tags indicating "character" or "starchless" finishes (86, 87). These help keep fabrics crisp in damp, humid weather.

Wear and Tear

If length of drapery life is important to you, remember that the best quality means the best service; it's a waste of time and money to buy sleazy fabrics. Here are lists of fabrics recommended for laundering (provided the dye is fact-tagged "washable"), others suitable for dry cleaning, and a few washables which do not require ironing. All are durable goods, which with proper care will stay fresh until you tire of them.

Washable: ninon, Nottingham lace, organdy, pongee, poplin, cotton rep, sailcloth, sateen, cotton taffeta, casement cloth, permanent glazed chintz, corduroy, cretonne, cotton damask, denim, cotton frieze, linen marquisette (cotton and rayon), monk's cloth, crash.
Need not be ironed: cotton nets, nylon, plastics (woven, film, coated), seersucker, waffle cloth, glass fiber.
For the cleaner only: brocade, brocatelle, non-durable glazed chintz, damask (rayon or mohair), rayon and cotton faille, frieze (rayon, mohair, or wool), rayon or wool rep, rayon satin, rayon taffeta, tapestry, velvet, velveteen.

Drapery Hardware: There are two types, stationary and traverse, and your preference will depend largely on the position and the uses of your draperies. But basic, simple hardware of each type is available.

Stationary Hardware

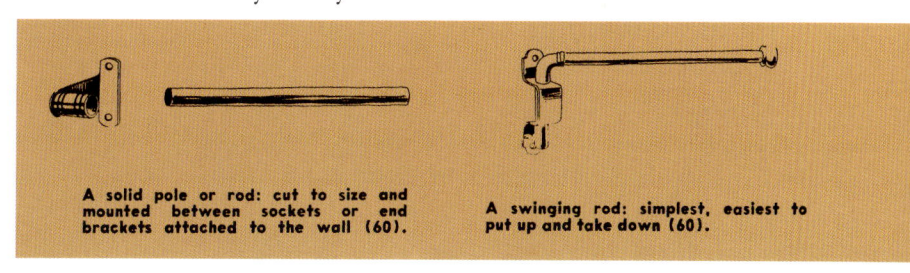

The simple principle of the stationary type is to run a rod through the hem in the heading of the drape. The rod can be mounted in a variety of ways:

A solid pole or rod: cut to size and mounted between sockets or end brackets attached to the wall (60).

A swinging rod: simplest, easiest to put up and take down (60).

103

Traverse Hardware

Extension type poles or rods, with end brackets, are not recommended; they are troublesome to adjust. If you insist on elaborate window trimming, use a double extension rod, which combines drapery with curtain or valance.

Rings (plastic ones are now available, and do not discolor like brass) and pins can be used to attach drapes to any of the mountings, instead of passing the rod directly through the hem, or through the new buckram heading, but the extra trouble is clearly not worth while for stationary drapery.

The use of pins or hooks to attach the traverse drapes to the runners is the principal difference. This is more bother than merely passing rods through, but is of course necessary if easy movement of the drapes is what you want. There is one basic type (see illustration). A possible variation, for greater simplicity, is to use this *without* cord controls; or merely use big rings on a wooden or metal pole—and draw the drapes by hand.

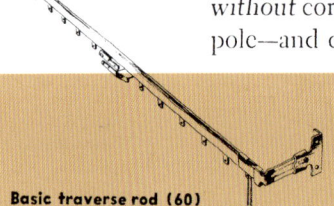

Basic traverse rod (60)  — **Pin-on hook** — **Sewn-on hooks**

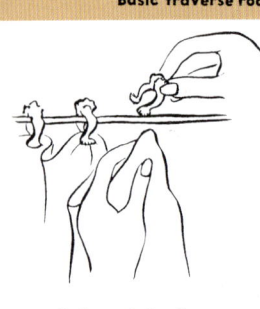

Cafe curtain clip speeds hanging. Pinch on and off, without sewing (60).

Pin-on hooks, used with rings, are much easier to put on and take off.

Sewn-on hooks hold their place better, and are preferable for heavy drapes.

If drapes are laundered at home, use pin-on hooks and remove when washing. Either type may be used on drapes to be sent out for cleaning; the better professional cleaners remove pin-on hooks and replace them afterward, and cover sewn-on hooks.

"Window-Dressing": This term has come to carry the general connotation of unnecessary showiness, and it is true that some housework could be avoided by eliminating curtains altogether—but actually very little work would be saved. Draperies are clearly much less of a housekeeping problem than the floors or the upholstery; certainly they are not constantly being sat on, walked on, or handled, and tend to be less dust-catching than horizontal surfaces.

Approached sensibly, the art of window-dressing can add much warmth and charm to the house. Yet it is a pity to lavish time, care and money on overdressing a window when underdressing it could achieve as good, and often a better, effect.

We trim a window to satisfy two needs: for color and to soften architectural lines. Admittedly, it's true that color can be concentrated in the rest of the room or can be painted into the window frame itself; a room with gun-metal walls could have window frames of coral-red, or jade-green, or any bright color. (We have seen handsome rooms that relied on such color devices and left their windows bare.)

But this would probably not satisfy most people, any more than do the schemes of some modern architects who for years have advocated the total abolition of window-dressing in favor of Venetian blinds and living plants. There would seem to be a need for drapery far too firmly imbedded in our civilization for us even to attempt to fight against it.

There is, however, no need to swing to the other extreme of conventional window-dressing: glass curtains, side drape, valance, tiebacks, and so forth. This sort of lavish self-expression *can* become a maintenance burden. The answer here—as elsewhere in the house—is to find a personal happy medium between utilitarianism and clutter. Study your room with the windows bare. Try not to think of the windows separately, but as part of the whole room, and attempt to imagine the simplest kind of treatment that would give the desired softening and color. Consider these examples:

Window-Trimming Suggestions

A pair of straight hangings at the sides, of pleasing color and texture, may be all you need.

The bedroom window of one of our friends is given neither drapery nor curtain, but simply a crisp nylon ruffle gathered on an elastic, stretched around the top and sides of the window on hooks at the four corners. These are little trouble, and give something of the casual effect of a country cottage.

Another friend has made handsome drapes of sacking, which she launders in her washing machine, runs through a mangle, and then twists tightly and lets dry—thus making dramatic-looking folds like those of the old "Fortuny" evening gowns.

A more formal treatment can be obtained with a simple length of yard goods swagged through two big rings, one at each corner of the top. The fabric falls gracefully down along the sides—no gathers, pinch pleats, or valances, no edgings or linings, no tiebacks, no hardware other than the two rings.

If you try to simplify, the chances are you will come up with something not only simpler but altogether happier than the conventional overadornment you might have bought in a hurry.

CHAPTER VI

OUTDOOR LIVING

MORE AND MORE living is being done outside the confines of four walls and a ceiling. American homes have been sprouting porches and terraces that range through every degree of shelter to no shelter at all: the removable-glass enclosed porch, the screened porch, the open porch with roof, the terrace, the patio, the lawn. These spots are often the best-liked in the home, comfortable and relaxing for family and guests, and usually the easiest to take care of. Even more important, the months during which the family is out of doors mean a great deal less indoor fuss and cleaning; it might even be a good idea to revert to Grandmother's practice of covering up furniture or even locking off some rooms during these months.

The screened porch, which many consider old-fashioned, certainly should be revived. It is the perfect living-dining room for summer, an outdoor room at night where your reading lamp won't make you an insect collector, and on rainy days the finest playroom for children.

Planning

1. Outdoors needs some housekeeping, however casual, so plan and furnish for the greatest comfort and the least maintenance. The outdoor "room" is apt to get hard use, and there are sun, wind, and rain to cope with.

We have an all-inclusive rule: Look at the walls, floors, and furnishings of any outdoor living area, and ask yourself whether you can wash them with a hose.

The Floor (unless you are on the lawn, where the grass is your floor): Hard-surfaced, *with a drain*, and no covering even on the roofed porch. Grass-fiber, jute, sisal, and hemp rugs, usually considered standard for the porch, take time to clean and are far less durable than a smooth, hard floor.

A screened porch was built onto the kitchen wing and provided with a fireplace. The living room and dining room of this house are closed off for the entire summer—all living and eating are done here. Ceramic floor tile; furniture of rattan, wrought iron, spar-varnished wood.

Outdoor Flooring

Terrazzo (1), magnesite (3), cement, with cove corners and baseboard, as easy to hose down as to sweep.
Masonry such as stone, brick, tile, less easy because of the rough surface.
Flagstone for the terrace; laid in cement so there are no cracks.
Flagstone laid in earth or sand, pesky if weeds grow between the flags, or grass, which must be clipped. Clover needs less frequent clipping but draws bees if allowed to blossom. Plant thyme, low-growing and fragrant when trod on, or dwarf (2-inch) alyssum.
Plastic tile for a softer surface and a less outdoor look, as on a glassed-in porch; washable, and requires no waxing.

Walls will get more soiled than in inside rooms, even on an enclosed porch. More practical here than any washable wall covering are walls that can be hosed, or brushed off with a broom. Consider: masonry, glass, cement, solid wood siding (not plywood). The Wall Chart has comparisons.

Outdoor Furniture

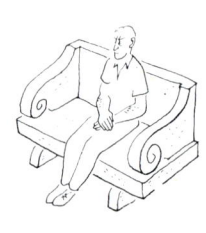

2. The ideal outdoor seating, from a housekeeping point of view, would require no caring-for and could be left out, unattended, all year round. This ideal does exist—in masonry furniture—but that offers absolutely *no* comfort, and certainly cannot be considered a solution to the problem. However, there are a great many types that can be left out all year, in all weather, and offer somewhat more comfort:

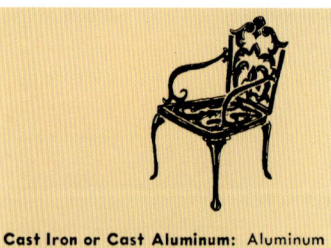

Cast Iron or Cast Aluminum: Aluminum is rustless, iron usually guaranteed so for about five years. Both require stripping and repainting after that time.

Baked Enamel on Steel—

"Baked enamel" is a somewhat misleading term; unlike your kitchen range, all these types will need occasional repainting. The steel-spring type has some of the comfort of upholstery. The "fiber" (actually treated paper) is much more durable than it sounds, and fairly comfortable, too. Also available are stationary types, in numerous designs, without springs.

Folding Chair (88)

with Woven Fiber (90)

with Steel Spring Seat and Back (89)

108

Note that all the following wood seating needs paint, varnish or creosote every two to five years.

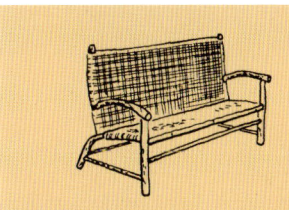

Hickory with Woven Rattan Slats: Somewhat more decorative and comfortable than the more common hickory-with-oak type, and having the same virtues.

Chinese Peel (93): Somewhat less fragile than it looks, its life expectancy is about three years, and since it is quite inexpensive, it offers you a good run for your money.

Steamer Chair: The old-fashioned all-wood kind, with no canvas or detachable cushions to worry about, but therefore somewhat less comfortable.

Rattan: Relatively expensive, very very good-looking. Practical, too, its open construction offering good drainage.

Hickory with Woven Hickory Splits: Similar to rattan in appearance, but though it can be left outdoors all year round, it should be under a roof, as the splits are too closely woven for quick drainage. Best used on covered porches.

Adirondack: A familiar style of wood seating—usually of fir, either spar-varnished or painted, sometimes folding. Open spaces permit drainage of snow, ice, rain.

Cypress—Rustic (92): In the same "family" as hickory, with the same advantages.

Hickory with Oak Slats (91): A very common, time-tested type; durable, sturdy, and treated to repel termites.

109

These new combinations of materials are also for year-round use:

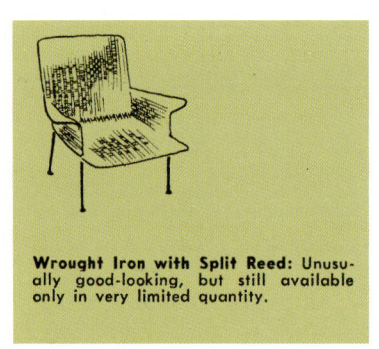

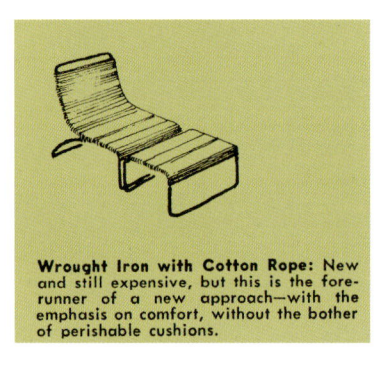

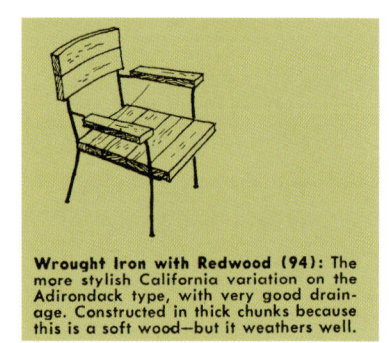

Wrought Iron with Split Reed: Unusually good-looking, but still available only in very limited quantity.

Wrought Iron with Galvanized Steel Mesh (96): Comparatively light and comfortable, the best idea so far in heavy metal seating, but just beginning to appear on the market.

Wrought Iron with Cotton Rope: New and still expensive, but this is the forerunner of a new approach—with the emphasis on comfort, without the bother of perishable cushions.

Wrought Iron with Redwood (94): The more stylish California variation on the Adirondack type, with very good drainage. Constructed in thick chunks because this is a soft wood—but it weathers well.

The following are not for year-round use, but may be left in the open for the summer season:

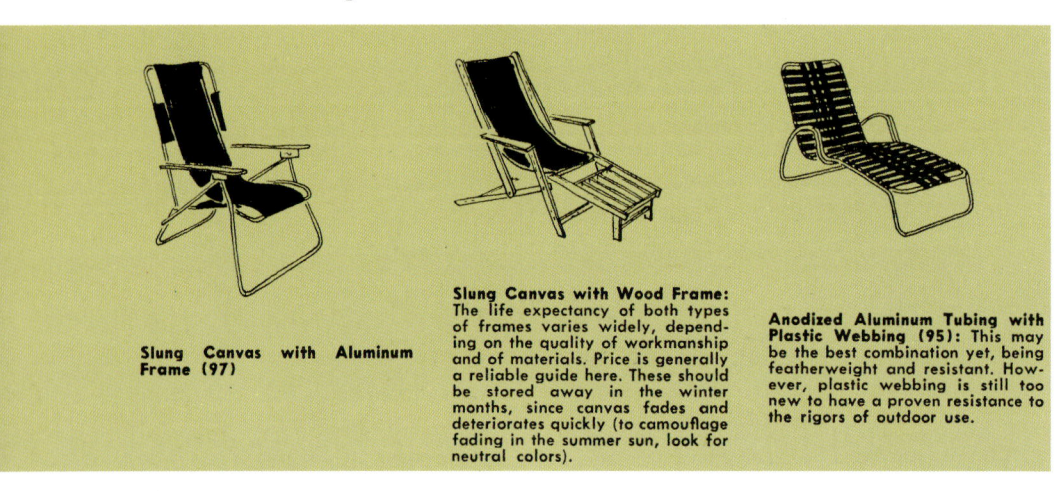

Slung Canvas with Aluminum Frame (97)

Slung Canvas with Wood Frame: The life expectancy of both types of frames varies widely, depending on the quality of workmanship and of materials. Price is generally a reliable guide here. These should be stored away in the winter months, since canvas fades and deteriorates quickly (to camouflage fading in the summer sun, look for neutral colors).

Anodized Aluminum Tubing with Plastic Webbing (95): This may be the best combination yet, being featherweight and resistant. However, plastic webbing is still too new to have a proven resistance to the rigors of outdoor use.

If you are looking for more comfort than unupholstered types give, get year-round frames that come with light, detachable cushions or pads. Or, for frames without cushions, you can buy or make inexpensive pads. These should be made of water-repellent canvas, duck, or sailcloth (which, however, are *not* waterproof), so that they can be left out most nights of the season, and need be carried under cover only in case of rain.

If you want additional comfort here, you must realize that you are taking on added work. With heavy, spring-cushioned pieces you run the risk of having the springs rust and the inner padding rot. Minimize the work of protecting them by attaching underneath, or in back, rolled-up rubberized "raincoats," and by buying pieces on wheels, easier to move when it rains. In any case, such pieces must be stored away in the winter months.

New designs, materials, and accessories are appearing all the time; measure them for comfort, convenience, ease of maintenance, and durability as against price. In fabrics, smooth and slick ones for easy brushing off are best. But realize that: there is no completely effective waterproofing for stuffed upholstery; all fabrics fade; all plastics become sticky, and eventually brittle, in the sun.

Outdoor Tables: The best for all year round use are tables with slatted wood tops—rain and snow can drain through. Baked-enamel types can be left out in winter, but paint-chipping and surface-denting from snow and ice must be expected. Glass tops are adequate for summer only; solid wood and plywood with unbroken surface are not practical for use, as they tend to warp and blister.

Porches and Sunrooms: Furniture can be selected with more consideration for comfort and decorative appeal, according to the degree of protection from weather. But ease of maintenance is still important. For glass-enclosed sunrooms, use any heavy seating described above, plus chromium-plated steel (not recommended for exposed outdoor use because of peeling and rusting and the high cost of refinishing). Woven-plastic, plastic-coated fabrics for spring cushions, which are often recommended for this type of furniture, are more practical here than out of doors.

Other Outdoor Equipment

Waterproof covers, "raincoats," for outdoor furniture, come ready-made to fit chairs, chaise longues, sofas, gliders; also in 6- by 9-foot rectangles.

Hudson Bay blankets, all wool, practically waterproof.

Tree hammocks of rope, with or without stretchers, for one reclining or two sitting.

Rubberized fabric ground mattress (98), for sun-bathing;

(99)
(98)
(100)
(101)
(102)
(103)
(104)
(105)
(106)

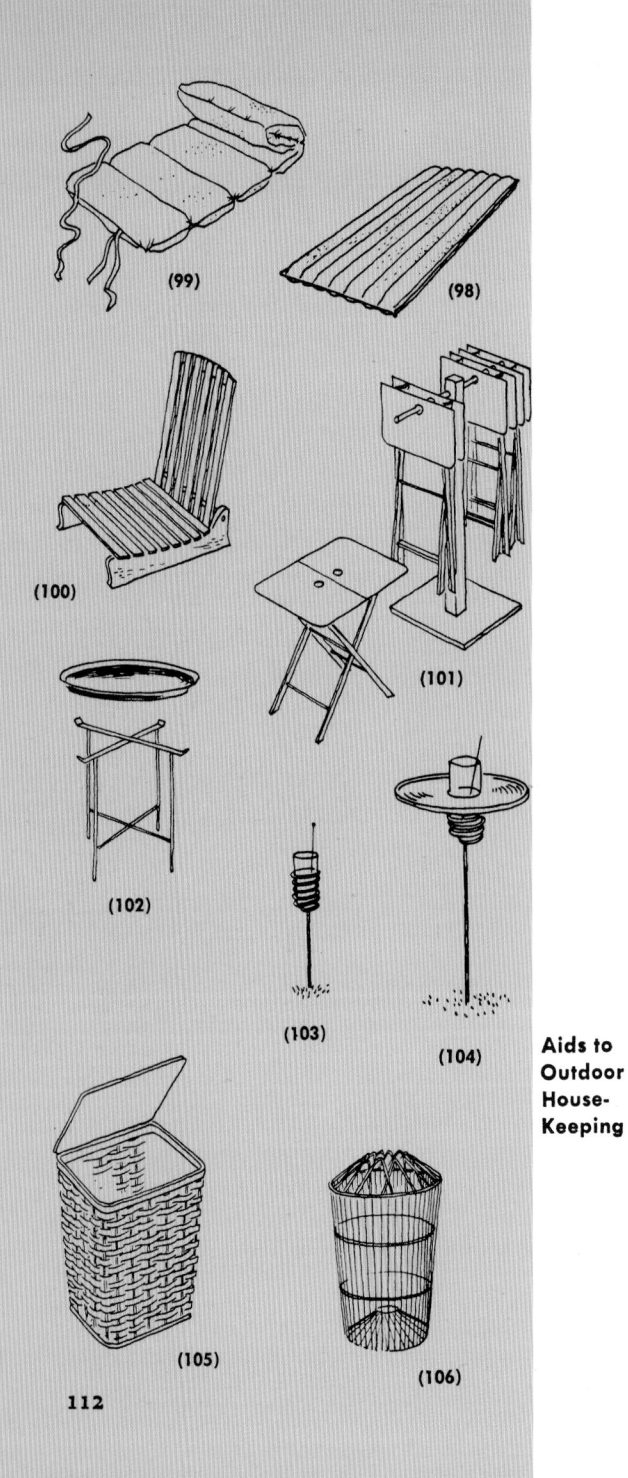

long lawn pillow or water float.
Kapok-filled canvas mattress, cartridge type (99), easily carried, for use on hard seating or on the ground.
Pads, for sitting on the ground or as upholstery for chairs: of tufted rubber, sponge rubber, foam rubber, inflated plastic or rubber-coated types.
On-the-ground chairs with back rest, either folding wood slats and canvas (100), or non-folding bent ash and rawhide lacing; aluminum tubing and canvas.
Occasional tables, small, of sheet aluminum and aluminum tubing, very light, rustproof (101).
Group of small, lightweight, folding tables of wood; complete with stand to hang them on when not in use.
Coffee tables whose tops are removable trays (102); enamel, lightweight, and of good size, on tubing or wrought-iron stands.
Lawn coasters: holder for glasses on a leg that spears into the ground (103). With aluminum tumbler, a good ash tray.
Small serving tray that sits on a metal frame (104), also mounted on a pointed leg.

Aids to Outdoor House-Keeping

Simple precautions and equipment can save a lot of steps—
Large rustic baskets (105) or painted metal incinerator baskets (106) around for trash, newspapers, bottles.
A minimum of furniture, permanent seating for a small group, and cushions, pads, light folding chairs to be brought out for the occasional crowd.
Storage nearby for these extra

seats, also for the furniture "raincoats."

Shelter nearby if you must carry pillows or push furniture out of the rain or in for the night.

Chairs with wide arms or drop-leaf arms to eliminate side tables and smoking stands; convenient for refreshments, too.

A whisk broom tied to the furniture for a quick brush-off of garden and insect debris; decorative little ones from a handcraft shop.

Sand-filled pottery pieces for cigarette butts.

An outdoor living-dining room, with slat-type wood furniture and inflated rubberized cushions and mattresses that can be left out rain or shine and will need little or no attention from the housewife.

Outdoor Dining

3. Meals on a porch or a terrace, or at a barbecue pit, or perhaps just a picnic supper on your back lawn, can be a very pleasant warm-weather variation in family routine. There is, unavoidably, more work involved in family outdoor dining, but this would seem to be one clear-cut instance of the pleasure involved, making added effort worth while.

But it is important to keep the additional work at a minimum. Your regular, everyday outdoor dining area should be near the kitchen, not a porch at the other end of the house or a romantic but distant clump of trees. If you have no convenient porch, consider the possibility of a terrace outside the kitchen; stretch canvas over it for protection from heat and rain.

Minimize Meal-time Housework

Paper plates, cups, and napkins—always suitable in this informal setting.

Furniture of a kind that can be hosed and scrubbed; the most practical, stone, glass, or slat-wood table tops; slat-wood benches and chairs.

A large sturdy serving cart to save trips to the kitchen; substituting large lightweight trays (possibly double-deckers) for the cart if the trip involves steps and turnings.

Individual trays, permitting cafeteria-style service.

Outdoor waste disposal—a can, a fireplace, or an incinerator.

A nearby spigot or hose, dishes to be washed off outdoors over a slatted or grilled grating.

A closed cupboard on the porch to hold outdoor tableware.

A weatherproof electrical outlet for cooking and warming equipment — coffee-maker, toaster, grill, etc.

To save work in outdoor dining, enlarge the window over the sink, add a small terrace adjoining the kitchen, tack screening to a frame of 2x4's, and roof it with canvas. Slat-type furniture, a big covered wastebasket, and you can clean all of it with a hose.

CHART OF WALL MATERIALS AND WALL COVERINGS

MATERIALS	HOUSEHOLD RATINGS	WATER	MILDEW	OIL & GREASE	OTHER HOUSEHOLD STAINS	SCUFFS & SCRATCHES	DURABILITY	DUST CAMOUFLAGE
WOOD - UNFINISHED ① ③								
Solid Hardwood	G-F	G	P	P	P	G	G	G ⑦
Solid Softwood	F	F	P	P	P	P	G	G ⑦
Plywood or Veneer ②								
WOOD FINISHES ①								
Spar Varnish	G	E	E	E	G	G	G	F ⑦
Phenolic Plastic, Liquid	G	E	E	E	G	G	G	F ⑦
Lacquer	G-F	P	F	E	G	F	G	F ⑦
Shellac	F-P	B	F	F	F	F	F	F ⑦
Paint, Water (Calcamine, Casein)	P	P	P	P	B	P	P	F ⑦
Paint, Resin Emulsion	F-P	P	P	P	B	F	F	F ⑦
Paint, Oil Base — Flat	P	F	F	B	B	B	P	F ⑦
— Semi-gloss	F	F	F	G	P	F	F	F ⑦
Paint, Non-Alkyd Resin Enamel	F	F	F	F	P	F	F	F ⑦
Paint, Alkyd Resin Enamel	G-F	G	G	G	P	G	G	F ⑦
Linseed Oil (Boiled, Rubbed In)	G-F	G	G	G	F	G	F	F ⑦
Wax	P	B	F	B	B	B	B	F
PLASTER ①								
Unfinished ③ ⑩	P	F	P	B	B	B	F	F
CONCRETE (Unfinished) ③	G	G	G	P	P	E	G	E
STONE (Unfinished) ③	G	E	E	P	P	E	E	E
BRICK — Natural Finish	G	E	E	P	P	G	E	E
WALLBOARDS (Unfinished) ① ③								
Acoustic Board	F-P	P	P	P	P	P	G	F ⑦
Plaster Board	P	P	P	P	P	B	F	F ⑦
Compressed Fibre - Unfinished								
Untempered	G-F	F	F	P	P	G	F	G ⑦
Tempered	G-F	G	F	F	F	G	G	G ⑦
Compressed Fibre - Factory Finished (Baked Synthetic Finishes)	G	G	G	G	G	G	G	F ⑦
Asbestos Board (Unfinished)	E-G	E	E	P	P	E	E	E
COVERINGS								
WALLPAPERS ① ⑤								
Non-Washable	P-B	B	P	B	B	P	P	F ⑦
Washable	F	F	F	G	F	F	F	F ⑦
Scrubable	G-F	F	G	G	G	F	G	G ⑦
FABRIC, COATED								
Oil Pigment	F	F	F	G	G	P	P	F ⑦
Vinyl	G-F	G	G	F	F	G	F	F ⑦
Pyroxlyin	G-F	G	G	F	G	F	F	F ⑦
FABRIC, UNCOATED ① ③ ⑥								
Canvas	F-P	F	P	P	P	G	G	P ⑦
Burlap	F-P	P	P	P	P	G	F	P ⑦
Grass or Fibre Woven	F-P	F	P	P	P	G	F	F ⑦
WOOD VENEER (Fabric Backed) ① ② ③								
THERMOSETTING PLASTIC SHEETS (Ex.: Micarta, Formica)	E-G	E	E	E	E	F	E	G ⑦
CERAMIC TILES								
Glazed	E	E	E	E	E	E	E	G ⑦
Unglazed - Vitreous	E-G	E	F	G	F	E	E	G ⑦
METAL TILES & SHEETS								
Baked Enamel Finish	E-G	E	E	E	E	E	G	G ⑦
Porcelain Enamel Finish	E	E	E	E	E	E	E	G ⑦
GLASS (Tiles, Sheets, Mirrors, Blocks)	E-G	E	E	E	E	E	E	F ⑦
HARD MARBLE POLISHED ①	E-G	E	E	G	G	E	E	G ⑦
ASPHALT TILE ①	G	G	G	G	G	G	G	G ⑦
RUBBER TILE, SHEET ①	G	G	G	F	F	G	G	G ⑦
LINOLEUM — INLAID ①	G-F	G	G	F	F	F	G	G ⑦
ENAMEL SURFACE (FELT BASE) ①	G-F	G	G	F	F	F	P	G ⑦
LEATHER ①	P	B	B	B	B	P	F	G ⑦
CORK TILE (RESIN BONDED) Unfinished ① ③	F	F	F	P	B	G	F	E ⑦

116

ASE OF LEANING	HEAVY CLEANING SPOTTING ⑧	OVER-ALL
P	naptha, sandpaper, steel wool	detergent
P	naptha, sandpaper, steel wool	detergent
G	naptha, steel wool	soap or detergent
G	steel wool	soap or detergent
F	steel wool	soap or detergent
P	steel wool	dough type cleaner
P	not recommended	not recommended
P	dough type cleaner	dough type cleaner
P	naptha	dough type cleaner
F	naptha	detergent
G	naptha	detergent
G	naptha	detergent
G	naptha	detergent
G	naptha	soap or detergent
P ⑨	sandpaper, steel wool	dough type cleaner
P ⑨	scrub brush, muriatic acid	detergent
P ⑨	scrub brush,	detergent
B ⑨	scrub brush,	detergent
B	not recommended	not recommended
B	dough type cleaner	not recommended
G	naptha, steel wool	detergent
G	naptha, steel wool	detergent
G	naptha, steel wool	detergent
G	naptha	detergent
B	dough type cleaner	dough type cleaner
G	cleaning fluid, detergent	detergent
G	cleaning fluid, detergent	detergent
G ⑨	detergent	soap or detergent
G ⑨	detergent	soap or detergent
G ⑨	detergent	soap or detergent
P	dough type cleaner	not recommended
P	dough type cleaner	not recommended
P	dough type cleaner	not recommended
E ⑨	detergent	soap or detergent
E ⑨	detergent	detergent
G ⑨	detergent	detergent
E ⑨	detergent	soap or detergent
E ⑨	scouring powder	soap or detergent
E ⑨	detergent	soap or detergent
E ⑨	scouring powder	detergent
G	Waterproof sandpaper, steel wool	detergent
G	scouring powder, steel wool	soap or detergent
G	scouring powder, steel wool	soap or detergent
G ⑨	scouring powder	soap or detergent
F	naptha	saddle soap
P	sandpaper, steel wool	detergent

In all charts where ratings are given by initials, these general classifications are indicated:

E – Excellent G – Good F – Fair
P – Poor B – Bad

① All materials and coverings on this chart are rated as unwaxed surfaces. When a surface is waxed, the wax film approximates the rating for *Wood Finishes – Wax.*

② Plywoods and veneered woods are either "regular" or "waterproof," and both come with hard or soft wood surface. The ratings are the same as given for solid hardwood or softwood, as the case may be, with the following exceptions: Regular plywood is rated *Poor* in resistance to water, *Fair* in durability, and has a household rating of *Poor*; waterproof plywood is rated *Good* in resistance to mildew.

③ If finished at home, refer to *Wood Finishes.*

④ The natural colors of these materials will resist fading quite well. Colored or dyed material will show varying tendencies to fade, depending upon the type of dye or color pigments used.

⑤ Commercial wall paper coating and lacquers are available for water-proofing wallpaper, which makes dusting and cleaning easier. In general, almost any type of wallpaper can be waterproofed, but it may cause some changes in color. Light and medium-colored paper is more easily waterproofed than darker shades. Application by spraying is recommended for dark-colored, hand-screened, and hand-painted wallpaper. If wallpaper is coated, refer to ratings of similar finish under *Wood Finishes.*

⑥ Canvas and burlap are more practical as wall coverings if they are painted with an enamel or varnish. This gives a smoother surface, which resists dust and can be more easily cleaned and washed.

⑦ These ratings are based on the 'natural' appearance of the material, but are subject to these conditions:

Color: White, pastel shades, black, and very dark colors will all show dust more quickly than shades which are closer to the color of dust, such as grey and tan. Medium value and medium intensity colors show more dust than grey, but less than pastels.

Pattern: Finely broken up, multi-colored patterns, such as those made by wood grain, natural brick, or a complicated wallpaper pattern will show dust less quickly than plain colors, or simple medallion patterns with large amounts of single-color background.

Surface Finish and Texture: A glossy, smooth surface, such as glass, will catch and hold less dust than embossed or sculptured papers, or heavily textured or woven materials. Color and variety of shading can sometimes be a compensating factor with textured materials, however.

⑧ Sandpaper, ordinary kind: 260 grit.

Waterproof sandpaper, if used with water: 330 grit.

Steel Wool: use #00 grade.

⑨ If you like extra work, you can wax almost any material. However, these items do *not* have to be waxed at any time.

⑩ Plastered walls should be allowed to dry for the longest possible time before painting. Some painters recommend waiting as much as a year.

117

CHART OF TABLE TOP MATERIALS AND COVERINGS

RESISTANCE TO:

MATERIALS	HOUSEHOLD RATING	WATER	BOILING WATER	OIL & GREASE	FOOD ACIDS & STAINS	ALCOHOL – BEVERAGES
WOOD UNFINISHED ①						
Solid Hardwood	F–P	G	G	B	B	P
Solid Softwood	F–P	F	F	B	B	P
Plywood, or Veneer ②						
WOOD FINISHES ③						
Varnish	F	F	F	P	F	F
Spar Varnish	G–F	G	G	F	G	G
Phenolic Plastic, Liquid	G–F	G	G	G	G	G
Floor Seal – Penetrating	F	G	G	G	G	F
Lacquer	F–P	F	P	G	G	P
Shellac	P	P	B	F	P	B
Linseed Oil – Boiled, rubbed in	G–F	G	G	G	G	G
Paint, Water – Casein, Calcamine	P	P	B	P	B	P
Paint, Resin Emulsion	P	F	B	F	B	P
Paint, Enamel – Semigloss	F–P	F	P	G	P	P
Paint, Non-Alkyd Resin Enamel	F	F	F	G	F	F
Paint, Alkyd Resin Enamel	G–F	G	G	G	F	G
Wax (Water emulsion & liquid types)	P–B	B	B	B	B	B
GLASS						
Standard	G	E	B	E	E	E
Tempered	E–G	E	E	E	E	E
SOAPSTONE	E–G	E	E	G	G	E
SLATE	G	E	E	F	G	E
ASBESTOS BOARD ①	G	E	E	P	P	E
MARBLE (Sound) ④						
Hard (Ex. – Verde Antique)	E–G	E	E	G	E ⑤⑥	E ⑥
Soft (Ex. – Light Glow)	G	E	E	P	G ⑤⑥	E ⑥
TERRAZZO	E–G	E	E	G	E ⑤⑥	E ⑥
COVERINGS						
PLASTIC						
Laminated Thermosetting ③						
Standard Grade	E–G	E	E	E	E	E
Cigarette-Proof	E–G	E	E	E	E	E
Tile & Sheet ③						
Vinyl	G–F	E	G	G	G	G
Cellulose Acetate	G–F	E	G	E	E	P
Methyl Methacrylate	G–F	E	G	E	E	E
FABRICS, COATED ③						
Pyroxylin	F	G	F	G	G	F
Vinyl	G–F	G	G	E	F	E
Oil Cloth	F	F	F	G	G	G
COMPRESSED WOOD FIBRE (Unfinished)						
Tempered ①	F	F	F	F	F	F
Factory Finished	G–F	G	G	G	G	G
CERAMIC TILE						
Glazed	E–G	E	E	E	E	E
Unglazed, Vitreous	G	E	E	G	F	E ⑥
METAL TILES & SHEETS						
Baked Synthetic Finish	E–G	E	E	E	E ⑥	E
Porcelain Enamel Finish	E–G	E	E	E	E ⑥	E
STAINLESS STEEL	E–G	E	E	E	G	E
LEATHER ③						
Tanned Natural ⑦	P	B	B	B	B	B
LINOLEUM – INLAID ③ ⑦	F	G	G	F	F ⑥	P
ENAMEL SURFACE (Felt-Base) ③	F	G	G	F	F ⑥	P
CORK – RESIN BONDED ③						
Unfinished ①	F–P	F	F	P	P	P
ASPHALT TILES ③ ⑦						
Grease-proof	F	G	G	G	F ⑥	F
Non grease-proof	F	G	G	F	P ⑥	F

118

RESISTANCE TO:				
CIGARETTE BURNS	OVEN-HOT UTENSILS	SCUFFS & SCRATCHES	DUST CAMOUFLAGE	EASE OF CLEANING
B	F	G	G	P
B	F	F	G	B
P	P	F	F	G
P	P	G	F	G
P	P	G	F	G ⑾
B	P	F	G	F
B	B	F	F	F
B	B	P	F	P
B	F	F	F	G
B	B	F	F	P
B	B	F	F	P
P	B	F	F	F
P	B	F	F	G
P	P	G	F	G
B	B	P	F	F
E	B	F ⑨	F	E ⑾
E	E ⑧	F ⑨	F	E ⑾
E	E ⑧	F	F	E ⑾
E	E ⑧	F	F	G ⑾
G	E ⑧	E	G	G
E	E ⑧	G	C	C ⑾
G	E ⑧	G	G	F ⑾
E	E ⑧	G	C	G ⑾
G	G	G	G	E ⑾
E	G	G	G	E ⑾
B	B	E	G	G ⑾
B	B	F	F	E ⑾
B	B	P	F	E ⑾
B	P	F	G	E ⑾
B	F	G	G	E ⑾
B	P	P	F	E ⑾
B	F	G	F	C
B	P	G	F	G
E	E ⑧	C	F	E ⑾
E	E ⑧	E	G	F ⑾
G	G	F	G	G ⑾
E	E ⑧	G	F	E ⑾
E	E ⑧	F	F	E ⑾
B	P	P	G	F
B	F	G	G	F
B	F	F	F	G ⑾
B	G	F	G	F
P	P	G	G	F
P	P	G	G	F

① If hand finished, see under *Wood Finishes*.

② Plywoods and veneered woods are either "regular" or "waterproof", and both come with hard or soft wood surfaces. The ratings are the same as given for solid hardwood or solid softwood, as the case may be, with the following exceptions: regular plywood is rated *Poor* in resistance to water, boiling and oven-hot utensils, and has a household rating of *Poor*.

③ These tests apply only if material is properly applied to surface.

④ Marble is described as "sound" or "unsound"; be sure to specify sound marble, as the unsound variety is not recommended for this type of use.

⑤ Note, however, that acid will eat into marble.

⑥ Mottles and textures will camouflage stains.

⑦ All materials and finishes on this chart are rated as unwaxed surfaces. If a surface is waxed, the wax film approximates the ratings given for *Wood Finishes — Wax*.

⑧ Oven-hot casseroles may be placed directly on these materials without noticeable effect.

⑨ Clear glass, although extremely hard, shows scratches very quickly. For colored glass, see 10.

⑩ A plain surface, light colors, bright or medium-dark colors on a shiny or glossy surface, all show fingermarks, slight soil, etc. much more readily than a semi-gloss, matte, or flat surface in a natural color, or a surface broken up by a pattern.

⑾ If you like extra work, you *can* wax just about every table top material. However, these materials do not ever have to be waxed.

CHART OF FLOOR MATERIALS AND FLOOR COVERINGS

MATERIALS (Unwaxed)	Household Rating	Cleaning — How (Usual)	Cleaning — How Drastic ④	How Often Usual	How Often Drastic ⑯	With What Material Drastic ④⑧
HARDWOOD - FINISHES						
FLOOR SEALS - Penetrating	F	Damp mop, Vacuum, Sweep	Scrub, steel wool, Mop ⑦	Weekly	6 - 12 Mos. ⑰	Soap, detergent, naptha for spotting
FLOOR FINISHES - Gymnasium Type	G-F	Dust, damp mop, vacuum, sweep	Scrub, steel wool, Mop ⑦	Weekly	6 - 12 Mos. ⑰	Soap, detergent, naptha for spotting
VARNISHES	F	Dust, damp mop, vacuum, sweep	Scrub, steel wool, Mop ⑦	Weekly	6 - 12 Mos. ⑰	Soap, detergent, naptha for spotting
VARNISHES - Modified ①	G-F	Dust, damp mop, vacuum, sweep	Scrub, steel wool, Mop ⑦	Weekly	6 - 12 Mos. ⑰	Soap, Naptha for spotting
SHELLAC	F-P	Dust, vacuum, sweep	Steel wool, damp cold mop ⑦	Weekly	6 - 12 Mos. ⑰	Alcohol for spotting
PHENOLIC PLASTIC, LIQUID	G-F	Dust, damp mop, vacuum, sweep	Scrub, steel wool	Weekly	6 - 12 Mos.	Soap, detergent
FLOOR ENAMEL	F	Dust, damp mop vacuum, sweep	Mild scrub, steel wool ⑦	Weekly	6 - 12 Mos. ⑰	Soap, detergent
MASONRY (Unwaxed)						
BRICK	E-G	Sweep, hose, vacuum	Scrub ⑤	Weekly	Quarterly	Detergent ⑩
TILE - Glazed - Gloss	G	Vacuum, dust, mop, hose, sweep	Scrub, wet mop	Weekly	Monthly	Detergent
- Matte	E-G	Vacuum, dust, mop hose, sweep	Scrub, wet mop	Weekly	Monthly	Detergent
- Unglazed	E-G	Dust, mop, hose, sweep	Scrub, wet mop	Weekly	Weekly	Detergent
TERRAZZO - Latex Bonded	G	Sweep, hose, mop, vacuum, dust	Scrub, wet mop	Weekly	Bi-monthly	Detergent
- Cement Bonded	E-G	Vacuum, sweep, damp mop, dust	Scrub, wet mop	Weekly	Bi-monthly	Detergent
MAGNESITE	G	Vacuum, sweep, damp mop	Scrub, wet mop ⑤	Weekly	Bi-monthly	Detergent
FLAGSTONE	E-G	Vacuum, sweep, hose, damp mop	Scrub	Weekly	Monthly	Detergent ⑩
SLATE	G	Vacuum, sweep, hose, damp mop	Scrub, wet mop	Weekly	Bi-monthly	Detergent ⑩
MARBLE (Hard)	E-G	Vacuum, sweep, hose, damp mop	Scrub, wet mop	Weekly	Semi-annually	Detergent, soft abrasive
CEMENT - Painted ②	F	Vacuum, sweep, hose, damp mop	Mop	Weekly	6 - 12 Mos.	Soap, detergent
- Unpainted ③	G	Vacuum, hose, sweep	Scrub ⑤ etch	Weekly	Bi-monthly Etch 5 to 10 yrs.	Detergent, Muriatic acid

① Modified, harder, more durable varnishes, such as Spar varnishes, Gym Varnishes, etc.

② Rubber, resin or copolymer-based paint.

③ Dusty or porous cement surfaces can be improved by the use of cement-hardening paints (such as "Lapidolith").

④ "Drastic cleaning" includes complete removal of any wax, followed by rewaxing, if necessary.

⑤ Porous masonry can be more easily cleaned by pre-wetting the floor before adding detergent solutions to prevent absorption of detergent into flooring.

⑥ Pile carpets should be vacuumed as soon as soiled, to keep dust from becoming imbedded in the carpet by traffic.

⑦ In general, #00 steel wool is recommended for spot cleaning, although coarser grades may be needed for special purposes.

⑧ These detergents include such trade names as *Dreft, Swerl, Vel, Glim, Tide, Fab, All.*

⑨ Detergents for shampooing are sold under special trade names, but certain of those listed in ⑧ above, and commonly available, are suitable.

⑩ Drastic cleaning to remove cement stains can be accomplished by etching with muriatic acid.

⑪ Non-rub waxes are the common, water-emulsion waxes. "Liquid" refers to the self-cleaning liquid waxes; both this type and the paste waxes require polishing.

⑫ "*Poor*" ratings in this category refer to difficulty of removing stains, to deterioration of the carpet, and to its susceptibility to becoming a site for germ and insect growth.

⑬ In this column, the ratings mean:
Good—Dust is not visible because surface is dull or matte finish, or (with any type of floor covering or material)

Frequency of Rewaxing (16) Usual	Recommended Wax (11)	Resistance to: Foods Acids	Foods Greases	Spilled Water or Rain	Cigarette Burns	Spilled Alcohol	Abrasion (Wear)	Scuffing (Mar)	Appearance Dust (13) Visibility	Ease of Removing Dust (14)	Length of Life (Of Material or Finish) (16)
3 Mos.	Non-rub or Paste	F	P	F	B	F	F	G	F	G	10 Years
3 Mos.	Non-rub or paste	G	F	F	P	G	G	F	F	G	5-10 Years
3 Mos.	Non-rub or paste	F	P	P	P	F	F	F	F	G	5-10 Years
3 Mos.	Non-rub or paste	G	F	F	P	G	G	F	F	G	5-10 Years
3 Mos.	Liquid or paste only	F	P	B	B	P	B	P	F	G	1-2 Years
3 Mos.	Non-rub, liquid or paste	G	G	F	P	G	G	F	F	G	10 Years up (New Product)
3 Mos.	non-rub or paste	F	F	P	B	P	B	P	F	G	1-2 Years
–	–	P	P	E	E	E	E	G	E	F (18)	50 Years up
–	–	G	E	E	E	E	G	G	P	E (18)	10-50 Years
–	–	G	G	E	E	E	E	E	G	G (18)	10-50 Years
–	–	G	G	E	E	E	E	G	G	G (18)	50 Years up
(Optional)	Non-rub only	G	F	E	F	G	E	E	E	G	10 Years (New Product)
–	–	F	G	E	E	E	E	E	G	E	50 Yrs. up (20)
–	–	F	G	E	E	E	E	G	E	G	50 Years up
–	–	G	G	E	E	E	E	E	E	F (18)	50 Years up
–	–	G	P	E	E	E	E	G	G	F (18)	50 Years up
–	–	P	G	E	E	E	E	G	G	E	50 Years up
3 Mos.	Non-rub or paste	F	F	F	P	F	P	F	F	F	1-3 Years
(Optional)	Paste	F	P	E	E	E	E (3)	E (3)	E	F	50 Years up

small mottles, patterns, and medium colors hide dust effectively; *Fair*–Intermediate; *Poor*–Dust particles are readily visible because surface is very glossy, or (no matter what the material or covering) large patterns, uniform dark and light colors show dust quickly.

(14) *Excellent* to *Good*–Dust readily removed because of smoothness of surface; *Fair*–Uneven surface which needs severe sweeping or vacuuming; *Poor*–Pile fabrics hold dust tenaciously; even severe vacuuming does not completely remove it.

(15) These ratings are based on the less strenuous use to which throw rugs or summer rugs are commonly subjected.

(16) Frequency of cleaning and waxing, and length of life, depends largely on location of flooring. Kitchen and bathroom floors need more attention than living room and dining room. "Drastic cleaning" for the living room might be the equivalent of "usual" for the kitchen. Much also depends on whether you live in city or country (city living is always dirtier) and on how heavy the "traffic" is through the room.

(17) For drastic rewaxing: we recommend using a professional service for best and most thorough results.

(18) Piece-laid floors (brick, flagstone, etc.) will be much easier to clean if joints are flush, making a smooth floor. If roughly laid, the joints will catch dirt, create a cleaning problem.

(19) Depends on sub-structure and installation.

(20) Brittle materials and coverings will not "give" with wood frame floors, and have a tendency to crack.

(21) A short-pile wool carpet with a sponge rubber backing is now available. Its characteristics are about the same as conventionally-backed wool carpeting, but it does not need an under layer or rug pad.

See next page for continuation of chart
(FLOOR COVERINGS)

CHART OF FLOOR MATERIALS AND FLOOR COVERINGS (Continued)

COVERINGS (Unwaxed)	Household Rating	Cleaning How (Implement) Usual	Cleaning How (Implement) Drastic ④	Cleaning How Often Usual	Cleaning How Often Drastic ⑯	With What Material Drastic ④⑧
CORK (Factory Finished) (If Hand Finished, see "Hardwood-Finishes")	G-F	Vacuum, sweep, dust, damp mop	Scrub, wet mop, steel wool ⑦	Weekly	6 Mos. ⑰	Detergent, naptha for spotting
ASPHALT TILE (Grease Proof)	G-F	Dust, vacuum, damp mop, sweep	Scrub, wet mop steel wool ⑦	Weekly	6 Mos. ⑰	Detergent
(Non-Grease Proof)	G-F	Dust, vacuum, damp mop, sweep	Scrub, steel wool ⑦, wet mop	Weekly	6 Mos. ⑰	Detergent
VINYL PLASTIC TILE AND ROLL (Plain)	G-F	Dust, vacuum, damp mop, sweep	Scrub, wet mop	Weekly	6 Mos.	Detergent
FLOOR SEALS-Penetrating	G-F	Vacuum, sweep	Scrub, wet mop	Weekly	6 Mos.	Detergent
RUBBER TILE	G-F	Dust, vacuum, damp mop, sweep	Scrub, steel wool ⑦, wet mop	Weekly	6 Mos. ⑰	Detergent
LINOLEUM - Inlaid	G-F	Dust, vacuum, damp mop, sweep	Scrub, steel wool ⑦, wet mop	Weekly	6 Mos. ⑰	Detergent
ENAMEL SURFACE (Felt Base)	G-F	Dust, vacuum, damp mop, sweep	Scrub, wet mop	Weekly	6 Mos.	Detergent
LEATHER (Waxed)	G-F	Dust, vacuum, damp mop, sweep	Polishing	Weekly	1 Year	Saddle soap, steel wool, naptha for spots
RUGS & CARPETS (Thick Pile) ⑥ ㉑ - Wool	G-F	Vacuum, sweep	Shampoo	Twice weekly	1 - 5 Years	Shampoo ⑨
- Cotton	F	Vacuum, sweep	Shampoo	Twice weekly	6 Mos.	Shampoo ⑨
- Flax	G-F	Vacuum, sweep	Shampoo	Twice weekly	1 - 3 Years	Shampoo ⑨
- Rayon	G-F	Vacuum, sweep	Shampoo	Twice weekly	1 - 3 Years	Shampoo ⑨
- Nylon	G-F	Vacuum, sweep	Shampoo	Twice weekly	1 - 3 Years	Shampoo ⑨
(Short Pile) ⑥ - Wool	F	Vacuum	Shampoo	Twice weekly	1 - 3 Years	Shampoo ⑨
- Cotton	F	Vacuum	Shampoo	Twice weekly	Annually	Shampoo ⑨
- Flax	F	Vacuum	Shampoo	Twice weekly	Annually	Shampoo ⑨
- Rayon	F	Vacuum	Shampoo	Twice weekly	Annually	Shampoo ⑨
Felt Carpet	F	Vaccum, sweep	Scrub	Twice weekly	Annually	Detergent
Flat Woven - Cotton	G-F	Vacuum, sweep	Launder	Weekly	Bi-monthly	Detergent
- Cotton & Flax	G-F	Vacuum, sweep	Launder, shampoo	Weekly	Annually	Shampoo ⑨
- Fibre (Paper) Plasticized	F	Vacuum, sweep	Damp mop only	Weekly	Monthly	Water only
- Wool & Fibre	G-F	Vacuum, sweep	Shampoo	Weekly	1 Year	Shampoo ⑨
- Wool & Cotton (Plast.)	G-F	Vacuum, sweep	Shampoo	Weekly	1 Year	Shampoo ⑨
- Hemp & Manila	G-F	Vacuum, sweep	Shampoo, scrub	Weekly	1 Year	Shampoo ⑨
- Sisal	G-F	Vacuum, sweep	Shampoo, scrub	Weekly	1 Year	Shampoo ⑨
- Rush & Grasses	G-F	Vacuum, sweep	Damp mop	Weekly	Monthly	Water only

① Modified, harder, more durable varnishes, such as Spar varnishes, Gym Varnishes, etc.

② Rubber, resin or copolymer-based paint.

③ Dusty or porous cement surfaces can be improved by the use of cement-hardening paints (such as "Lapidolith").

④ "Drastic cleaning" includes complete removal of any wax, followed by rewaxing, if necessary.

⑤ Porous masonry can be more easily cleaned by pre-wetting the floor before adding detergent solutions to prevent absorption of detergent into flooring.

⑥ Pile carpets should be vacuumed as soon as soiled, to keep dust from becoming imbedded in the carpet by traffic.

⑦ In general, #00 steel wool is recommended for spot cleaning, although coarser grades may be needed for special purposes.

⑧ These detergents include such trade names as *Dreft, Swerl, Vel, Glim, Tide, Fab, All.*

⑨ Detergents for shampooing are sold under special trade names, but certain of those listed in ⑧ above, and commonly available, are suitable.

⑩ Drastic cleaning to remove cement stains can be accomplished by etching with muriatic acid.

⑪ Non-rub waxes are the common, water-emulsion waxes. "Liquid" refers to the self-cleaning liquid waxes; both this type and the paste waxes require polishing.

⑫ *"Poor"* ratings in this category refer to difficulty of removing stains, to deterioration of the carpet, and to its susceptibility to becoming a site for germ and insect growth.

⑬ In this column, the ratings mean:
Good—Dust is not visible because surface is dull or matte finish, or (with any type of floor covering or material)

| Frequency of Rewaxing (16) Usual | Recommended Wax (11) | RESISTANCE TO: ||||||||| Appearance Dust (13) Visibility | Ease of Removing Dust (14) | Length of Life (Of Material or Finish (16) |
| | | Foods || Spilled Water or Rain | Cigarette Burns | Spilled Alcohol | Abrasion (Wear) | Scuffing (Mar) | | | |
		Acids	Greases								
1 - 3 Mos.	Non-rub or paste	G	P	G (19)	B	F	G	G	G	G	10 Years up
1 - 3 Mos.	Non-rub only	G	G	G (19)	P	G	G	G	F	G	8 - 12 Yrs. (20)
1 - 3 Mos.	Non-rub only	G	P	G (19)	P	F	G	G	F	G	8 - 12 Yrs. (20)
–	–	G	G	G (19)	B	G	G	F	P	G	5 - 15 Yrs.
–	–	G	G	G (19)	B	G	E	E	E	F	10 - 50 Yrs.
1 - 3 Mos.	Non-rub only	G	F	G (19)	P	G	G	F	P	G	10 - 15 Years
1 - 3 Mos.	Non-rub, liquid or paste	G	F	G (19)	P	F	G	G	F	G	5 - 15 Years
(Optional)	Non-rub only	G	F	G (19)	P	F	P	G	P	G	1 - 3 Years
Annual	Paste only	F	F	B (19)	B	P	F	F	G	G	15 Years up
–	–	P (17)	P	F	P	P	G	E	G	P	10 - 20 Years
–	–	P	B	F	B	P	F	E	G	P	4 - 5 Years
–	–	P	P	F	B	P	P	E	G	P	4 - 5 Years
–	–	F	F	F	B	P	G	E	G	P	4-5 Years
–	–	F	F	F	B	P	G	E	G	P	10 Years up (New Product)
–	–	P	P	F	B	P	F	E	G	P	2 - 10 Years
–	–	P	P	F	B	P	P	E	F	P	2 - 5 Years
–	–	P	P	F	B	P	P	E	F	P	2 - 5 Years
–	–	P	P	F	B	P	P	E	F	P	2 - 5 Years
–	–	P	P	F	B	F	P	E	F	F	1 - 3 Years
–	–	P	B	G	B	F	F	E	G	F	3 - 5 Years (15)
–	–	P	P	F	B	F	F	E	G	F	3 - 5 Years (15)
–	–	P	P	P	B	P	B	E	G	F	1 - 2 Years (15)
–	–	P	P	P	B	P	F	E	G	F	3 - 5 Years (15)
–	–	P	P	F	B	P	F	E	G	F	3 - 5 Years (15)
–	–	P	P	F	B	P	F	E	G	F	5 - 10 Yrs. (15)
–	–	P	P	F	B	P	F	E	G	F	5 - 10 Yrs. (15)
–	–	P	P	P	B	P	P	E	G	F	1 - 5 Years (15)

small mottles, patterns, and medium colors hide dust effectively; *Fair*—Intermediate; *Poor*—Dust particles are readily visible because surface is very glossy, or (no matter what the material or covering) large patterns, uniform dark and light colors show dust quickly.

(14) *Excellent* to *Good*—Dust readily removed because of smoothness of surface; *Fair*—Uneven surface which needs severe sweeping or vacuuming; *Poor*—Pile fabrics hold dust tenaciously; even severe vacuuming does not completely remove it.

(15) These ratings are based on the less strenuous use to which throw rugs or summer rugs are commonly subjected.

(16) Frequency of cleaning and waxing, and length of life, depends largely on location of flooring. Kitchen and bathroom floors need more attention than living room and dining room. "Drastic cleaning" for the living room might be the equivalent of "usual" for the kitchen. Much also depends on whether you live in city or country (city living is always dirtier) and on how heavy the "traffic" is through the room.

(17) For drastic rewaxing: we recommend using a professional service for best and most thorough results.

(18) Piece laid floors (brick, flagstone, etc.) will be much easier to clean if joints are flush, making a smooth floor. If roughly laid, the joints will catch dirt, create a cleaning problem.

(19) Depends on sub-structure and installation.

(20) Brittle materials and coverings will not "give" with wood frame floors, and have a tendency to crack.

(21) A short-pile wool carpet with a sponge rubber backing is now available. Its characteristics are about the same as conventionally-backed wool carpeting, but it does not need an under layer or rug pad.

123

CHAPTER VII

THE HOUSEWIFE-ENGINEER

SOMETHING UNDREAMED-OF is happening to American women—their housework, which has always been statistically recorded as unskilled labor, has now become the subject of scientific study!

Although our recommendations in the preceding chapters of this book have been largely concerned with *preventing* housework, by planning and by the use of laborsaving materials, we realize that —no matter how simply or practically your home is furnished —some maintenance work will always be necessary. And even our preventive measures cannot, by themselves, miraculously eliminate the major share of the huge and apparently endless job of housework. We believe that reducing the work is a threefold proposition, of which preventives are only one aspect. So we decided to deal in this chapter with housework itself, and with the two remaining means of decreasing its drudgery: simplification of methods, and the development of a *new* attitude toward home maintenance—for we consider the traditional standard of immaculateness completely unrealistic for our times.

With this in mind, we started to investigate, and found that methods developed in industry are now being applied to the home. The drudgery of housework is now being attacked in a scientist-conducted revolution: the battle cry is "Work simplification" and the weapon is the "time and motion study." The home is considered a small industry, and every housewife its production engineer.

However, the leaders of the new approach are finding that, like most revolutions, this one is meeting a great deal of opposition. Most housewives of our transitional age are apparently firmly rooted in traditional standards. So we interviewed many people—from universities, from industry, the home-furnishings press, our friends—with the idea of combining in this chapter the most convincing energy-saving and time-saving approaches to housekeeping. (And we found, incidentally, that we had stumbled into a hotbed of divergent opinions.)

This chapter is not intended as a complete treatise on all problems of housework. What we offer here are some scientifically tested examples, plus simplified methods we have evolved or uncovered ourselves. Many housekeeping tasks are not discussed here, simply because we've been unable to devise or discover any good short cuts for them. (However, you'll find many housekeeping source books on the market offering unshortened routines for all tasks.*) We believe that what we do offer here is the beginning of a whole new approach—a stride in a new direction.

Time-and-Motion Studies

1. "If housewives would plan *how* to do their work, as well as *what* to do, they would all save an appreciable amount of work," says M. E. Mundell of Purdue University, an engineering professor and one of the pioneers in methods research in the home. Time-and-motion studies are a principal tool of such investigators, a means of determining by concrete example just how much simpler even the simplest of household tasks can be made.

The basic idea is itself simple: Eliminate unnecessary steps and motions in your work, combine, rearrange, make them easier. The desired result is housekeeping minus all that is unnecessary, unduly arduous and time-consuming. Certainly this is a most desirable aim; no housewife, no matter how immaculate-minded, *wants* to be worn out at the end of the day. Don't misunderstand us; time and energy given to those parts of housekeeping you really like and consider essential are not wasted, but an improved approach and simpler methods can conserve your energies for just such tasks.

The value of time-and-motion studies can probably be made most clear by an actual example. Even in a task like preparing potatoes for baking, the time and motion expenditure can be cut down substantially. Revisions like these make the difference: keeping a week's supply of potatoes in the sink cupboard instead of going to a distant bin each time; using both hands simultaneously (turning on the water with the left hand while reaching for the brush with the right), carrying all the potatoes to the oven in a pan in one trip instead of taking them by hand, one or two at a time.

*We recommend: *How to Keep House*, by Mary D. Gillies, Harper, 1948; *Woman's Home Companion Household Book*, ed. by Henry Humphrey, Doubleday, 1948; *The Good Housekeeping Housekeeping Book*, ed. by Helen W. Kendall, McKay, 1947.

These findings, you might think, are absurdly obvious. But any housewife, if she is honest with herself, would confess that she could probably find equally obvious ways to shorten her work merely by watching and criticizing herself for a few days.

Timing an operation from start to finish is an incentive to work simplification. Checking with the clock, being conscious of the passage of time while getting breakfast on the table, stimulated us to simplify our routine here, so that the time was cut from 15 minutes to 8. To help get the idea across to yourself, make a few test-case time-and-motion studies:

Timing Household Tasks

Choose a single small job comparable to potato preparation; for real labor-saving incentive, select one that irks you.

Make a simplified "Process Chart" like the one below and get an observer to keep the record—your husband or an older child (it's a good, constructive family game).

Now begin the task. The observer records time, motions, and number of separate steps in the task, like this:

Step	Motion (details)	Time begun - 3:44
Goes to range	Turns on heat	
Goes to cupboard	Opens door (right hand) Takes out pan (left) Transfers to right hand	
(Goes to sink, oven, etc.) Total steps: __	(etc.) Total motions: __	Time ended - 3:53 Total time: 9 min.

When the task is completed (the potatoes in the oven, perhaps), total motions, steps, and elapsed time. Now analyze every step, every motion. See what you can eliminate as unnecessary, combine, or rearrange in more efficient order.

If you let this result in hurrying, you're defeating your own purpose, and merely adding one more pressure to a job already full of pressures. But the placing of utensils, the use of both hands, carrying more than one thing at a time, setting up a second operation while performing the first—all these are motion-savers that can contribute to timesaving *without* hurry.

Work Simplification

2. Now we'll consider the housekeeping job as a whole, and the methods that may be applied to ease it. Here is a work-simplification catechism worked out for this book, especially for the use of housewives, from industrial, engineering, and home economics sources: (A) Question the job; (B) Question the setup; (C) Question the tools; (D) Question the working conditions.

(A) Question the Job

Why do it? Does it contribute to your family's health, comfort, happiness? Measured against the expenditure of time and energy, does the task show a profit? If the answer to this isn't a firm Yes, don't do it.

Who should do it? The housewife, another member of the family, or the maid, if any? Should it be done at home or by professional services (such as laundries, dry cleaners)?

When should it be done? (Out of this aspect of planning a schedule is born.) Start a big job after lunch, or save it until morning, when you're fresh? Change beds just before washday or the laundryman's call? Defrost and clean the refrigerator when it's almost empty, just before your big marketing?

How should it be done? This brings up the matter of techniques and routines for specific tasks; detailed suggestions are offered in Section 6 of this chapter—Household Tasks, beginning on page 141.

(B) Question the Setup

This involves selection and pre-positioning. Selection is the step of picking out the tool and the material with which you are going to work: the potato and the knife to peel it. To go on with the potato, you'll peel it at the sink, so store it near there, and have knife, garbage disposal, work counter, all at the sink; also the utensil in which it gets cooked, and the salt to season it. This is pre-positioning. Check over all your storage arrangements for pre-positioning:

In the kitchen, the old system of putting all of your pots, pans, and lids in one cupboard, dishes in another, all kitchen cutlery in another, dry groceries in another, only *looks* efficient. It's really much more efficient to store things at the places where they are first used: foods which require washing, near the sink, but those which go directly into a pot of boiling water, near the range; a saucepan, to be filled first with water, near the sink, but the lid near the range; dinner plates in the dining area, but platters near the range. Duplicate small utensils used in different places, such as measuring cups and spoons, and make other duplications in the kitchen and dining area.

Kitchen Storage Hints

Have some saucepans and other utensils hanging on the wall above the work counter where they are mostly used first, in plain view and within easy reach—like the copper pots in an old farm kitchen.

Store frequently used utensils at counter height, those infrequently used on higher and lower shelves.

Have mixing bowls and platters placed separately where they are used—not nested—if space permits, so you don't have to lift all to get at one.

Have knives in a wall rack within easy reach of the counter; one kind is a magnetized bar (107) which holds knives slapped against it.

A multiple-tier Lazy Susan (108) built into a corner provides more easily accessible shelf space than corner cupboards.

Have slot storage for cookie sheets, muffin pans, all shallow baking tins, pot lids, serving platters, at the range. This is done by putting adjustable vertical dividers in a deep shelf.

Have shallow shelves, about 6 inches deep, for single-row storage of packaged and canned goods, so nothing is stored out of sight.

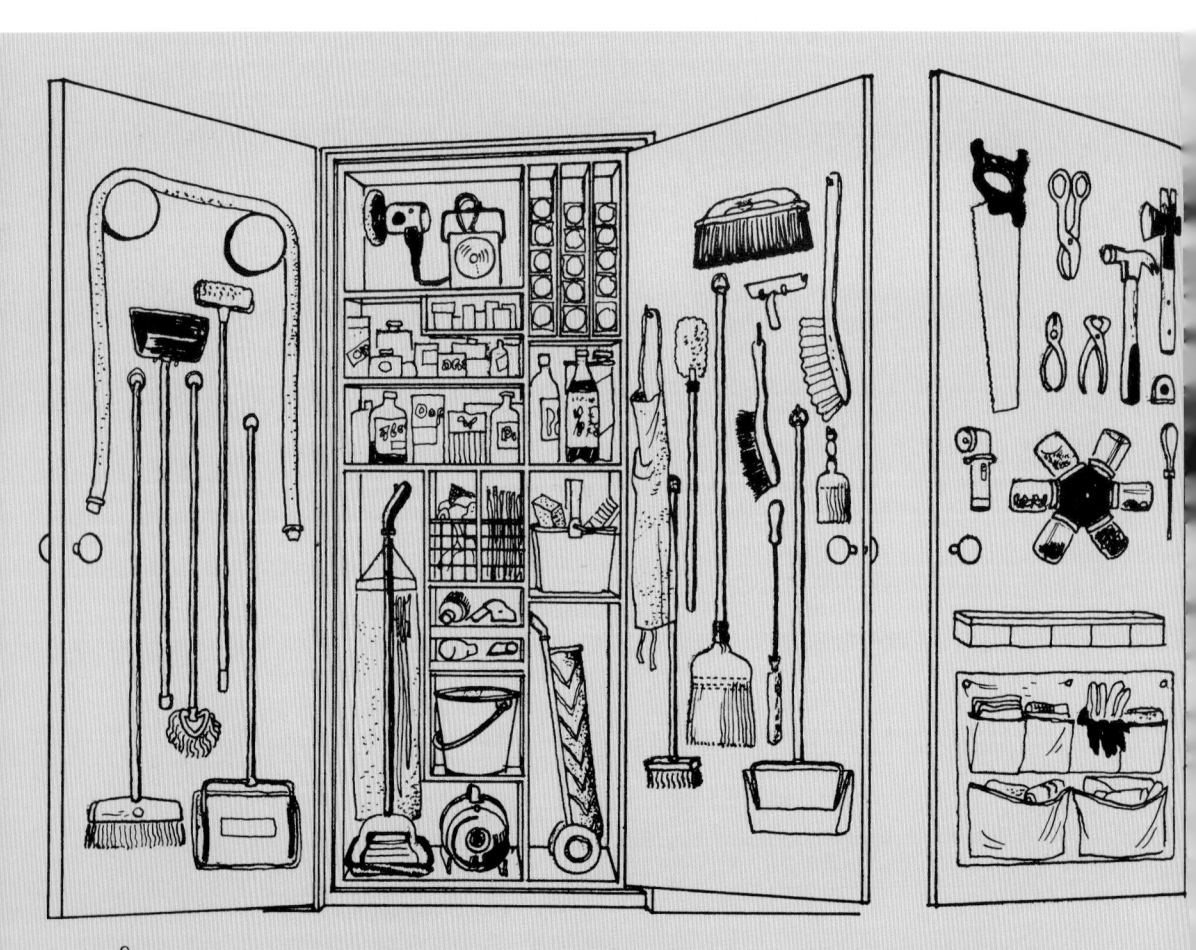

You'll find that most kitchen storage space is not adequate for really labor-saving pre-positioning, and that you'll have to do a lot of improvising. We recommend Cornell University's inexpensive descriptive pamphlet, *Functional Kitchen Storage (Bulletin 846)*, with working drawings—not too difficult for a home carpenter to execute. Write to Cornell University Agricultural Experiment Station, Ithaca, New York.

Pre-positioning cleaning storage—having your cleaning tools and supplies stored together, wherever you need them—will save many steps, much time and motion.

Storing them where they are to be used may mean not one big cleaning closet, complete with everything, but several small storage places — in the bathroom, the kitchen, hallways, on stairs.

If possible, duplicate supplies that are needed in different parts of the house: a second carpet sweeper, a junior or hand vacuum cleaner upstairs, brushes and cleaners in each storage space, etc.

GENERAL CLEANING CLOSET: You may not have the space to store all cleaning equipment, supplies, and tools together (and in a large house you'll probably find it convenient to have duplicate items in various parts of the house). But if you can turn over one large closet to cleaning material, you'll find it a great saver of time, steps, and bother. The closet shown here is 30 inches wide; in addition to its shelves and hanging space on the back of the outer door, additional space is provided by an independent hinged panel directly behind the door—in effect, an inner door, with hanging space on both its surfaces (the outer surface of the panel, with space for hanging tools, is shown to the right of the closet).

In such a closet can be stored the great variety of items on the following check list:

GENERAL CLEANING CLOSET CHECK LIST

Equipment:
Vacuum cleaner and all attachments and/or hand vacuum
Carpet sweeper
Dry mop—washable, extension type
Wet mop—cellulose or rubber-sponge recommended
Floor brush—long-handled
Dustpan—long-handled
Scrub brush—long-handled
Wax applier—long-handled (sponge mop can double for this)
Wall brush—swivel type, for corners
Scrub pail with perforated, removable squeeze-out ledge, or mop bucket with roller (dolly for bucket)
Rubber gloves
Electric work lamp (bulb in a wire cage on a long cord) or flashlight (lantern type)
Apron or overalls, with large pockets
Notebook and pencil (in apron pocket)

Supplies:
Drain cleaner, ammonia, washing soda, bleach
Detergents (washing, cleaning, and scouring types—see page 134)
Self-cleaning wax
Non-rubbing wax
Glass cleaner (nonrinsing, in spray-top bottle)
Silver polish
Treated dust and polishing cloths
Metal polish
Plastic spray for metal
Furniture polish

For Cleaning Basket, Tray, or Cart:
Plain or lintless dust mitts
Dustcloths (lintless) and rags of all kinds
Cellulose sponges of various sizes
Whisk broom
Paper bags
Paper towels and tissues
Treated polishing cloths
Art-gum eraser
Wallpaper cleaning pad, dough type
Dry cleaner for spots on upholstery or rugs
Detergents (see page 134)
Bottles or jars for detergents
Scissors

Tools and supplies that can be kept elsewhere:
Box of household tools: hammer, plane, screwdriver, pliers, scissors, pocket knife, sandpaper, steel wool, box of assorted nails, scotch tape
Hand electric buffer and sander
Box of electrical supplies: bulbs, fuses, plugs, extension cords

(C) Question the Tools

A craftsman loves best those tools which serve him best—especially those which are most versatile. Tools are just as important to you; choose carefully to get the most out of them, and to suit your own ways. If you're new to housekeeping, buy sparingly and experimentally. The stores are full of wonderful tools, some of them a far cry from such old staples as straw broom, string mop, and cotton dustcloth, all of them designed to make your household labors easier and quicker. Here are just a handful of which we're particularly fond:

Modern Cleaning Tools

The cellulose sponge, which replaces the dishrag; soft when wet, doesn't drip, doesn't trail edges or threads, squeezes out clean, and can be boiled for sterilizing. Have several, for dishwashing, woodwork, bathrooms, etc.

Sponge-rubber or cellulose-sponge mop, instead of the old cotton or string type; it rinses clean with a few squeezes under running water. Some have devices for self-squeezing (109).

Long-handled tools for the floor. Your broom has a long handle so that you can sweep without stooping; get dustpans, scrubbing brushes, etc., with long handles, too.

Long-handled, reversible wax applier (110). One side is a cleaning pad, for applying wax; the other side is a polishing pad.

Roll of cloth, pieces of which can be torn off for dusting, dishwashing, and cleaning mirrors, windows, stoves; it's washable (111); assorted cloths (130).

Copper-mesh balls for scouring pots, pans. *Also "Tuffy" and S.O.S. Magic Scouring Pads*

Spray attachment, plus hose, to be placed on the kitchen-sink faucet for easier rinsing in dishwashing.

Aluminum foil. It's amazingly all-purpose. Use it for lining broilers, casseroles, roasters (saves cleaning pans), wrapping vegetables like cabbage for boiling (eliminates odor), wrapping food to be warmed over (holds in the moisture), wrapping and covering food in the refrigerator, wrapping to protect against moth damage, wrapping clean paintbrushes (keeps them soft). Placed under the ironing board cover, it reflects heat; under the ice tray it prevents sticking.

Plastic refrigerator bags (112) are wonderful for leftovers, fresh foods, and paintbrushes. Turn inside out to wash. They take up practically no storage space.

A dish drainer with a section for draining eight glasses (140).

A kitchen timer—with bell—for timing food during cooking. Can be set as easily as an alarm clock (141).

A jar opener designed for quick, effortless opening of vacuum-sealed jars (131, 132).

Appliances: Watch for new appliances, major and minor, but watch out for them, too. An appliance might turn out to require more labor before and after than it saves during the job, so don't buy it just because it seems like a good idea, but try to get an opportunity to test it before buying. A most important point to consider is whether you can get neighborhood service on the appliance.

Study the manufacturer's directions for the use and care of any appliance you buy, and carry them out to the letter. Be willing to spend time practicing, so that you can develop real skill with these tools.

New models and improved variations make their appearance on the market so frequently these days that it would be impossible to catalogue in detail the "latest" or the "best." So we are limiting ourselves here to describing the general laborsaving features of the most useful major appliances now available to the housewife.

Vacuum Cleaner: This is probably the most important laborsaving appliance in your home. With its attachments, it can rid the room of dust from ceiling to floor, including furniture, books, lamp shades—even bureau drawers; some can wax the floor, and spray paint and moth-repellent. New timesaving attributes are continually being added as the range and versatility of attachments increases.

Dust-bag nuisance in emptying the vacuum cleaner has been minimized by the addition of disposable paper bags; others replace the dust bag entirely with a concealed cone (114), or with a sealed paper cone that is automatically ejected when the bag is full (134).

The choice of model—whether it's upright, canister, or cylinder—depends on the amount of carpeted area versus hard-surface floor area in the home. The two latter types have swivel arrangements that permit one to reach all parts of a room from one central position. For large carpeted areas, the upright is preferred because motor-driven brushes get deeply embedded dirt out of the rug fibers.

Refrigerator: We believe "high-humidity" types save you the most time, not only as compared with the greater time and nuisance of conventional defrosting methods (whether automatic or not), but also by eliminating the necessity for covering foods.

Before buying, decide what you want of the refrigerator with regard to your own storage needs. Do you need it to store frozen foods for any length of time, or should more space be available for shorter-storage foods? In any case, *buy a refrigerator that's large enough.* Much time can be lost in hunting, spilling, and constantly rearranging foods in a box that's too small for your needs.

Range: Today's best ranges provide many features that help free the housewife from "slaving over a hot stove all day." These provide pilot lights or electric switches throughout the entire range, automatic time and heat controls—on some, ovens can turn themselves off at the required time when you're not there to do it (115), ovens raised to convenient heights, two or more ovens (42, 115, 116), smoke and draft control, provision for deep fat fryers and rotisseries. The new "decentralized" types—sectional range units plus storage drawers—permit flexible arrangements that are especially helpful in a cramped kitchen area.

In buying a range, well-known brand names are a particularly important guarantee of quality, and of convenience in servicing.

Dishwasher: The ideal in mechanical dishwashers, if you're building, is the electric sink, complete with dishwasher and garbage grinder. Here is machine-made pre-positioning, saving time in both steps and motion.

Dishwashers may be portable (42, 83, 120) or installed. Undercounter types, with doors that drop down like an oven door, have sliding racks and are easiest to load. Square tubs are better than round because corners can be used for pots and pans. Vinyl-coated racks preferred to metal for greater dish protection. Silverware basket that permits silver to fan out for most effective cleansing. Heating element to boost water temperature always to the desired 180° insures best cleaning (118, 138). The greatest time-saving value of this appliance is realized in accumulating dishes throughout the day and washing all at one time, so buy the largest size.

It's true that hard incrustations of food on pots, pans, and baking dishes must be dislodged before putting these utensils in the dishwasher. But if, after removing food deposits, you soak pots and pans for a while, preparatory to placing them all in the dishwasher together, it's still easier and quicker to do them this way than entirely by hand.

With a dishwasher, be sure to use only the detergents recommended by the manufacturer.

Freezer: Meal-planning in terms of quick-freezing and zero storage is such a new concept that the surface hasn't even been scratched yet. In addition to the obvious advantage of laying in substantial supplies of food and thus saving much marketing time, a freezer enables you to prepare entire meals or parts of meals weeks ahead of time, and all at one time.

Important cooking needn't be done each day, but only at certain times during the month, and then in a really "mass-production" way. Using a home freezer in this manner would, of course, tend to change your other kitchen arrangements. For instance, you'd need a supply of larger pots, pans, and casseroles, and more storage space for them. But on the other hand, your refrigerator might not need to be as large as otherwise.

Freezers demand relatively little upkeep, defrosting being necessary only every few months.

Garbage Disposal Unit: Of course having such a unit saves time and also eliminates one of the most disagreeable housekeeping tasks. But before considering the idea, first determine if it's legally permissible to install one in your vicinity. And note also that the unit will require much additional plumbing, and possibly a different type of sink (unless the appliance has been provided for, in a new house). Be sure to purchase from a reliable outfit that can promise quick service if necessary.

Air-Filtering Systems: Air-conditioning, with its filtering action, is an important saver of housework—for those who can afford it.

A unit for a single room, which may be installed in the window area, now costs from $300 up, with monthly operating expenses about $10. This type is rated high in ability to remove dust and other particles from the air, which it draws in directly from outside. Some makes both cool and warm the air.

Air-conditioning for the entire house (which can be used all year round) may be connected to a forced-draft hot-air system of heating. It is far more expensive; for installation in an average 6-room house, during construction, the cost now runs upward from $1200, with operating expenses about $60 per year. We know of an office in an air-conditioned building that has not needed a thorough cleaning job in three years, despite its upholstered furniture, pile carpet, and draperies!

A system that only filters air is the Electrostatic Precipitator (119). One type hangs from ceiling; floor model takes about the same space as a small refrigerator; cost from $385, and must be hooked up to an outside blower or to a forced-draft hot-air system. It filters dust, smoke, and particles from the air, but—unlike true air-conditioning—has no effect on temperature or humidity. One hundred housewives, reporting on test installations, needed to dust only once a week; clothes, furniture, draperies and rugs stayed clean for long periods.

There are many other appliances and systems on the market to make your work easier, and there are certainly many more to come. Others worthy of mention are: electric ironers, automatic washing machines, and dryers; electric floor waxers, if you have floors that require waxing; an electric hand buffer and sander for furniture surfaces that aren't spotproof; water-softening systems, if hard water is your problem; garbage incinerators.

Cleaning Agents: New work-saving preparations and cleaning materials are constantly being developed, which help to do away with old-fashioned scrubbing and elbow grease. Here are some we've found useful. In most cases, several brands are available in neighborhood groceries or hardware and department stores. We've mentioned some trade names here merely as a guide.

Soaps and Detergents

Whether to use soap or detergent depends on the degree of hardness of your water supply and the type and amount of soil. If the water is soft, soap is fine. For hard water, a detergent is better. Non-sudsing detergents should be used for dishwashing machines and automatic clothes washers *(Finish, Thanx, All)*. There are two types of soap and detergent products:

Mild or *light-duty products* are intended for fine fabrics and dishwashing *(Vel, Dreft, Lux)*; liquid detergents belong in this category.

All-purpose or *heavy-duty products* are intended for family wash and general household cleaning *(Surf, Tide, etc.)*.

Cleansing and Scouring Powders

Cleansers which do not require rinsing or wiping dry save considerable time in cleaning painted walls, woodwork and other surfaces *(Spic and Span, Soilax)*. Abrasive scouring powders for pots, pans and porcelain surfaces differ in their action. Some are relatively gentle, others stronger. It is best to try the mildest powders *(Bon Ami, Sunbrite)* before resorting to a more abrasive one. Harsher scouring powders *(Ajax, Kitchen Klenzer)* are fine for marble or terrazzo floors, unfinished wood surfaces and cement walls and steps. They should not be used on surfaces where smoothness is to be preserved. They will scratch the surfaces, thus making them pick up dirt more easily and require more scouring.

Other Cleaning Agents

A metaphosphate water-softener, if you're using soap, that eliminates bathtub rings and similar marks *(Calgon)*.

A liquid, self-polishing floor wax that requires no rubbing *(Glocoat)*.

A window or glass cleanser that doesn't need rinsing *(Windex, Glaspray)*.

Silicon-impregnated dry-polishing cloth—especially useful for interior glass and mirrors. Dusts, polishes, and protects surface all in one operation *(Cornelia Cloth)* (121).

Dustcloths impregnated with a small amount of furniture polish *(Glad Rag)*.

Treated cloth or paper for quick, touch-up metal polishing *(Silver Cloth, Silver Sheet and Glo Pad)*.

A coating for cooking utensils (122) that retards food sticking and water-spotting of aluminum utensils *(Pantastic)*.

(D) Question the Working Conditions

Industry long ago took note of fatigue factors that affect the worker's efficiency—light, ventilation, temperature, order instead of clutter—and went on to consider the value of pleasant colors, elimination of glare and noise, and the installation of wired music. The housewife's working conditions are pretty much her own choice. The radio as a companion for her long hours of solitary work is no novelty now, but here are some other obvious, often neglected angles:

Improve Your Working Conditions

Have enough light for the task; a work lamp on a long cord if the normal lighting of the room is inadequate for housework purposes; or a large flashlight for dark corners.

An open window staves off fatigue; when the work is strenuous, turn down the heat as well.

Sit down to work whenever possible—when preparing food, ironing, sorting clothes. Have chairs or stools of the right height for your various tasks; adjustable, "posture" types are the best. (The whole subject gets a good going-over in *Posture in Housework*, a booklet by the Department of Agriculture, Washington, D. C.)

Wear work clothes. A long housecoat and mules are nice for relaxing, but a hindrance for work. Some women go in for dungarees and work shirts, or the comfort and convenience of coveralls. Play suits or slacks give freedom of movement. An apron with big pockets, which are extra hands for carrying, is fine for some tasks. And wear comfortable low-heeled shoes.

Your frame of mind is an important working condition. You might feel better if you realize that the housewife's job demands skill and competence, and is no longer looked upon as mindless drudgery. Looking for ingenious ways of doing the job more easily, you may find yourself no longer resentful, but interested, perhaps even enjoying yourself.

Division of Labor

3. If a woman has no children at home, no outside job, and a fair amount of modern mechanical aids to household efficiency, it's hardly fair to ask a working husband to share much of the burden of housework. But especially with a larger family, and under harder circumstances, it's important to have everyone share in the work to some extent.

The classic example of dividing the work is furnished by the Gilbreths,* who were among the first so-called efficiency engineers. They not only applied time-and-motion study techniques to their home, but also organized their six boys and six girls into an efficient working democracy.

Cheaper by the Dozen, Crowell, 1949; and Dr. Lillian Gilbreth's *The Homemaker and Her Job*, Appleton-Century, 1927, 1938.

We know a family, of more conventional size, where the loss of a maid was turned into such a good source of creative effort in the home that the mother decided against having a maid altogether. The eleven-year-old daughter took special delight in helping with dinner preparations, particularly when she was allowed to mix sauces, stir pots, and occasionally even cook a dinner, under her mother's supervision. The son was no more eager to perform household chores than any other thirteen-year-old boy, but used his wits to devise the most efficient routines for table-clearing, garbage disposal, and keeping his own room in order. The father enjoyed using a mechanical tool like a vacuum cleaner, as a change from his sedentary daily job, and discovered in addition that he had an unexpected talent for cooking sea food. The mother still had a full-time job, with an old-fashioned house to maintain, but she found herself freed from the greatest mental hazard of housewives —the feeling of being a persecuted drudge. With everyone picking up after himself and helping with dinner, not only were her spirits lifted, but her job was made materially easier. She rates the habits of neatness, co-operation, and considerateness that her children are learning, as well as the actual skills they have gained, as of far more importance than the luxury of having a maid.

The Family Council: Of course it's easiest to set the pattern of dividing the work early in family life, but a family of older children can also learn to help, provided they understand the need and are given an opportunity to discuss and plan the work. Therefore the family council is essential in dividing the work. The mother, as household manager and chairman, brings her list of tasks to be done, and suggestions as to who is best suited by inclination, ability, and time to do the various jobs, but the family as a whole makes the decisions. It is important, if the rest of the family—particularly the children—are not to feel they're being imposed upon or coerced into drudgery, that the council unearth the special talents and interests of each member, and discover how to use these for the benefit of all. Tradition needn't act as a stumbling block: the father may be the best interior decorator or pie-baker, a daughter an incipient plumber.

Beyond the actual division of work, basic rules for all to follow should be agreed upon. Those who share the benefits of the home should also share in all aspects of the work: planning, preparation, cleanup. For instance, everyone should clean up after himself, and leave the bathroom, in particular, in order.

As for family wages, we've always considered it close to "exploitation of labor" to make children's allowances dependent on the housework they do. An allowance should be a share of the family income, perhaps decided on by the Family Council; wages should be a separate, additional payment—if the family can afford it. Of course young children are paid less than an outside adult helper, but their pay should be fair, and relative to the work they do and the results they accomplish.

Even small children will undertake tasks—within the limits of their strength and skill—if parents let them handle tasks that can also be fun, be patient while they develop skills, and let them use their own ingenuity, with a minimum of supervision. (A detailed sample division of work, which may help you in organizing your family routine, may be found in Appendix A, pages 192-193.)

Scheduling

4. Many women we know reject the whole idea of scheduling, claiming with indignation that it puts them under constant pressure for time. Our claim is that systematic, intelligent organization of your work week is one of the most essential of timesavers. Our recommendation is to at least give scheduling a two-week trial.

Planning a Schedule

First list the tasks; break them down into daily, weekly, when-necessary, seasonal.

Next estimate as best you can the time each task takes. (Of course you'll have to adjust these estimates somewhat in the light of actual experience.)

Then fit the tasks into your week, in a workable order.

Schedule tasks when they are actually indicated by family requirements, not on arbitrarily chosen days.

Develop logical sequences. If Friday's the best day for your big marketing, the logical time for defrosting the refrigerator would be Thursday evening, or while you're out marketing on Friday.

Plan tasks in combinations: giving the baby his airing while you do the marketing is an obvious example.

Include in your schedule the time it takes to prepare work for others to do: sorting laundry to go out, getting a part-time maid started on a special job.

Provide time for planning: household office work like planning menus, making marketing lists, doing cookbook research, schedule-making itself.

Include definite rest periods.

Provide "elasticity stations" to take care of small emergencies and routine, unavoidable interruptions (a telephone call, an especially persistent door-to-door salesman), or just to take the pressure off. Manufacturers often add 20 per cent for "unforeseen" in estimating the time to complete a contract.

After a time-consuming interruption that you just couldn't sidetrack, be elastic yourself. Don't grimly try to crowd the still unfinished task into your existing schedule. Instead, defer the less pressing items on your agenda, and ease them into the schedule later on. A schedule isn't a race you have to win every day.

Of course your own schedule must be tailor-made to your household; we could not hope to provide an ideal work breakdown that would apply for everyone. But if you've never made a schedule, you may be helped by the two samples that follow, one for a full-time, the other for a part-time, housewife; neither depends on regular paid help.

Schedule for a Full-Time Housewife: This is planned to get through the bulk of the weekly housework by lunch, and also to leave weekends as free as possible. This housewife has a baby and one school-age daughter; she does all her laundry at home, has a small four-room house, and no help except an occasional cleaning woman and what her husband and the older child contribute in their free time. She is at the peak of her work load; if anyone needs to be a production engineer, she does. Fortunately, she is also at the peak of her energies.

```
EVERY DAY:
            Get Breakfast. (Daughter packs her own school
            lunch.
            Feed baby; put him in play pen, within seeing
            and hearing distance.
            Soak diapers.
            Fix baby's formula; start long-cooking dinner
            dish(roast, stew,etc.) - to be reheated later.
            Wash breakfast dishes (put in rack without
            drying).
            Wash diapers and hang them to dry.
            If baby is restless about now, pick him up,
            change him, and put him in his crib for
            morning nap.
            Put house in order - pick up, straighten, do
            a quick dusting job.
            Get baby's lunch. Then eat own lunch; stack,
            soak own and baby's dishes.
            Rest - while baby is in crib for afternoon nap.
            Out for walk with baby; marketing if needed.
            Home again; put baby in play pen; bring in
            his diapers and fold them.
```

Bathe and feed baby; husband home about now to take over baby's before-bedtime play (on some days he is also to take over bath, feeding, putting to bed).
Finish preparing dinner; daughter helps with setting the table.
After-dinner clean-up, with everyone helping - wash lunch dishes now, too.
Set tomorrow's breakfast table; made advance breakfast preparations.

ADDITIONAL ONCE-A-WEEK TASKS:

<u>Monday</u> - Change bed linens; thorough-clean bedroom if necessary (if not, use this time for putting closets, bureau drawers in order, or other when-necessary tasks).
<u>Tuesday</u> - Family laundry (do quick bedmaking while clothes are soaking). Prepare dinner dessert while tending washer. Come home earlier from afternoon walk with baby to bring in wash before getting dinner.
<u>Wednesday</u> - Ironing in the morning (if there's too much, finish on Thursday).
<u>Thursday</u> - Thorough-clean in living room (do when-necessary tasks: clean woodwork, blinds; dust books; vacuum floors; etc.). Get cleaning man or woman to help with this?
<u>Friday</u> - Kitchen and planning day: next week's general menu scheme and when-necessary work; check supplies; complete market list while defrosting refrigerator. Clean refrigerator, range, if necessary. Major marketing in afternoon; home early to put groceries away before preparing dinner.
<u>Saturday</u> - Minimum housework; everyone makes own bed, straightens up. Cold lunch. Sitter (or husband or daughter) for baby in afternoon.
<u>Sunday</u> - Minimum housework: brunch, or one meal out, or picnic (taking baby along). Same after-supper schedule as on weekdays.

Schedule for a Part-Time Housewife: Both husband and wife have full-time jobs. They have a two-room apartment, send the laundry out, use as many professional services as they can afford, but have no paid "help." They do some housework together, some separately, but *planning* together is an absolute necessity.

WEEKDAYS Before work	Both: Tidy up after yourself in bathroom. She: Get breakfast. He: Put away leftover breakfast food. She: Scrape and soak breakfast dishes. Both: Make beds; pick up, put away in bedroom.
After work	Both: Put house in order - dust, straighten. She: Prepare dinner. If there's time, do some advance cooking for tomorrow's dinner. Both: Set table; finish dinner preparation. (Remember to buy frozen foods, packaged raw salads, desserts, on way home.)
After dinner	She: Wash dishes (including breakfast dishes) and put them in rack to dry. He: Clear up kitchen; put food away. Set table, do other advance breakfast preparation.
SATURDAY	Both: Get breakfast (defrost refrigerator at same time). Plan next week's menu scheme and marketing list. (Check on supplies, to avoid any weekday marketing.) She: Soak or wash breakfast dishes; clean range, refrigerator, if necessary. (If guests tonight, start long-cooking dinner dish now.) He: Clean kitchen floor; vacuum-clean, do other necessary thorough-cleaning. She: Change bed linens; sort laundry and all clothes to be sent out for cleaning and pressing; do personal laundry. Both: Snack lunch, or out for lunch and afternoon. Do marketing in afternoon.
SUNDAY	Both: Brunch, or out for the day. Minimum chores. <u>After dinner</u>, same as weekdays.

Household Tasks

5. No two women do the same task exactly the same way; no two households run exactly the same way. But even though task methods can't be standardized, a new approach to an old task can often mean greater efficiency. So use your best energies—not on your knees scrubbing the floor, but "on your toes" figuring out how to make the task less work! Take time out to examine your methods objectively; try to rid yourself of old household reflexes.

Good work habits can help greatly in simplifying tasks:

Train yourself to do all there is to do at one place at one time. For instance, if you're putting something in the refrigerator, while the door is open, try to think of what you have to take out. (What if you do leave the door open a few seconds longer?)

Use both hands at once. To continue with the refrigerator, use both hands to carry out what you need—close the door with your elbow.

Plan "wholesale." Consolidate the work, don't do it piecemeal. Use trays to carry all the dishes when setting the table. Market less often, but buy for longer times. Cook less often, doing as much advance food preparation as possible at one time.

Dovetail the work. Combine and ease one task into another. Since "a watched pot never boils," don't wait for it, but do something else in the meantime.

Here are a series of household-task *routines*—some examples of the application of work-habit principles we have devised ourselves, and some that have been worked out by our friends or in home economics testing laboratories. In most cases we have limited ourselves to those household tasks for which we have found short cuts. You can use these routines as models from which to work out routines best adapted to you and your home.

In the Kitchen

Dishwashing by hand is one of the most time-consuming of all tasks. (A Westinghouse report finds that it takes, on the average, almost *nine* hours per week.) Certainly it's highly important to do this job more efficiently. Here's a list of the materials you'll need:

Scouring powder
Soaps and Detergents (see page 134)
"Tuffy" scouring balls
Cellulose dishmop and sponge
Bottle brush

Rubber spatula
Dish drainer (metal rack type)
Dishpans (or sink stopper)
Spray attachment for faucet (with a hose if your faucet isn't the swinging type).

The ideal arrangement is to have a double sink-well unit, one for washing, the other for rinsing—and of course a generous water supply. A drainboard or a counter on each side is preferable, but if you have only one, let a table, a wheeled cart, or a pull-out shelf serve as the second surface.

The routine actually begins well in advance, while you are preparing food for the meal. Cleaning and putting away as you go will give you three dividends: decks will be cleared for action; the task of cleaning utensils will be made easier if they are washed or put to soak soon after use; and you're left with less work after dinner. Now follow these steps, *in order:*

Dishwashing Routine

1. Organize the cleanup at the table, scraping all food onto one plate, stacking scraped dishes with filled ones on top, putting all silver together, all glasses together.
2. Bring scraped tableware into the kitchen and place on the drainboard. Place it in this order: all glassware nearest the sink; next to this all silver; then all stacked dishes. (Use a tray to cut down on the number of trips.) Empty liquids into the sink, garbage into the container. Put the dish drainer on the other side of the sink.
3. On one of your trips, start filling both sinks with hot water. Arrange the stopper in the sink on the drain rack side so that this one will drain slowly, ensuring an ever fresh supply of water and no danger of overflow.
4. Collect all leftover food at this time and put all of it away, in the refrigerator, etc., at one time.
5. When you have emptied any utensils still left with food in them, fill them with hot water, shake in the detergent and stand together, out of the way, so they won't clutter the drainboard.
6. When washing sink is filled, add detergent.
7. Using a cellulose sponge or mop, wash the glassware (insides first) and put it into the rinse sink, holding the sponge in one hand, the glasses in the other. When they're all done, use both hands to lift them out of the rinse sink and put them, upside down, into the dish drainer. Or a helper can shake out the water and put them right back on the shelf, right side up.
8. Next wash all the silver. The best technique here is to hold the sponge in one hand, a few pieces of silver in the other, and wipe with a downward motion. Put the washed silver into the rinse sink.
9. Wash all dinnerware. Here's where developing a rhythm in doing each piece is important: use the mop in a circular motion, rather than many short up-and-down strokes, on both sides of the dish. Use a rubber spatula for hardened food deposits, a bottle brush for spouts, etc. Put each piece into the rinse sink, and then use both hands to take out several pieces at a time and place in the dish drainer.
10. Now take the silver out of the rinsing sink and put it in its compartment of the dish drainer.
11. Wash and rinse the remaining serving and cooking utensils in a similar manner, using a rubber spatula, scouring balls, and sponge as needed. Make this a separate project, but you can use the same soapy water, unless it's exceptionally dirty. Use scouring powder where needed, too.
12. Put crockery, glass, and stainless-steel utensils away upside down, so that they can drain and dry. (Aluminum ones, too, unless water-spotting them worries you.)
13. Rustable items, such as iron pots, pans, knives, should *not* be put away wet or placed in the rack with air-drying pieces—they'll make hard-to-remove stains. Iron or cast-aluminum pots can be dried over a stove burner.

If two sink wells are an impossible luxury for you, there are several alternatives:

a. If your sink is large enough and the amount of dishes is small, fit two small dishpans (or two rectangular porcelain-enamel, hydrator-type pans) into it—one with soapy water, one with clear—and wash and rinse as above.

b. With a small sink, fill with water, add detergent, wash and stack unrinsed tableware in the dish drainer *without* rinsing. Then, if your counter has built-up sides, you can rinse everything at once by spraying with a hose attached to the faucet. But be sure to have plates, bowls, and cups with the open face up! (This method saves water.)

c. With a drainboard without built-up sides, empty the sink after washing, place the entire rackful in the sink, and rinse by spraying. But this strong-arm method calls for a husky woman, or a male assistant. As an alternative, remove the soapy pieces from the dish drainer several at a time, and rinse in the sink by spraying or by filling sink (or dishpan) with clear hot water—our own method.

d. If there are few dishes, as for a family of two, you can try what we call the "pell-mell" system, which saves carrying dishes to the sink on a tray. Bring a large porcelain-enamel pail to the table and fill it with all the scraped tableware. Bring it to the sink, add detergent and hot water, and do your dishwashing directly in the pail. Transfer washed, unrinsed dishes to the dish drainer or the sink, and then rinse according to "b" or "c."

If you have an abundant supply of tableware—or just have finished a small meal—there's no need for dishwashing after every meal. Leave everything (*except* plastic-handled utensils, woodenware, and rustable items) to soak in detergent-filled water, to be washed with the next batch.

With all of these methods, the use of a detergent means that almost everything can be left in the dish drainer, to be dried by the air, which frees the person formerly assigned to drying by hand. That person can now save time by putting food away, setting the table for the next meal, sweeping the kitchen, emptying the garbage, and so on, while you're washing.

Kitchen Care: The most important thing to remember here is that you save time in the long run by wiping up every spill or spatter *when* it occurs (always keep a sponge handy for this purpose), and by sandwiching in any cleaning and straightening tasks that you can while you're in the process of regular meal preparation. But we do suggest a daily over-all brush-up.

The frequency with which you'll have to clean furnishings and equipment varies widely, and depends largely on the sort of use you make of your kitchen. Out of the great number of common cleaning tasks, we are listing only a few for which we've found short cuts, to show how work can be cut down in the kitchen.

Care of the Range: Use low oven temperatures (325°-350°) as much as possible, to minimize spattering and discoloration of the oven from moisture. You can also protect against spill-overs and spattering by following such general rules as placing aluminum foil under foods that might run over (casseroles, pies, sweet-potato dishes), and never filling containers so high that they might boil over. Leaving the oven door open after every use, to let it cool, helps prevent rusting. These cautions, and daily wiping of burners and washing of outside range surfaces, plus washing of broiler pans and racks after use, is just about all that the range needs. (And don't be overfussy about burners—remember that the heat keeps them sanitary, and unless they are actually clogged, they will operate properly.)

Cleaning the Range: If conscience drives you to this monster task, you can clean the burners of your gas range by boiling them in a hot soda solution (½ to 1 cup of soda in a pan filled with water). Then scrub off stubborn spots with a vegetable brush while they're still in the solution, and pierce any clogged holes with wire. If the oven is badly discolored, apply household ammonia to all inside surfaces with a cloth; let it stand overnight (with the oven door closed); then scrub thoroughly with steel wool or a sponge and a mild scouring powder.

Floors: We consider waxing a particularly silly and useless practice in the kitchen. The "easiest" way to do this task is to dispense with it; if possible, have surfaces that don't require waxing: ceramic or plastic tile, terrazzo, flagstone. (See the Floor Chart for others.) A rubber mat at the sink is easy on the feet and easy to clean. Where floor care is necessary, see page 147.

Walls: Check the Wall Chart to find easy-to-wash materials, such as ceramic tile, plastic-coated fabric, glass, porcelain enamel. For washing, a cellulose sponge is the best all-round tool. (You can get one with a long handle for cleaning from the ceiling down to within arm's reach.)

Proper ventilation above the stove will minimize grease deposits, keep walls clean longer. If you have unwashable, flat-painted, or papered walls, you can cover the area near sink and stove with a roll of plastic film (123) developed for this purpose; this plastic is non-combustible and easy to wash, and can be secured with masking tape.

Work surfaces and adjacent areas should also be of materials requiring little care: non-inflammable plastic (4) or ceramic tile, porcelain enamel, Formica (27), stainless steel.

Care of Living Room and Bedroom

The tasks of caring for these rooms fall into three main categories: daily room-grooming; weekly cleaning; and "when-necessary" tasks.

We advocate doing away with the upheaval and toil of "spring and fall cleaning" by occasionally working some of the bigger jobs into your weekly cleaning routine. We don't, however, recommend including *weekly* cleaning tasks in your daily procedure. It is more of a time-saver to establish these as two completely separate routines, which can then become such habits you can practically do them in your sleep.

Daily Grooming: This should be short and snappy, a superficial cosmetic job. It can be greatly simplified if the family agrees on a few work-saving customs:

> Before retiring, everyone helps tidy up the living room—emptying the ashtrays, and putting away all books and magazines, games, records, glasses, dishes, etc. he has used.
> Before leaving the bedroom in the morning, everyone puts away his own clothes and personal belongings (combs, brushes, make-up), and straightens his desk, bureau top or dressing table.
> If possible, everyone makes his own bed, or at least pulls back bedclothes for airing.

Such assistance helps to give the housewife a cheerier attitude, for certainly half the dreariness of housework lies in constantly picking up after others. For the daily job, we suggest here a labor-saving routine applicable to both living room and bedrooms:

Daily Cleaning Routine

1. Assemble cleaning equipment. Put small tools in a "cleaning" basket or cart. An apron with large pockets for tools helps, too. Include a whisk broom, treated dustcloths, dampened tissues or paper towels, a cellulose sponge dampened in washing-detergent solution, a paper bag for rubbish. Also have a carpet sweeper or a dry mop, or both, plus sprinkler bulb or can.
2. Water plants; wet down ashes in the fireplace and push them back with hearth broom.
3. Open windows (both top and bottom, if they're not the casement type).
4. If in the bedroom, pile any night clothes that might still be left on or around beds on a nearby chair, so that you can put them all away together in the closet —stopping there to give the closet a quick straightening-up, if necessary. Then make the bed (see page 150).
5a. Do a quick over-all pickup job before beginning your light cleaning—putting odds and ends away, rubbish in the wastebasket. Gather together all articles that belong elsewhere in the house, and set them and the wastebasket outside the door of the room.
5b. Or else do a combination straightening and light cleaning job. On a once-around-the-room route, carrying both a "cleaning" and a "catchall" basket (the latter for gathering up out-of-place articles), do the following things as you come to them—thus saving many side trips:

   Upholstered furniture and other seating. Brush upholstery; plump pillows; dust, dry-polish, or sponge all wood surfaces.

   Tables, desk tops, etc. Empty ashtrays of dead ashes; put them and other rubbish in the paper bag. Clean ashtrays with dampened tissues. Remove out-of-place articles and place in the catchall basket. Now push all other small articles that belong here to one side of the top surface, or place on a nearby surface. Then dust, dry-polish, or sponge the top of all surfaces. Finally replace all small articles in proper arrangement — also putting back any articles from your catchall basket that belong here.

   Windows. Dust or sponge sills. In cold weather, close windows while you're here. Lightly shake draperies and line up blinds or shades.

   Put the paper bag you've filled with rubbish into the wastebasket.

   Put the wastebasket, cleaning basket, and catchall basket (with articles that belong elsewhere in the house) at the door. (Later on, empty all wastebaskets in the house at the same time.)
6. Only if necessary, carpet-sweep rugs and dry-mop exposed floor areas—putting each piece of furniture back in position after you've finished with the floor under or around it.

Weekly and When-Necessary Cleaning: These are the "thorough-cleaning" operations, inevitably your hardest work. So dress for work, checking working conditions (window open, heat off, lots of light), and above all taking advantage of every laborsaving device at your command, from long-handled cleaning tools to the ever important vacuum cleaner (remembering that vacuum "dusting" is a thorough operation). It's an important work-saving concept to avoid making yourself into an overfussy housewife who attempts these arduous tasks too often. (For a suggested weekly cleaning routine, and additional list of tasks see Appendix A.)

Here are some of these when-necessary routines, for which we have uncovered short-cut techniques:

Floor Mopping: (Some surfaces *cannot* be wet-mopped, so consult the Floor Chart first.) As equipment for mopping, you'll need:

A long-handled floor brush and a dustpan; or a vacuum cleaner.
Detergent (see page 134).
#oo steel wool, or very fine waterproof sandpaper (for asphalt tile).
Long-handled scrubbing brush.
Cellulose-sponge mop or a string mop.
If you use a cellulose-sponge mop, you'll need a pail with a perforated squeeze-out ledge. For a string mop you'll need a bucket with wringers attached; two buckets are preferable (one for detergent-filled water, one for clear rinsing water). For a very small area, you can use the new rubber-sponge mop (126), and dampen it in the sink. It's constructed to be rinsed by self-squeezing, and can be squeezed into sink.

Mopping Routine

1. Remove as much furniture as you can from the room; have the heavy pieces on casters for easier movement.
2. Brush or vacuum the floor.
3. Tackle very dirty spots first, using scrubbing brush. Where marks (like rubber-heel marks) resist, use steel wool or sandpaper, depending on the surface.
4. The general procedure is to dip the mop into the detergent solution, squeeze out on the ledge or through wringers; carefully go around floor next to baseboard first, to avoid slopping against baseboard and walls. Then quickly wash the rest of the floor, using long, overlapping strokes and pressing the mop down to loosen the dirt. Do a small area at a time, repeating the dipping and squeezing process, until entire floor is finished. Rinse the mop in a pail of clear water each time before immersing in the detergent-filled pail.
5. For a drastically dirty floor, mop it *quite* wet; allow it to stand for about ten minutes, and then mop with sponge mop squeezed out of clear water. The dirt should come up with the water.

Floor Waxing: For floors that are to be mopped *and* waxed (see Floor Chart), this routine follows mopping:

Make sure the floor is dry before waxing. We recommend self-polishing liquid wax and a cellulose-sponge mop. Instructions are on the can; we find it best to do the edges of the area first, following along the baseboards carefully, to avoid spotting the walls.

For floors that can't be mopped, use a self-cleaning wax and a special applicator (110). As with mopping, do the hardest-to-clean areas first. This waxing method is just about as easy as mopping plus self-polishing wax, if it's suitable for your floors—check the Floor Chart again. However, it does need follow-up polishing, for which a waxing machine is recommended. (We timed a professional: with self-polishing wax and no machine, the job took slightly more time—but less expenditure of energy—than with self-cleaning wax and a machine.)

If you do need a polishing machine, many hardware stores rent them; or you might buy one in partnership with neighbors (prices start at about $50).

Wall Cleaning: Check the Wall Chart, to see if your walls are washable. Dust or vacuum the walls first, using a long-handled wall brush or the dusting attachment of the vacuum cleaner.

Use either a rinseless-type liquid wall-cleanser (117), or, if the walls are very dirty, a cleansing detergent (see page 134). Begin by tackling badly soiled spots and stains, using a sponge, a brush, or a cloth on water-soluble stains (carbon tetrachloride for greasy spots). Then go over the entire surface with your rinseless wall wash or cleansing detergent, starting from the bottom and working up; but experiment with a small area first.

Of course we're opposed to non-washable wallpaper, shellacked walls, and other surfaces that can't be cleaned in this manner. But if you do have such coverings or finishes, we recommend a special clear lacquer for the walls (127), after which you can wash. Lacquer can be applied over a thin "sealer" coat of shellac, but a heavy coating of shellac should be removed with alcohol. (First make sure, however, that the alcohol won't harm the actual wall surface.)

Woodwork Cleaning: Check the Wood Finishes portion of the Wall Chart, to see if your surfaces can take washing. Dust or vacuum first, then start with the hardest-to-clean spots, holding a cellulose sponge in one hand and a bottle of rinseless wall wash (117) or cleansing-detergent solution in the other, and apply the liquid directly to the sponge, again experimenting with a small area, for safety's sake—a good general rule.

After doing the hardest-to-clean spots, do the entire surface, using long strokes and following the grain of the wood. Reapply the liquid to the sponge as needed. Get into corners and fluting by using the edges of the sponge.

If your woodwork has been long neglected and the over-all job seems likely to be a dirty and difficult one, for best results have a second sponge handy, wrung out of fresh water. After applying the liquid to your cleaning sponge, put the bottle down and pick up the rinsing sponge. Follow up the cleaning sponge with this second one, to wipe off the dirt you may have missed.

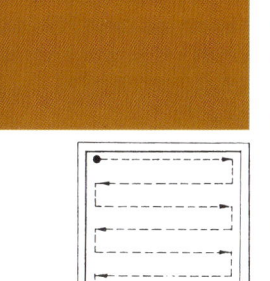

Window Washing: The required tools are a bottle of rinseless cleaner for windows, which comes in a bottle with a spray attachment, and a good supply of clean, lintless cloths. If necessary, first wash the window frames and the moldings according to the instructions for cleaning woodwork.

Squirt the fluid onto a large pane, or two or more panes at a time if they're small. Wipe clean in the pattern shown in the diagram. Use both hands, holding a cloth in one and the bottle of the fluid in the other. For inside panes that are not too dirty, try also the new dry-polishing method mentioned below.

For the outsides of windows above the ground floor, other than pivot-swinging (casement) types, it's best to have a professional do the job. However, there is a long-armed, adjustable, double-jointed tool, a combination sponge and squeegee (128), that enables you to wash from inside.

Glass and Mirror Cleaning: In addition to using the no-rinse method mentioned above for windowpanes, try also the more laborsaving, new dry-polishing with Silicone-treated Cornelia Cloth (see page 134). Like "Sight Savers," this cloth not only polishes and dusts in one operation, but also leaves a protective film behind it. Try it also on picture glass and frames, furniture and other woodwork. If surfaces are very dirty, sponge off first, then use cloth.

Rug Cleaning: This is better done by professionals, but if you must clean rugs at home, here's the easiest no-stooping method we could devise:

Buy a bottle of good-quality rug shampoo of the type that can be used with a vacuum cleaner, and mix with water (according to instructions) in a vacuum-cleaner spray-bottle attachment. Spray out on the rug, starting in one corner and working back and forth until the whole surface is damp, with some froth visible. Let stand until the rug is almost dry (opening the windows speeds this); reverse the vacuum-cleaner action and vacuum carefully with the carpet-cleaner attachment.

Polishing Furniture: The fastest thorough polishing method we know of is to use nonrubbing wax sprayed right out of the container.

Cleaning Venetian Blinds: Put them in the bathtub and scrub with a washing detergent.

Cleaning Books: After books are removed from the shelves, clean them with the *soft-brush* vacuum attachment—and while you're at it, thorough-clean the shelves.

Five stages of making "hospital" mitered corner.

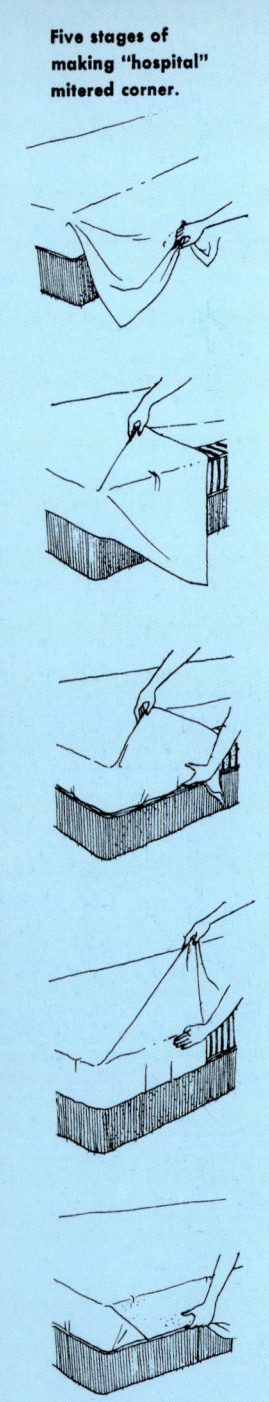

Bedmaking

Stripping and completely remaking a bed every day is obsolete! Turning back the covers after getting up in the morning (warn your family against yanking the bed apart) gives the bedclothes all the airing they need by the time the bed gets put together again. If you make the bed *well* once a week, with all corners mitered (see marginal diagrams), all you have to do daily is:

Remove pillows and fold back all covers to the foot of bed.

Tighten up on both sides of bottom sheet (not the top and the foot).

Pull up and smooth upper sheet and blankets, folding back about 9 inches of top sheet over blankets. (If the sleeper desires, tuck upper sheet and blanket in at sides of bed.)

Plump, straighten, and replace the pillows.

Replace the spread.

Once-a-Week Bedmaking: Using old methods, a housewife may take a walk of up to 262 feet in making a standard-size double bed! That's what the University of Vermont Agricultural Experiment Station staff found in developing their "once-around-the-bed" routine, which cuts the walk down to 23 feet, and reduces the time, which may be as much as 6½ minutes with conventional methods, to as little as 2¾ minutes. The basic idea is to make the bed *one-fourth* at a time, doing all you can at one position before moving on, instead of completing each item individually.

Here's their quick, labor-saving routine for a bed with headboards and footboards.* First place all the bedding on a chair within easy reach, folded, and piled in the order in which it goes on the bed—the bottom sheet on top, and so on. Begin at the right-hand corner of the head of the bed—note that the right side is designated as "side A," the left as "side B"—and move counterclockwise. (We're reproducing the instructions exactly as given in the University of Vermont's pamphlet, to offer you at least a taste of the specific, scientific, "methods research" approach to housework problems):

---

*From Marianne Muse's booklet *Saving Time and Steps in Bedmaking*, Bulletin 551, Agricultural Experiment Station, University of Vermont, Burlington, Vermont. It is also described in *Easier Homemaking*, Station Bulletin 529, a most helpful general pamphlet on household tasks published at Purdue University, Lafayette, Indiana.

'Scientific' Bedmaking Routine

Each corner of bed is completely made in turn. The worker makes one trip along side A, the foot, and side B of the bed and does no other walking (except stepping from the center to the head of side A because the sheets, blankets, and counterpane were thrown from the center of side A. This was done to accommodate a comparatively short woman. Others could easily stand at the head of side A).

1. Get lower sheet, unfolding on bed
2. *Step to head of side A*
3. Pull, tuck (A half of head), miter, and tuck (head half of side A) lower sheet
4. *Step to center of side A*
5. Get upper sheet, unfolding on bed
6. Get first blanket, throwing over bed
7. Get second blanket, throwing over first one
8. *Step to head of side A*
9. Straighten blankets. Fold back upper sheet (A half of head)
10. Get counterpane, throwing over bed (folded twice crosswise)
11. Toss edge of counterpane toward foot of bed
12. Get two pillows and cases. Lay them on bed, tossing one case aside. Pull case on first pillow, lay it on A side of head
13. Turn counterpane over pillow
14. Pull case on second pillow, lay it on first pillow
15. *Walk to foot of side A*
16. Toss back upper sheet and blankets
17. Pull, tuck (A half of foot), miter, and tuck (foot half of side A) lower sheet
18. Pull, tuck (A half of foot), and half-miter upper sheet and blankets
19. Pull counterpane into place
20. *Walk to foot of side B*
21. Toss back upper sheet and blankets
22. Pull, tuck (B half of foot), miter, and tuck (foot half of side B) lower sheet
23. Pull, tuck (B half of foot), and half-miter upper sheet and blankets
24. Pull counterpane into place
25. *Walk to head of side B*
26. Toss back upper sheet and blankets
27. Pull, tuck (B half of head), miter and tuck (head half of side B) lower sheet
28. Pull upper sheet and blankets. Fold back upper sheet (B half of head)
29. Place the second pillow on B side of head
30. Turn counterpane smoothly over pillow

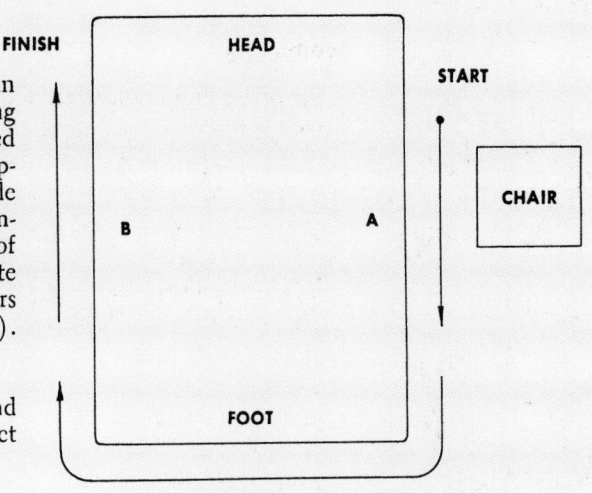

An even simpler version of the once-around technique is possible with a bed having no headboard or footboard, at wrist height from the floor* (which is a height we recommend; see page 53). With this method, the sides of the blankets and the upper sheet are not tucked in.

*Method devised by Helen E. Halbert, at Purdue University.

The bed is made largely in two steps, rather than four, since the routine calls for a somewhat narrower bed (about 40 inches wide), where two corners of the bed can be reached from one position. It's best for single beds, but we have found it feasible even with wider beds. Start at the foot, with bedding piled on a chair within easy reach. (Again, the wording is that of the methods researchers, from Purdue University's *Easier Homemaking*.)

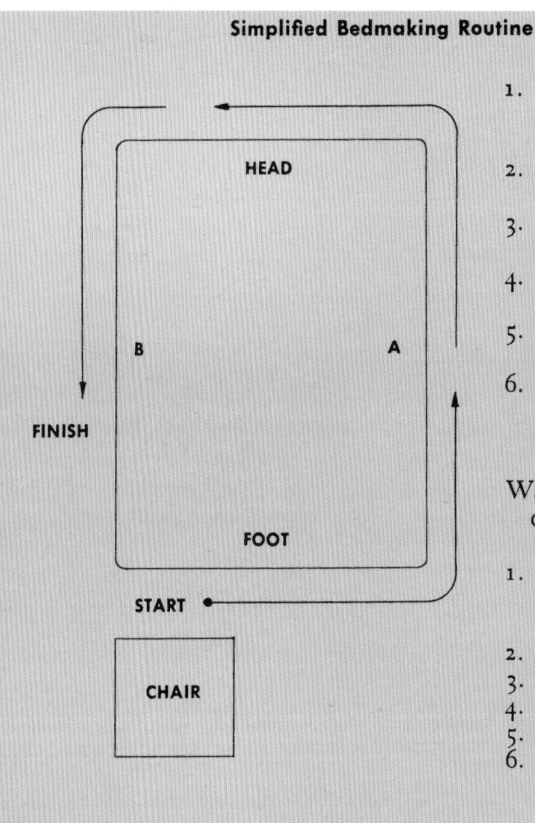

Simplified Bedmaking Routine

FOOT OF BED

1. Place the lower sheet on the bed, unfold, flip it to the top of the bed, tuck in at the bottom, miter, and tuck at the sides.
2. Place the upper sheet on the bed, unfold, flip it to the top of the bed.
3. Place the blanket on the bed, unfold, flip it to the top of the bed.
4. Tuck the blanket and upper sheet at the bottom, and miter the corners.
5. Place the bedspread on the bed, unfold, it over the foot of the bed.
6. Place the pillow and pillowcase on the bed, slip the case on the pillow, and toss the pillow to the center of the bed.

SIDE A OF BED

Walk to center of side A of bed and tuck center of lower sheet under mattress.

HEAD OF BED

1. Pull lower sheet into place, tuck at the head, miter corners, and tuck at the sides.
2. Pull upper sheet into place.
3. Pull blanket into place.
4. Fold upper sheet edge over blanket.
5. Put pillow in place.
6. Place bedspread over pillow, tuck it under pillow front and smooth.

SIDE B OF BED

Walk to center of side B of bed and tuck center of lower sheet under mattress.

Of course you can vary or combine these once-around systems to suit yourself. Some people like the sides of the upper sheet and blanket tucked in, others don't. Some like the bottom of the bed left untucked, which shortens your job.

Some tall people are apt to kick out the foot tucking. To help avoid this, tuck the top sheet under *deeply* at the foot—so that it barely turns over the blanket at the top. A bed made this way will really hold together firmly.

Bathroom Care

A great deal of work can be saved if everyone picks up after himself in the bathroom; puts all articles he has used back in place, throws soiled towels in the hamper, wipes the basin clean, washes the bathtub, spreads the shower curtains open to dry, hangs up the bath mat, and his personal towel, and facecloth on racks, and so on.

But all of us, and particularly children, are likely to forget sometimes; so it's well for the housewife to develop the habit of giving the room a daily touch-up. Here is a routine, worked out in sequence, that does the job quickly. (A separate bathroom cleaning closet is most helpful; see the Bathroom Cleaning Closet Checklist, in Appendix A, page 192.)

Daily Bathroom Cleaning Routine

1. Give the room a quick survey; determine what cleaning tools you'll need, and get them out.
2. Remove all articles from surfaces that are to be cleaned, putting away those which belong in medicine chest and putting others all in one place—so that all surfaces can be cleaned at one time.
3. Put soiled towels and clothes in hamper, rubbish in wastebasket.
4. Go over toilet bowl quickly with a long-handled brush. (A daily "swish" eliminates need for weekly cleaning.)
5. Wipe mirrors with treated polishing cloth.
6. Fill basin with hot water and washing detergent of the rinseless type.
7. With this water and a cellulose sponge, wipe off any dust or surface spots on shelves, metal fixtures, the wall near the basin, etc.
8. Refill basin with hot water and washing detergent and soak glasses, ashtrays, soap dishes, etc.
9. Pour small amount of detergent into bathtub; add hot water, and wipe all tub surfaces with long-handled sponge. Start with the edges, work down the sides, and finally, while water is draining out, clean the bottom. (If you use a water-softening detergent, or water-softening bath salts, each time you take a bath, there'll be no "ring" around the tub to remove.)
10. Rinse articles left to soak in the basin, wiping the water from ashtrays, soap dishes, etc., with a paper towel, and return them to their places.
11. Wash the basin with a hand sponge; if it's very soiled, use scouring powder. Dry off flat surface with paper.
12. Replace and put in order everything kept on shelves, etc. Replace on the racks, or straighten the towels.
13. Gather up your tools and wastebasket. Return tools to the bathroom storage closet, or else set them outside the door.
14. Now mop the floor or, preferably, vacuum it. A quick daily job will cut down materially on your weekly thorough cleaning.

If you follow this daily routine, about all you'll have to add to the weekly job is a thorough mopping of the floor (using a long-handled mop and a rinseless type of cleaning detergent), plus cleaning the toilet bowl with scouring powder or ammonia. In addition, here are a few extra when-necessary tasks to be fitted into the weekly routine:

Additional Bathroom Tasks

Dust and — less frequently — wash woodwork, doors, walls, fixtures, bulbs.

Wipe soap spots from shower curtains. If you hold the curtain against the sides of the tub, this can be done easily, using a sponge. Less frequently, remove and wash off or launder curtains, according to type.

Clear out all cabinets, washing shelves and rearranging the contents. This is the time to throw out those old bottles that accumulate. (Have a pad attached to the back of the cabinet door to jot down prescription numbers, and also to check your staple supplies.)

Clean rubber tub or shower mats.

Things Professionals Can Do Better

6. Outside services are really invisible servants. Being professionals in their fields, they do many things better, and in some cases may actually be more economical, too, if you consider the time such tasks would take away from your other tasks and the upheaval they would cause.

Laundry. For all the wash, or just the more difficult items (sheets, men's shirts) — by piece or by pound, ironed or not. Also for large cotton rugs, summer blankets, etc.

Dry Cleaning. Use the corner tailor for cleaning — and pressing — suits, dresses, topcoats. To clean them at home is to run the risk not only of damaging them, but also of fire, explosion, or injury to your health from fumes. Drapes, upholstery, rugs, can be sent out or done inside the house by special services. Doing them yourself may mean leaving dirt or soap in them, so that they'll soil more quickly, rot, or even change color.

Mothproofing. Dry cleaners can do this along with cleaning.

Summer storage. Not only for furs, but also for winter coats and bedding, if your storage space is limited.

Window-cleaning. Professionals are advisable if your windows are above the ground floor and not the casement type. Use them, too, to scrape off stains after a big paint job — on mirrors as well as windows.

Cabinetmakers. For repairing and refinishing furniture.

Exterminators. For acute situations; and several times a year in order to avoid these. If you have young children, or pets, make sure the insecticides used are safe.

Floors. Professionals do scraping, waxing, polishing; use them occasionally to spruce up exposed floors.

Housecleaners. For a once-a-year, extra-thorough job, there are services to wash walls, ceilings, and other hard-to-get-at places.

Appliance servicing. Have major appliances checked and cleaned occasionally — preferably by the company's own servicemen.

Housekeeping Standards

7. We pointed out, strongly, at the beginning of this book that the traditional ways of furnishing a home are not in keeping with the facts of modern life. Many etiquette and housekeeping books still promote an equally outmoded traditional way of keeping house, which is impossibly meticulous and far too laborious for our times. They thereby give millions of housewives bad consciences.

It should be quite apparent by now that our standards are considerably different. Dusting by hand, for example, merely succeeds in temporarily removing dust to a higher level, from which it just settles into another place, and it's silly to attach undue importance to it. But as a daily "cosmetic" treatment, it's clearly preferable to the labor of constant scrubbing and polishing. Actually, we prefer as much as possible to select furnishings that camouflage dust.

We think it often justifiable to sweep dust under the rug for a while, or to let dirty dishes pile up in the sink temporarily.

We consider it virtually a form of insanity to insist on floors that require waxing and polishing when you can choose—from materials available today—floor surfaces that don't have to be waxed. The traditional ideal of mirrorlike floors *is* pretty, but the smooth sheen of a nonrubbing wax and the mat surface of stone or terrazzo also have their own kind of beauty, and by requiring a great deal less work, leave you more time to enjoy their good looks.

We don't ask you to swallow our standards whole, either; but we do think you'll be a lot happier if you give the entire matter of housekeeping a thorough going-over in your mind, and decide on a practical standard of your own, one that's attainable without drudgery.

Tricks of the Trade

8. Here's a grab bag of miscellaneous work-savers and trouble-savers—in addition to the many presented elsewhere in this chapter—gathered from experienced housewives, from home economics laboratories, and from industry. Many of them may be familiar to you, but others are likely to come as a surprise.

Muscle savers

To move a heavy piece of furniture, lean against it where it's heaviest, using your weight as well as your muscles.

To lift something heavy, bend your knees and use your leg muscles as well as your back.

Don't stoop to work at a low level; bend your knees (good for your figure as well as your back) or sit on the floor.

If your sink is too low, put a block of wood under the dishpan; if too high, have a floor platform with a rubber mat on top.

For Laundry

Don't soak clothes too long; they begin to take up dirt again from the water after about 15 minutes.

Shake out and hang clothes carefully on the line; pull into shape: pin at seams. "Well hung is half ironed" is an old housewife's adage.

Don't iron sheets. Stretch and fold them as you take them off the line; four hands for this—get a family assistant on washday. (If this troubles your conscience, iron only the top one-third, for turning back over the blanket.)

To avoid ironing slip covers, fit them carefully back on chairs and sofas while still a little damp, pulling pleats into shape. (Do this only on furniture where slip covers are intended to hide upholstery, not to protect it.)

Use fabrics that don't require ironing (knitted or sheer nylon, seersucker, terry cloth) for many household furnishings such as table mats, drapes, bedspreads.

Buy night clothes and underwear that don't need ironing; dress children in play clothes that don't need ironing: cotton knit T shirts, seersucker, dungarees—fold them seam to seam right off the line.

Use nylon, dacron, and orlon household linens—and fiberglas curtains—to speed drying and reduce ironing.

Instead of ironing a few handkerchiefs, press them while wet against the sides of the bathtub, or against tile bathroom walls.

Everyday Kitchen Tips

Use kitchen shears, or surgical scissors with blunted points, to cut parsley, chives, and the baby's meat; wet them to cut dates, figs, marshmallows. (Attach them to a cord, or they'll always be missing!)

Clean vegetables on an open bag or a newspaper; roll up with parings and throw into garbage container.

Feed the baby out of the jar his food comes in. Stand it in hot water to warm.

Save warming pets' food to room temperature by taking it out of the refrigerator beforehand—but put it out of their reach.

Keep a dish, a sheet of aluminum foil, or a thick-folded paper towel handy to rest mixing spoons, etc., so you won't have to wash them off while cooking.

Use plastic or stainless-steel spoons or forks for the breakfast eggs, to avoid tarnishing your silver.

Try the electrolytic bath for a quick way of cleaning silver—solid or plated flatware (not hollow ware or knives with hollow or bone handles, nor silverware with oxidized design). Line an enamel pan with aluminum foil; add 1 tablespoon each baking soda and salt to 1 quart water. Bring the solution to boiling point and put the silver in it, making sure that each piece touches the aluminum foil or each other. Boil from 2 to 5 minutes, depending on the degree of tarnish. Wash, rinse and rub dry.

Especially for oxidized or embossed silver; saturate a cellulose sponge with a paste silver polish; tarnish is removed in about half the time it takes with a cloth, and you don't have to keep dipping the sponge into the polish. As each piece is finished, toss it into a hot water and washing-detergent solution. Rinse all together in clear hot water and rub dry.

Lacquer silver display pieces with clear lacquer to keep them from tarnishing—the same for brass and copper.

A rubber faucet guard or spray attachment on the sink faucet allows faster dishwashing without danger of chipping.

Cooking fat may be poured down the sink if mixed with detergent and flushed with plenty of hot water.

To avoid washing of baking dishes, and to salvage leftovers, make "meat and vegetable pies" in individual paper casseroles of the very new *Bondware* (33).

Keep some leftovers (like stewed fruits, salads) in the refrigerator in the same container in which they were served (never woodenware), along with all-plastic serving utensils. Saves washing of utensils as well as container.

Always have a few dozen paper cups and plates stacked in with your regular glassware and china. If it's handy, you're likely to use paper service more often than if you have to make special trips to the place where you store your big supply.

Keep a water-filled dishpan in the sink at all times, for between-meal dishes and glasses, etc. that you don't feel like washing until later.

Use an inexpensive pair of tongs—ice-cube tongs are good—for innumerable kitchen jobs: taking things out of the back of the oven, turning potatoes while baking, stirring foods that need to be lifted gently while cooking, etc.

Keep a supply of rubber bands in a dish for many wrapping jobs, particularly for items wrapped in wax paper.

To save innumerable stoopings to the garbage container each day, enamel the inside and the outside of a coffee tin, fit it with a dime-store pot lid, and use on the drainboard for small kitchen waste, plate scrapings, etc.

A large kitchen wastebasket, preferably of metal, for empty bottles, wrappings, etc., to eliminate more stooping.

Rubber mats, placed in front of stove and sink, are practical. They catch drippings and splashings, save much floor-scrubbing time.

Have a desk, or a writing surface and drawer, in or near the kitchen, so you can sit down to do the thinking and paper work for your job. Tie a pencil here with a string, and have a pencil-sharpener here, too. This is also a good place for a telephone.

Handle With Care

Keep pets off furniture with a powder sold for the purpose (*Chaperone*—especially for dogs), harmless but discouraging to them. Spray shrubs and flower garden with the same in liquid form.

To prevent a dust line forming on the wall behind pictures and mirrors, place a small rubber bumper between their bottom edge and the wall, to permit air to circulate freely.

Clean ivory piano keys with rubbing alcohol on a cloth. Rest cloth and bottle on folded newspaper, not on the piano, and watch out for drippings.

For speed in hand-washing your best china and glassware, have a rubber pad on the bottom of the sink or the dishpan. A Turkish towel on the drainboard saves chipping and nicking.

To keep fireplace ashes from flying all over the room, wet them down before cleaning, and really soak them before removing with a shovel.

To cut down on trips to empty ashtrays, use a large "silent butler."

If no one is at home during the day, and in unused rooms, keep windows closed to keep out dust; keeps them cooler in summer, too, especially if the shades are drawn.

For Children and Patients

Hang a small bell on the baby's crib or on the carriage on the porch, to warn you of restlessness, and to save you many unnecessary checkup trips back and forth.

During illness use a third sheet on the bed, over the blanket or quilt, to protect it from food or medicine spills. For a child patient, use a plastic tablecloth or shower sheet.

Have the baby's play pen or toddler's play area within hearing as well as seeing distance if possible, and talk to him as you go about your work; he'll interrupt your work for attention less frequently that way.

Save old magazines for a young child, or a sick one, for scribbling and cutting out, to save you time in entertaining him.

Put the Telephone To Work

Have the phone near the kitchen, or an extension in the kitchen.

Phone as many errands as you can, even some marketing.

The telephone company can install an excellent, inexpensive, non-twisting cord on your phone.

Plug-in telephones can be taken into whatever room you're working in; they're less expensive than an extension in every room.

Look into the possibility of an intercommunication system to be installed on your telephones. Especially if your house has more than one story, it saves much running around—and shouting.

Have an engagement pad or calendar by the phone, or a family bulletin board, for messages to and from busy members of the family. They can save you work if they will learn to let you know in advance of lateness to meals, absence, changes in plans.

Save time in looking up telephone numbers with an alphabetized book or gadget in which you can write all frequently called numbers and emergency ones: hospital, doctor, fire department, etc.

For Yourself

Dig your nails in white soap before tackling housework, to keep them clean.

Keep an assortment of adhesive bandages, burn remedy, antiseptic for small accidents, in a kitchen first-aid box.

A small auxiliary make-up shelf and mirror in the kitchen will help your morale. Keep hand lotion there, too.

If you haven't room for a sofa in or near the kitchen, at least have a comfortable chair or rocker.

Have all keys labeled (varicolored tags are a good idea) and keep extra labeled sets on hand—saves annoyance and hunting time. In the country, have an outdoor hiding place for an extra house key.

If you like to save things you may find useful someday, keep a filing system of what you store and *where*.

. . . And last and best of all is the trick of catching, and adding to your repertoire of tricks, those which you hit upon more or less unconsciously. Send them to us to pass on to others.

CHAPTER VIII

TODAY'S SERVANTS

WE MIGHT as well face it: the old-fashioned family retainer is extinct, lingering on only in fiction and old jokes. But even though the household slavey is gone, probably forever, the household-help situation is actually not nearly so grim as it's generally cracked up to be. For it stands to reason that among the millions of paid workers in this country there will always be an appreciable number suited by inclination, or moved by circumstances, to take up occupations as basically natural as the domestic ones.

So the "servant problem" lies not so much in lack of manpower as in the absence of a trained class of "career" servants. But there are available people, and professional services, with x number of hours and x talents, ready for domestic jobs. The resourceful housewife can find help of many kinds, though she may have to search for it, and she will need to plan wisely to get the most value out of it. She must be ready to make the most of what is available, and not expect the old-fashioned impossible. Above all, the housewife must realize that the status of servants has changed—today's domestic workers, like any other job-holders, have lives of their own outside the job.

Individual Help and Professional Services

1. There is a great variety of *auxiliary* help available to you, either "on call" or by a standing arrangement. Individual helpers include:

Older children to take care of your younger ones, and to do all kinds of chores, ranging from errands and dog-walking to ground-floor window-washing.

College students to do all kinds of part-time work: some will sleep in and baby-sit for a small salary plus room and board.

Men for heavy chores in and outside the house: cleaning, window-washing, gardening, odd paint jobs, simple carpentry, or driving the family car or station wagon. (The last is important these days as a means of calling for and returning country help.)

Women for general and special housework—cooking, cleaning, laundering, mending, canning.

Butlers and waitresses complete with uniforms—if you still want them—to serve at a fancy party.

Available professional services (in addition to such staples as laundries, cleaners, window-washers—as listed in the previous chapter) include:

Day nurseries and pre-kindergarten groups to take care of the youngest children part of the time.

Registered or practical nurses for the new baby and for home illnesses.

Caterers or restaurants, who not only prepare food for your parties, but often supply the personnel to serve it as well.

Telephone services, in larger cities, to receive messages when there is no one at home.

Errand services, in larger cities: mostly for emergencies.

The Maid —and How to Get Along with Her

2. Not to be considered as auxiliary help, but as the most important of domestic aids, the maid rates a section all her own. Today's general housekeeper-maid is the more fortunate successor to yesterday's "girl"—the drudge who was possessively alluded to as "one of the family," largely because she never had time, energy, or money enough to be "one" of anything else. These days the maid isn't wedded to the family; the tables being turned, the family is more dependent on her than she is on it. So don't expect gifts of free time from your maid. Plan her time for the greatest benefit to your household; don't squander it, for instance, by leaving the house a continual mess for her to pick up. And keep remembering that your maid isn't your nursemaid.

Whether she is a full-time or part-time worker, if you expect her to give value received, and if you want to get along with your maid—be a fair boss.

Have a fair, clear understanding about the job and stick to it: duties, hours, wages. Pay prevailing wages; have an agreement about paying for extra time (don't try to squeeze it out of her).

Have an agreement about sick pay, and arrange an annual vacation with pay, as is given in most businesses.

Like a good executive, learn to allocate the work, steadily increasing responsibilities and diminishing your supervision as she learns the particular problems of the job.

After she has learned the job, avoid working together, as much as possible. Do your own job instead of watching or nagging her; she'll enjoy the feeling of working independently and it'll save you the time that supervision takes. Encourage her to use her head, as well as her hands, in her work—even if she does skip corners occasionally.

Make the most of her special assets, encouraging any skill—such as a talent for cooking.

However, remember that most people can do, or can learn, good "plain" cooking and at least adequate housekeeping. If you want more—if you want her to take on real responsibility—qualities like good sense and willingness will be of far greater value to you than special skills. Cherish those qualities; don't kill them by pettiness over occasional mistakes.

Make things easy for her: give clear and easy-to-follow directions, simplifying wherever possible. Don't confuse her with old-fashioned nonessentials. (For example, few houseworkers these days are trained in conventional waiting on table. Instead, simply have her carry the food to the table for you to serve while seated.)

Be resourceful, prepared to cope with emergencies. Have a reference file of on-call help in case your maid is sick, or if she just can't stay to do all the work of a last-minute party.

Don't crowd her. Nothing is so unnerving as the pressure of more work than there is time for. If anything special comes up, cut out or rearrange something else.

Be human. Servants are people; expect them to have moods and whims like anyone else. If your maid is ill, don't assume she's malingering. Adults rarely do—do you? Assume that she wants to please you; people prefer to work in a pleasant atmosphere.

Remember that your maid is most probably a housewife in her own home and it's reasonable to assume that she knows as much about housework as you do (or more). Your methods may differ—but you can probably learn from each other.

Don't expect your maid to last forever. It isn't in the cards these days. The best proof that you've got along is if, when you decide to part, she helps you find her successor.

The Maid Plus Auxiliary Help

3. Full-time or part-time, the maid belongs to herself and not to the family she works for. So in a sense you can consider all maids part-time these days, their longest working week usually not exceeding 48 hours, and the few who are still willing to sleep in often doing so only on certain nights and expecting other free time during the day.

Expecting all-or-nothing assistance is what keeps so many women from accepting available help these days, even when they are well able to afford it. Often they talk themselves into accepting the myth that "really, it's easier to do it all myself than to have it 'half done' by someone else." This defeatist attitude is clearly not justified. Even though you can't get *all* of any servant's time, if you make use of auxiliary help to fill in the gaps, if you use your new housekeeping know-how, and if, above all, you cultivate a more casual attitude toward housekeeping—then of course life can be easier for you with servants than without them.

With a maid for the main job, there are many additional combinations you can make:

Extra-help Combinations

An evening baby-sitter, the most obvious auxiliary of all, to take over in the evening after the maid has gone.

Other auxiliary child care, such as nursery schools, organized play groups, or a high-school girl or boy to take care of the younger children after school or on Saturdays.

Especially for a large family where one maid can't possibly do all the work, get additional help with housecleaning, cooking, and the inside or outside laundry.

If there are young children and you can only get a maid for mornings, a home laundress certain afternoons, who will help keep an eye on the children while she works.

Extra help in addition to your maid when enough company warrants it. For large parties, professional help if possible.

The Invisible Servant

4. Bachelors can give most housewives lessons in household management—away all day, they almost never see their servants. They give instructions in writing, and of necessity are specific. Perhaps for this reason, or just because they are not around while the work is being done, they manage to avoid most of the crises of the housewife-maid relationships. There's no reason why a woman with a job or other outside interests shouldn't settle for this remote-control way of running a home.

Here's a practical Invisible Servant plan for a working couple who live in a small apartment. Their maid gives them about 5 hours a day. They leave too early to see her in the morning, and get back after she has left to get supper for her own family.

Part-time Help Plan

The maid puts the apartment in order and cleans; does light laundry; sends out, checks, and puts away the heavy laundry; does all the marketing on an expense account, keeping a record.

She handles the entire supper preparation, except the cooking of last-minute things.

She sets the supper table for serving without getting up.

She leaves in the refrigerator everything that cannot go on the table in advance (water in a pitcher, butter in its dish, sliced bread on a plate, salad and dessert), leaving meats, stews, etc., in or on the range.

She also sets trays for breakfast, and organizes in the refrigerator everything needed for breakfast.

She washes the dishes, which have been left soaking in the sink.

Thus only a short assembly job for dinner and breakfast is left for the working couple to do.

This shows that the work can get done without having the housewife and the maid on the job simultaneously. The Invisible Servant idea may be modified and adapted to other arrangements:

Other 'Invisible' Combinations

If you're away during the afternoon, have your maid come at noon, clean up and prepare supper, staying on to serve it and wash up afterward. This works well when there are older children; she is home when they return from school.

For a family with children where the housewife is absent all day, the maid comes early and gets breakfast, takes care of the entire household job, including marketing, and although she doesn't stay for supper, prepares it and sets the table.

If your family and house require it, your maid might also manage whatever auxiliary help is needed.

If you can't get or afford a maid, have a cleaning woman or man come in occasionally while you're away at work (and have them wash the dishes, too).

And don't forget that the telephone, and many other professional services, are invisible servants, too — use them to make life easier for yourself.

Following the principles expressed in this book should make your home simpler and easier to care for, make your entertaining more informal and therefore less of a strain for you, as well as for your household help. As for the relaxed, more realistic housekeeping standards advocated in the previous chapter, don't make the mistake of applying them only to yourself and continuing to expect immaculate results from those you hire to assist you. Don't ask the impossible of servants—any more than you ask it of yourself—and the chances are you'll find the help available today adequate for today's housekeeping.

THE NEW HOSPITALITY

OF COURSE you love your friends. But do you still love them when the party's over? When you've slaved to prepare for them, and still have to clean up after them when they're gone? When you say brightly at the door, "So glad you could come!" don't you really mean, "Wish you'd stayed home!"?

Take for example one of those nice young couples just getting started in life. They live in a tiny apartment with no servant, but they are determined to measure up to that fiction of "gracious living" handed down to them by their nice parents and perpetuated in the standard books of etiquette.

The hostess in her dinner gown brings the Vichysoisse to the table, disappears immediately to change the baby, returns in time to take away the soup and place plates and fetch in the roast beef and Yorkshire pudding. Two more trips for the vegetables and the hot dinner plates, and then perhaps she can sit down long enough to pick up her stemmed crystal goblet of Beaune 1932 before the baby cries again.

The host, stiffly wearing an unaccustomed and perhaps slightly threadbare dinner jacket, juggles the carving tools, trying to remember meanwhile to keep one of your two wine glasses filled (he would be slighting his guests if he served only one wine). Later, you will see him carrying out the garbage in the same dinner jacket!

And when it's time to clear the table, the hostess jumps up, saying firmly, as the etiquette books prescribe, "No, please don't get up, it's no trouble," and carries out the plates two at a time.

No wonder it's just about impossible to have any dinner conversation, or for the hostess to enjoy the dinner over which she has worked so hard. We'd like to know why otherwise sensible people think they must imitate the forms of an English manor house in a three-room, birdhouse-size apartment—or anywhere else, for that matter—without benefit of servants.

The picnic is the prototype of all informal entertaining. Everyone helps to prepare and serve the meal and make the entertainment.

In sharp contrast, the party we recall as the best we ever went to was one at which the hostess greeted thirty friends with the announcement that it was up to them to get dinner from scratch. The result was a superb dinner, and an evening that all the guests remember with pleasure to this day, because they helped to create the party. These, as it happens, were artists, the most rugged individualists of any society. We're certainly not advising this for your routine party-giving, but we are mentioning it here as an example of the best kind of party spirit—an informal spirit of fun in just sharing and being together.

We'd all like to be able to throw our homes open to our friends with this sort of ease, grace, and enjoyment—and without drudgery. Certainly entertaining at home is bound to mean some extra work; so do children, pets, gardens, and most of the better things in life. But the question is: Why so *much* work?

The New Etiquette

1. A new style of party-giving *is* beginning to grow up, even while the etiquette books cling to the same number of forks on the table and put into the hostess's mouth the insincere words with which she begs her guests not to lift a finger. We are making a new etiquette, with a new set of manners for both hosts and guests. They are better manners, more truly gracious, because they are sincere, not a counterfeit of a vanished aristocracy but an honest product of our times. What they demand, more than anything else, is a new and more relaxed attitude on the part of *all* concerned.

The new hostess is one who can stay within the limits of her home budget, hours, and energy and still give her guests a good time. She feels flattered, rather than nettled, when guests join her in the kitchen to help clean up, perhaps bringing their after-dinner coffee along. But, you may protest, guests never know where to find things or put things; a kitchen just isn't geared for a lot of strangers wandering in and out.

But it can be arranged—much more easily than you may think. We can plan for that informal, relaxed kind of entertaining in which host and hostess are both freed from a continuous round of duties so that they can enjoy their guests and help the guests enjoy each other. After all, the traditional forms of entertaining have hundreds of rules and dictates, whereas the new etiquette has only one basic principle: to make entertaining less work and more play for everyone concerned.

To go along with the new hostess there's a new-style host, whose talents are not limited to mixing drinks. He is equally likely to shop for the dinner, cook it, or serve it. He and the hostess *plan the work in advance*, deciding, for example, which of them will answer the door and take coats, fix and pass refreshments, tend to the children. They determine who will be responsible for specific duties in serving and carrying away cocktail glasses, dinner dishes, and so on. And in making their plans, host and hostess also decide on how much they can count on their guests for help.

For of course the new hospitality cannot function smoothly without the *new-style* guest. He may be recognized as the friend you invite most often because he (or she) is so easy to entertain. This guest knows that using the right fork is less important than helping with the party. He may be capable of doing many things, from merely serving himself to perhaps cooking the meal, which a talented guest is sometimes delighted to do. On the other hand, the guest who avoids helping in a servantless home is being downright rude. New manners for guests would include some of these (you'll no doubt have special preferences of your own to add):

Manners For Guests

Offer to help with whatever preparations are still to be made when you arrive, like mixing cocktails (and bringing one to the kitchen if the host or the hostess is still busy there), or fetching wood for the fire, or carrying dinner to the table.

Serve yourself and volunteer to serve other guests.

Carry dishes out to the kitchen, and don't wait to be handed a dish towel—get it yourself.

Volunteer to mix the salad dressing, make the steak sauce, or some similar service (but don't insist, especially if the ingredients aren't in the house).

Especially on weekends, remember that your hosts are not your servants; you'll find things much more relaxed and pleasant if you pitch in and help than if you just sit by and wait to be attended to.

Make your own bed when weekending with a family who make their own. Take the sheets off and fold them on the morning of your last day.

Don't, if a man, settle back with the host in the living room and leave all the work for the women (the new-style host knows better than that, too.).

Simplification: This is perhaps the most important consideration of all in the new etiquette. The first step is to simplify the *kind* of entertaining. It makes no sense, and isn't even good taste, to attempt more elaborate entertaining than you can afford in either time or money. Sharing a meal is the warmest kind of hospitality, but it is also the most work. Today it isn't always necessary to ask people to dinner, or always to serve food; there are other types of entertaining included in the various examples we've listed here (they're listed according to amount of work involved for you, beginning with the easiest):

Entertain With Ease

Entertain away from the house: movies or a theater, a ride in the country, swimming, skating, etc.

Entertain after dinner with an evening of bridge, television, home movies, music, games, or just talk. Serve a drink, not necessarily alcoholic, with or without a snack.

Picnic away from or at home, with everybody bringing part of the meal, as at the old-fashioned Sunday picnic.

Give a joint party, where several hostesses share work and expenses of a gathering at the home of one.

A barbecue—at home, outdoors.

A cocktail or tea party, outdoors or indoors.

A company meal — luncheon, brunch, or dinner—for large or small groups.

Eating and drinking don't make up *all* of hospitality; but they are nevertheless basic factors. For the rest of this chapter, therefore, we're confining ourselves primarily to detailed suggestions for handling food and drink in less laborious ways, yet in ways that best serve the purposes of hospitality. The goal is still *simplification*—simplify the menu, and simplify service (including the cleanup afterward).

Let's start with meals.

Meals for Small Groups

2. Almost all kinds of mealtime occasions for small groups of people have enough in common in their basic handling to be considered together. Adapting a standard family meal to meet the requirements of a company dinner is not so much a matter of adding to the number of courses served as one of the choice of food, and its preparation. The suggestions here are made mainly to simplify the work and make meals run more smoothly, and more enjoyably, when there are no servants, or only one.

Simplify the Menu: Think of your menu in terms of the easiest service. Our key menu plan, which is endlessly variable, is a one-dish main course (nutritionally well balanced as to protein, carbohydrate, and a non-starchy vegetable—or with a salad or a relish as a substitute for the vegetable, or as an extra), plus a simple dessert, preferably one that doesn't require cooking. There'll be times when you'll want to add a soup or an appetizer course—but ask yourself first if it's really worth the extra work. Whenever possible have only a one-dish main course. Classic examples are:

One-dish Courses

- Stews or casserole dishes.*
- A naturalized version of an exotic foreign dish: chop suey, chow mein, sukiyaki, curry.
- If it's a roast, serve the potatoes and vegetables (the gravy too, if the platter has a gravy well) all on the same big platter.
- If it's steak or chops, prepared at the last minute, these too can be put on a platter along with the vegetables.
- Or make a substantial soup your main course: a thick chowder, or an oyster stew, with salad or a relish as your vegetable.

Fresh fruit, and cheese and crackers make the simplest desserts. Frozen fruits, refrigerator-made ice cream, and jelled desserts are easy, too.

For hot weather meals, serve your cold course on one platter, too: cold meats or fish, with vegetable and potato salad or potato chips. There are all sorts of well-balanced combination salads: tuna fish, or chicken salad with greens are the most obvious. An aspic that combines meat, potatoes, and vegetables is a good idea; it can be served in the container in which it's been jelled.

Simplify Service: This probably calls for even more courage on the part of host and hostess than simplifying the menu. How far can you go? Would you dare let your best business prospect help set the table and present him with paper cup, plate, and napkin? How far you can go is of course up to you—and depends, quite understandably, on how far you feel your guests can go along with you. But we believe that your degree of nonconformance to useless convention determines the extent of your meal's smooth service, plus meaning less work for you. Any of these simplifications, if executed thoughtfully, can be in good taste, can even have "style."

We will suggest several varieties of simplified small-group service, but first here is a list of maximum time-and-labor savers for you to consider in all cases, both before and during the meal:

*Casserole Cookery by Marian and Nina Tracy, Viking, 1941, has some fine ideas for one-dish meals.

Before-the-Meal Labor Savers

The basic principle is to have everything (except such last-minute items as hot or chilled food) on the table in advance—or on the serving counter if it is a buffet meal.

This includes a general butter dish, salad and dessert, a filled water pitcher (the kind you can fit into the refrigerator between meals, to do away with last-minute ice-cube struggles). If you're serving milk or a soft drink, have it ready in a pitcher, too; if wine, have it on the table, uncorked.

Have coffee waiting in a utensil you can make it in. Or have an electric or alcohol hot-water pot and serve prepared coffee. (We keep ours in a tea caddy for swank.)

Have the hot course ready, too (whether you've cooked it earlier in the day or finished just a short while before the guests arrived), and leave it waiting in a slightly warmed oven, ready to be served. Even steaks and chops will keep for a while if covered and left in an open oven or on top of the stove.

Use stove-to-table ware (or any kind that withstands warming and is good-looking enough to come to the table) and refrigerator-to-table ware, to save general handling and clean-up time (see page 189).

Use mats instead of a tablecloth—they can be every bit as attractive and decorative (and if your table top isn't heat-proof, don't forget to provide tiles, or straw or asbestos mats, for the hot course).

Paper cups and plates cut dish washing labor to the bone. Even partial use of paper helps—we often use good-looking, solid-color paper plates for desserts, or paper cups for water. Solid-color paper napkins are attractive enough for most company meals, too.

A maximum of three pieces of silverware for each place: knife, fork, and a spoon or a fork for dessert. At buffets, have food that requires no knife. Then, with a dessert that can be eaten with the fingers, you'll only need one piece of silverware per person.

Two, or at most three, dishes for each person: one for main course and salad, one for dessert, a possible third for extra soup or appetizer course.

Have an extra side table nearby for used dishes, and for anything else that can't be placed on the main table without crowding.

Just before the guests are due to arrive, make a last-minute checkup to see that nothing's been forgotten.

Now you can relax! You have everything at the table; the food is cooked. If you and your guests are having a good time over cocktails, there's no need to break it up abruptly and rush everyone in to dinner. If there's no one waiting to hurry you to and from the table, make the most of your freedom from servants! And after you're seated, there are further labor-saving considerations:

Meal-time Hints

Serve the main course covered, so that food will stay hot between servings without trips to the stove.

Rest dish covers on a side table between servings if your table isn't large enough to hold them.

A prearranged serving routine between husband and wife is important, to avoid duplicating jobs, leaving others undone, and a general state of disorganized inefficiency.

And—if the thought doesn't horrify you—it's a good idea to scrape plates into a large "silent butler," or a good-looking covered utensil, before stacking them on a side table. (This, more than anything else, aids the clean-up later on, especially if your guests are to assist.)

Our specific suggestions for small group service are of two general types, which we have labeled All-at-the-Table (seated meals) and Bring-it-to-the-Table (buffets). Variations within each group are to help meet the special demands of greater or less formality, the size of the dining area, the number of guests and how well you know them, and so on. But each variation makes use of most or all of the general labor-savers we have listed above.

All-at-the-Table Service

'Co-operative' Meal: Simplest and most informal meal of this type, this gets its name from the emphasis on having guests as well as hosts help take care of serving the food. If you follow our general principle of having as much as possible of the food and equipment on the table in advance, you need make only one trip to the kitchen; when you call your guests to dinner, take the host or a guest out with you, bringing the cocktail glasses out to the kitchen at the same time, on a tray or wagon, and return with the covered main course, warmed dinner plates, and rolls.

The serving routine can be arranged in several ways. If you have a large-enough round table, preferably with a Lazy Susan center, everything can be arranged in the middle—in the style of the old-fashioned farmhouse dinner—within easy reach of everyone at the table. Or the serving dishes can be placed between each place setting, so that each diner serves the course that is placed at his right. Or host and hostess can sit at opposite ends of a rectangular table, with the food divided before them (uncarved roast in front of the host, perhaps; vegetables and salad bowl before the hostess), and do the bulk of the plate-filling themselves, with everyone passing filled dishes on to the right.

'Don't Get Up' Meal: Suggested for less intimate guests, or a more

"Co-operative" table setting on a marble-top table. At the four corners are the main course, bread, coffee, water. Each person serves the course placed at his right. Down the middle are salad, dessert, butter. Careful arrangement makes the table attractive—and division of labor keeps the service smooth. (Table setting by Russel Wright; photo courtesy of McCall's.)

"Don't Get Up" table setting, by Mary Wright. The main course is placed in front of the host, salad in front of the hostess. Other food and service equipment are on the top of two side tables; courses are served by host and hostess. Lower shelves on side tables are for stacked dishes. (Photo courtesy of McCall's.)

172

festive occasion—still without servants or with only one, yet without a great deal more work for yourself. Here host and hostess do all the serving, do not have the table laden with food and dishes, yet do not have to leave their seats to serve or clear off. And more people can be seated at a smaller table this way.

Again, the food and equipment is set out in advance. But only the main course is set at the table, before either host or hostess. Beside each of their places is a serving table or cart: on the top shelves of this are placed the salad bowl, the dessert, the stacked dessert dishes. The coffee-maker and service can go on whichever shelf has more room. On the lower shelves are a covered container and paper napkins for scraping and stacking used dishes. (If dining space is limited, or if you have no side tables, you can make use of a low buffet, a wall shelf, a desk, or even the top of a bookshelf, by arranging your table within easy reach of them.) The serving routine calls for host or hostess to serve the main course, and thereafter for each to serve the course on his or her side table. Guests pass filled plates along and used plates back.

Prearranged routine is an essential here; it means that hot food gets on plates as promptly as possible, the table doesn't get to be an unappetizing mess of dirty dishes, and host and hostess don't conflict embarrassingly about who's to do what. So, for the sake of smoothness and efficiency, decide ahead of time who is to carry in the main course, who is to carve, who is to fill plates, suggest second helpings, stack plates on the side table, serve wine, keep bread and butter passed, and so on and so on. After a while you'll both get so expert at this kind of teamwork that you'll even learn to follow each other's improvisations when things don't go as planned—like practiced dance partners. (If there's only one of you, get a guest to pinch-hit.)

The Cafeteria Table: A third All-at-the-Table idea; it looks festive and saves table-setting work by letting the guest set his own place. In effect it is a small sit-down buffet meal in which the dining table holds everything you need for the meal and doubles as the place where you eat it. We have shown this as a work-saver for family meals (page 34); it is easily adapted to company meals.

Set the table in T-shape. Cutlery and dishes are across the top of the T; serving dishes are down the center of the table—the stem of the T. The diner gets his own dinner plate, silver, napkins; puts

The Kitchen Buffet is really cafeteria procedure. A stack of trays and tableware is laid out on the counter, and food is taken directly from the stove by the guests.

Bring-it-to-the-Table Service

roll and butter on his plate, pours his glass of water, and sits down at a place along the side of the table. He serves himself—or is served by the person nearest each platter or bowl. A side table or shelf for used plates is helpful here, too.

This is, in effect, buffet service. Our chief recommendation for large-group meals is a form of buffet service; it is treated in detail in the following section of this chapter.

The Seated Buffet, also described in that section, can be used for small-group service, too.

The Kitchen Buffet: This is quite the most unconventional and informal variation, if your kitchen is large enough to permit it. A kitchen-counter cafeteria, complete with cafeteria trays, this is one of the greatest work-savers for the hostess.

Everything is laid out on the counter in the proper order for the easiest self-service: napkins, silver, plates, water and glasses, bread and butter, salad bowl, dessert. At the head of this design are the trays. You can buy fiber or aluminum cafeteria trays, of the right size for an individual diner, from a hotel-supply company; these are light and can be neatly stacked. The routine is obvious: everybody takes a tray, fills it, and lights wherever he pleases to eat his dinner.

174

The Clean-Up: This is basically the same after any type of small-group meal. Above all, don't rush the clean-up. Make the most of your servantless leisure, for with no maid whisking things away, after-dinner talk is apt to be freer, more relaxed.

Especially if your dining area is in the kitchen, you will have cleaned up as you prepared the meal. A good part of facilitating after-meal clean-up with guests assisting lies in putting your kitchen in order *before* the meal. Moreover, it's an illustration of present-day good manners; your guests are doing their best to help you, so don't go so far as to inflict your unwashed before-dinner pots and pans on them.

When you feel the time has come to clean up, often the host can start the ball rolling, so that even the most imperceptive guests get the idea of pitching in to help. If you haven't already served it, have after-dinner coffee or your after-dinner drink during the clean-up—or carry them from the table with you.

When guests help, make it fun. Never order them about, or belittle their efforts. And don't oversupervise them. Make it easy for them to help.

Co-operative Clean-up

Arrange for clean-up right through the meal by having dishes already scraped at the table, and dishes, silver, and glassware waiting on trays to be carried to the sink counter.

Keep like things together, to avoid meal-end clutter both at the dining table and on the kitchen counter.

Provide plastic aprons for men as well as women.

If you expect guests to help put things back in their proper places, *label* those places clearly. Don't forget to disclose, by labeling, the location of your garbage disposal.

Salvaging food to go back into the refrigerator, and putting it in containers, can be the host's job. (There's no reason why platters or casseroles with enough food still in them can't be put back in the refrigerator for another meal.)

To shorten clean-up time, don't have the dishes dried, but let them drain, if you have space for a large-enough dish drainer, or two. Of course you'll have to put them away yourself later on, but the main work will have been done.

It's a good idea for host and hostess to get together in advance about a clean-up routine, too. If they can work well together in organizing and dividing their main jobs of dishwashing and food-salvaging, that makes it easier for guests to share the rest of the work.

Meals for Larger Groups

3. The line of demarcation between procedures and occasions for small and larger group meals is, of course, flexible. Each borrows from the other, and many of the suggestions that follow are equally suitable for smaller gatherings. However, entertaining larger numbers does produce some special problems.

Buffet Service: This is our principal suggestion for a large company dinner. Fundamentally informal, with guests and hosts sharing the work, we know of no better way to give large mealtime parties without a bevy of servants.

Choose food in terms of the simplest service. We urge the least possible variety of foods—don't have a groaning smörgäsbord, but on the contrary, make it easier for yourself by making your menus even shorter than those we've suggested for small groups.

Plan your meal so that it can be eaten standing up, perched on the arm of a chair, from an end table, or on the floor.

Cleanup can even be a part of the evening's pleasure, if managed properly.

Buffet Menu

Foods that require no knives (hot rolls being buttered all at once on the table by a guest or the hostess).

Foods that have a minimum of liquid and won't spill off plates: combination foods that don't have to be cut with a knife, or casserole dishes to be served along with a relish or a shredded salad.

For a hot-weather buffet, combination salads or aspics for the main course.

Ice cream, kept cold in a thermos jar, is an excellent buffet dessert and can be served in low wax cups.

Cakes or fruit tarts that can be eaten in your fingers or on a paper plate are good, too. (If the dessert is a dry one served on a plate, you won't need a coffeecup saucer.)

Simplified Service

Minimize flat ware to two pieces each: fork and spoon, or two forks if the dessert requires one; preferably, just one fork, if the dessert can be eaten in the fingers.

Two plates; or preferably one for the main course, a paper plate or none at all for dessert.

One tumbler each.

Large paper napkins (preferably solid-color ones).

To point up the laborsaving values of paper service at a large gathering, a test study was made for us at the experimental apartment maintained by New York University School of Education. At a buffet dinner for 42 people, using china and glassware service (2 glasses, 2 plates, cup and saucer, for each guest), the time expended in "labor"—largely dishwashing—was 4 hours. There was also the matter of 2½ hours for laundering 42 napkins. With paper service, "labor" (in this case mostly washing the silverware) amounted to only ½ hour. The cost of paper plates, cups, and napkins was $4.00. So whether you measure in terms of labor saved, or balance the outlay for paper against the cost of professional dishwashing and laundering help (plus the inevitable breakage of china and glass), use of paper service shows a decided advantage.

Buffet serving ware should be chosen with an eye toward self-service. Electric hot plates, candle warmers, help keep food warm during the party; even a good-looking double boiler is fine (fill the bottom compartment with hot water to keep the food in the top part warm). A thermos jar for hot or cold dishes is a good idea, too (see Equipment List, Appendix A, pages 193-194).

Lay out your table to facilitate self-service, too; plates stacked near the containers that serve their food, tumblers near their pitchers, napkins and silver placed where most easily reached. Leave free spaces near plates, so that guests can fill them on the table, not in mid-air. Have trays, away from the table, for used dishes, and covered utensils into which food can be scraped from plates before they're stacked out of the way.

If you don't have one dinning table large enough to serve as your buffet counter, use several, including folding bridge tables, dividing the various courses between them. This works especially well on a porch or a terrace, where there is usually no large table.

A buffet party belongs to the guests as much as to host and hostess, everyone taking a share not only in serving themselves but also in entertaining each other. Thus you'll often find your most successful buffet parties splitting into small, self-sufficient groups —with talk apt to be more spontaneous than the general discussion at a seated dinner table. Don't spoil it by managing; now that you don't have to worry about what comes next, relax and have as good a time as your guests.

Buffets are wonderful for outdoor meals, too, if food is kept covered. But for very large barbecues, where food is prepared after the guests arrive, we advise at least one paid helper, unless you'd rather play chef than host.

Even after feeding a big crowd, don't dread getting guests to help you with the clean-up. If you've planned your menu and table with an eye toward simplifying clean-up, the work may be far less than your worried expectations. And by all means accept assistance from those guests who volunteer to help you; some always will, especially if there's no servant around.

Seated Buffet: This variation of the buffet meal is for those occasions on which you feel that more formality is necessary, but still want to avoid excessive fuss and labor. It's particularly helpful if the group is not too large to be seated all at one table. The table is fully set except for food, which is on a separate counter or buffet; guests fill plates there and take them to their places at the table.

Bridge Luncheons, and other purely feminine daytime functions, can usually best be handled as buffets. We single them out for special mention only because the hostess is all on her own here, with no husband to help, and at the same time her table is on display before female friends and neighbors. You may be tempted to "make an impression" on such an occasion, but our advice here is to keep the menu and the service as simple as you possibly can— let the efficient success of your meal speak for itself.

The Seated Buffet can be used to serve a medium-sized group with no servants, or only one—even if you want to do it with more formality.

For *indoor* company meals, we have three other suggestions:

Impromptu Meals: These are the ones whipped up on the spur of the moment, when guests are in the house and you decide to keep them there for a meal. This should be largely a matter of drawing quickly from a variety of canned and packaged goods, but it should not mean that they are disorganized, hit-or-miss affairs. Plan for such unexpected meals by making sure you're always well stocked with canned goods—and an extra supply of paper plates and cups. If all this is carefully planned, it will probably seem like magic to your guests and be much more impressive than many an ornate dinner. If you have the space, you may find it advisable to cache the supplies in a separate storage space. And, as special equipment, have a wall-type can opener, mounted waist-high.

Your problem is minimized by the fact that just about everything comes in cans these days, from a stew to a whole roast chicken. Even salad ingredients can come out of cans—our favorite quick salad is a combination of mixed canned vegetables plus chicken, lobster, shrimp, or tuna. Many big city department stores and "fancy" grocers stock a wide selection of remarkably out-of-the-ordinary canned goods (including the canned specialties of many famous restaurants).

Snack Meals: This is our even more casual version of the Impromptu Meal—our favorite Sunday meal and also a good "potluck" way of feeding a few close friends who've just dropped in. It's partly gleaned from odd bits of food in the refrigerator, plus food in jars, packages, and cans. There's usually an embarrassment of riches, and though many foods can be served together on a large platter, paper plates and cups are almost indispensable here for individual service and as auxiliary containers. Cold vegetables, made into salads with bought dressing (have a pot of growing chives around to dress up such salads), cold cuts, miscellaneous icebox leftovers blended in a soup, crackers and cheese, fruit—such things make a fine spread that you can produce with great speed and little effort.

Brunch: A meal to save a meal, this is most usually a late, extra-big, extra-leisurely Sunday breakfast that eliminates lunch. Have a hot main dish, and make the menu substantial enough to really fill in for the extra meal—not a number of courses, but enough of one good main course.

Snack Meals made up of leftovers and canned goods, and using paper service, can be much more fun than a formal meal. With a little planning and organizing, the food on the table—with its great variety of different shapes—can take on the appearance of a generous and amusing smörgäsbord.

Brunch Menu

Eggs of any kind, with Canadian bacon, ham, country sausage, or kippers.
Corned beef hash with fried or poached eggs.
Scrambled eggs made with stewed tomatoes or chicken livers.
Waffles and sausages—if you have an efficient waffle iron and not too large a crowd.
Pancakes, or French toast, with sausage or any smoked meat.

Plan the meal for laborsaving and ease. If it's a big breakfast for a few, make it a *Don't Get Up* meal; for a crowd, a buffet meal or a barbecue.

Electrically heated equipment helps guests to help themselves, especially if they are invited to eat at their convenience between certain hours rather than all at one time: electric coffee-maker, egg cooker, toaster, hot plates.

Here are two suggestions for *outdoor company meals*:

Barbecue: This can have the same basic pattern as hot indoor meals (although the vegetable usually appears as the relish). Substitute rolls or bread, to be toasted over the fire, for a starchy vegetable. Fruit, and cakes like brownies, make the easiest barbecue desserts.

Your fire being a natural incinerator, you can usually burn up all traces of this meal, including paper plates. Done simply, the barbecue can be the greatest work-saver of them all for a fairly small group. So much has been written on this subject that we won't go into detail here—except to warn you to evaluate what you read about barbecues in terms of the simplest possible procedure. The fussy, full-paraphernalia barbecue can involve a tremendous amount of labor and expense.*

Picnic: This is really the prototype of the informal meal, with everyone sharing in the work, and frequently involving several families, with each providing a prearranged share of the food. Paper service and forks of course, and a minimum even of these, and disposable containers for the food wherever possible—so that you're left with practically nothing to carry back from a picnic in the country, and a minimum of items to wash.

A picnic doesn't have to mean sandwiches, which are so much work. Take some foods in their original containers, and let the picnickers make their own sandwiches on the spot:

Cook It Outdoors by James Beard, M. Barrows & Co., Inc., and *The Sunset Barbecue Book*, Lane Publishing Company, have much valuable information.

Picnic Menu

Cold sliced meat or chicken.
Cheeses. Take along a knife, put the cheese on wax paper on a clean board, and let guests cut their own wedges.
Hard-cooked eggs in their shells, the classic picnic food and the least trouble.
Raw vegetables, cool and thirst-quenching: celery, carrots, tomatoes, whole cucumbers.
Oranges. Instead of peeling, hit the fruit against a rock until it is soft, then cut a deep hole and suck the juice.
For dessert, individual portions: brownies, apple turnovers rather than a pie, cupcakes.

If you're hiking or motoring, thermos bottles and jugs for liquids are necessary equipment. Also dry ice. Order it in advance from your drugstore soda fountain and keep in its original packing to preserve it; avoid burning your fingers, and keep it from getting into the food—it can be poisonous. Lining the basket holding the dry ice and perishables with newspaper creates a handy, featherweight icebox.

Refreshments

4. This general heading covers the snack that you prepare for a few friends who drop in before or after dinner or after the theater, as well as the food and drink for a large dance, a cocktail party, or a tea party—in other words, all between-meal service. The only important difference is the size of the crowd, but all such occasions can be kept informal, more enjoyable, and less work if you follow three basic principles: simplify the menu, simplify service, and arrange things so that guests can help themselves.

Cocktail Parties: We start with what is often the largest kind of gathering—where it is most important to avoid undue work and trouble. The procedures that serve you best here in preparing and serving food and drink are easily adapted to smaller gatherings; this might be considered the blueprint for all parties at which people constantly come and go.

Use prepared foods as much as possible. You can really be creative about this between-meal larder.

Party Menu Hints

Have a collection of canned and packaged snack foods to draw from, not forgetting potato chips, pretzels, peanuts, and other cocktail staples.
Go on food hunts in the foreign delicatessens. Swedish and Italian stores, for instance, have wonderful cheeses, put-up hors d'œuvres, and relishes.
Look for unusual crackers, too: matzohs, sea toast, celery-flavored crackers.
Buy unusual foreign breads—Jewish rye, Italian and French bread, heated a few minutes in the oven, are wonderful with spreads, cold cuts, cheese.

Cocktail parties can be the easiest way of entertaining large groups with refreshments. Placing the

You don't have to make canapés yourself. Put the ingredients in bowls and let your guests spread them on crackers, toast, bread, or potato chips.

Have hors d'œuvres that require little or no work for you: green or ripe olives, chilled raw vegetables (carrot "needles," white radishes, celery), or shrimps to be dipped into bowls of mayonnaise or other dressing. Small hot cocktail sausages, fish balls, or anchovies plus olives on toothpicks. Or you can serve salamis and other sausage meats, sturgeon and other salt fish.

And don't forget to include cheese and crackers—on trays designed especially for this combination.

Serving equipment should be selected to make it easier for guests to serve themselves: large subdivided bowls and trays. Sandwich humidors, for keeping fresh canapés made ahead of time, are excellent equipment. For other suggestions, see the Equipment List, Appendix A, pages 193-194.

One of the greatest causes of confusion among guests, and added work for hosts, is to offer a great variety of cocktails and liquors. Preparing one kind of cocktail (plus one kind of highball, if you feel it's necessary), may not *look* as bountiful, but experience has

...ood in one room and the drinks in another is a ...ood device for making the guests circulate.

shown us it satisfies almost everyone, and is far more practical.

Good equipment is another key to easier serving. Provide yourself with an efficient group of accessories, as multipurpose as possible and chosen for durability and practicality (not gag appeal, or you'll end up with a mess of pornographic bottoms-up glasses, cute bar aprons and drink thermometers—all destined for the junkman). There's so much on the market in the way of useful drink gadgets that we won't go into much detail here. But it is important to get yourself a good drink-recipe book.

If the table (or other flat surface) being used as a bar isn't alcohol-proof, cover it permanently with glass, or with a plain-colored plastic cloth for the occasion. If it's a really large party, several such drink stations will make it easier for guests to serve themselves. Depending upon the size and degree of informality of the party, you may want the guests to serve themselves entirely, or it may be necessary for host, hostess, or a volunteer friend to alternate at the bar. A routine, decided on in advance by host and hostess, is especially important here, so that the serving of drinks doesn't get out of hand.

For large cocktail parties we find it a good idea to make up large, uniced batches of cocktails. Keep them in ordinary half-gallon demijohns (for which you'll need a funnel). Then you or your guests can mix up smaller batches with ice, in small big-topped pitchers; a number of quart-sized mixing pitchers will serve you well. Have plenty of ice near your uniced batches of drinks and serving pitchers, in any large bowls you have around—we find a large punch bowl makes a fine oversize ice bucket, eliminating constant trips back and forth for more ice. And if you can buy ice cubes from a supplier, don't try to provide your own.

Snacks and Drinks for a Few: This can be treated as a sort of cocktail party in miniature; the food table becomes a food tray, the bar a drink tray. Select your food from among the suggestions made above; a cheese-and-cracker platter may be enough. Drinks need only be tea, coffee, beer, or soft drinks; if they're alcoholic drinks, you can probably reverse our advice on the cocktail party—it's not much added work to offer a full choice of liquors and cocktails to a small gathering. Bring out all drink supplies on one tray: liquor, mixes, ice, all pouring and mixing accessories. Serve the first round, and then let everyone serve himself.

Tea Parties: Whether large or small, these are really buffets, and are an easy way to entertain a large group. Having two teapots going, or one teapot and a coffee-maker, helps make the service flow. Get several of your guests to help pour, so that no one person has to bear the brunt of the work. Recommended:

Tea Party Hints

- Old-fashioned alcohol-burner teapots, equipped with strainer, still make the best on-the-spot tea unit.
- Electric hot plates or candle-type warmers on the tea table are fine for keeping hot such hors d'œuvres as fishballs on toothpicks, or cheese-spread toast.
- Think of canapés as open sandwiches and they'll be less work. For instance, cucumbers or tomato slices on buttered, thin-sliced white bread without crusts; ham or turkey sliced very thin on buttered bread.
- Avoid painfully achieved decorative masterpieces; after all, they are soon to be swallowed in one gulp. Hard-cooked eggs aren't daisies.
- For small teas, old-fashioned cinnamon toast and English muffins toasted and buttered on the spot are still excellent fare. A more substantial variation is our idea of *blini*—iced red caviar topped with a spoonful of sour cream on hot English muffins.
- Try store-bought lady fingers or chocolate leaves—any cakes or

cookies that can be held in your fingers save using extra plates.
For sweets (other than candy) try large strawberries — to be dipped into a bowl of powdered sugar—or kumquats on toothpicks.

Dances, and large gatherings like young people's parties, should also be planned to allow guests to serve themselves easily. Refreshments should be in another room than the one used for dancing: the kitchen for real work-saving, the porch or the terrace in mild weather. Food and drink depend on the age of the group, but you can't go wrong if you keep it simple: a barrel of beer and a supply of pretzels for an adult square-dance party; soda pop and frankfurters for a teen-age dance; fruit juice and fancy-looking store-bought cookies for younger children. At parties where dancing, games, or music is the important thing, service as well as refreshments can be simple—decorative, colored-paper service can be adequate.

Clean-up: This is usually up to the hosts, especially if it's a large party or tea, with guests staying varying lengths of time. Protect yourself as much as possible by having food that doesn't need plates, or that can be served on paper ones. If possible use paper cups (this is most feasible at outdoor summer cocktail parties); otherwise we recommend an oversupply of inexpensive dime-store glasses and teacups—we've been able to find good-looking, simply designed ones — to eliminate dishwashing during your parties. These extra cups and glasses can be packed away afterward in a dustproof box, ready for the next party.

Some clean-up assistance from friends can probably be counted on, though; if it's a large gathering, you might ask a few of your more intimate friends to help, and to stay on for a simple supper afterward.

House Guests

5. After the weekend is over, if you and your guests still like each other, then in our opinion you've been successful hosts. You face a major problem in sharing two relatively unfamiliar sets of lives, even for a few days.

Don't expect the impossible of guests who aren't used to the ways of your household. On the other hand, don't be afraid to suggest, if there's wood to be gathered, that two men are better than one, or that if there's no maid everybody makes their own beds. We live in a transition period in which there are few established rules; if a guest doesn't automatically pitch in it doesn't necessarily mean he doesn't want to. But make it pleasant for your guests to help, especially where meals are concerned. Experience has taught us that unpleasantness over meals and their preparation can wreck a weekend.

If possible, prepare some of your main foods beforehand—your roast, for instance, which can do double duty as cold cuts at another meal. Plan meals so that you can assemble them, rather than cooking them from scratch.

Have at least two impromptu or snack meals during a weekend, so that less cooking is required.

Whether breakfast is to be eaten in a group or separately in the order of people's getting up, have everything on the table, including electric table cookers for coffee and eggs, juice squeezers, etc.

Use as much paper service as you can, to cut down dishwashing. Try to plan so as to have only one dishwashing a day.

As one meal gets put away (with everyone helping), set your table for the next, or set trays with service for a next outdoor meal.

Try to avoid the cabin fever that comes from being with your guests *all* the time. Set the example by reading if you feel like it, or by leaving your guests on their own for a while.

A successful weekend requires some sort of over-all plan—no matter how flexible—as to how time is to be spent, and it also calls for division of labor and responsibility between host and hostess. Decide in advance, as you would at any party, who's to handle dishwashing, table-setting, the preparing of drinks and between-meal snacks, and so on. And it's particularly unfair social practice for the host to monopolize the more interesting guests (it's worse of course if it's a female guest), leaving the hostess stranded in the kitchen with the less attractive ones, and with more than a fair share of household chores. Advance decisions to share work and social responsibilities are bound to create a happier atmosphere than if one member of the family feels singled out for special drudgery.

What about Looks— and Taste?

6. After all this talk about paper plates, kitchen utensils on the table, and dime-store glassware, you may think we've forgotten all about looks. We haven't. Though in our scheme of things you can't expect the elaborate elegance of the past, the table you set for your guests can still have its own kind of good looks, and often

beauty, without benefit of priceless china and crystal stemware.

Table-Settings: Good taste is largely a matter of fitness and appropriateness. Who would think of wearing an evening gown on the golf course? Isn't it just about as ridiculous to set a traditional table, complete with starched white damask and all the trimmings, in the dinette, or in a combination living-dining room? Whether or not you've ever been really sure of your taste, if the basic rule of *fitness* is strongly enough ingrained, we're willing to bet you won't go far astray by following the vagaries of your own taste.

Since most dining tables are in or near the living room or the kitchen these days, *harmony with their surroundings* becomes a major consideration. Think of your table accessories as integral parts of the decorative scheme of the room. Let your setting pick up the room's predominant colors—either by the main color used, or by carefully chosen color accents.

Tableware: Table decoration needn't be confined to flowers and candles. Think of everything that goes on your table as part of the decorative whole. An unusually handsome salad bowl, for instance, can "make" a table if you plan your setting around it. Have a few favorite serving accessories as key pieces: a really good-looking casserole, perhaps an antique soup tureen.

There is still little refrigerator-to-table ware and stove-to-table ware, designed as such, on the market. But it's possible to improvise. For refrigerator-to-table pieces, we've used good-looking low, rectangular bowls, of colored pottery or glass, for frozen desserts and salads, and a hand-made, bubble-glass water pitcher with a small neck that stays in the refrigerator between meals.

For stove-to-table ware, look for utensils that are good-looking and simple in design. Tin-lined copper pots and pans can look wonderful on the table, as can chrome-finished ones, especially the double boilers (to keep food hot on the table). Some heavy aluminum ware is simply designed, too, aluminum Dutch ovens being particularly useful. When using cooking ware on your table, it's best not to mix metals: don't use chrome-plate with copper, for instance. You can use pottery stove-to-table ware, too. The French peasant bisque type is practical and can lend a gourmet touch to your table. Our own design of heavy "Casual China"—ovenware with matching flatware—is glazed in soft, appetizing colors, and looks well on the table.

Paper Napkins, Plates, and Cups: You may have to hunt for them, but do try to find undecorated, one-color types. If you can't, avoid corny decorations and settle instead for plain white. There is an infinite variety of possibilities—a table with which we were particularly pleased had dark-brown cotton mats, light-blue paper plates with matching paper napkins, and plain white waxed cups. The red-handled plastic flatware we used with this, plus a few bright red geraniums in a pewter bowl, combined with the rest to make a table setting for which no one would ever have to apologize.

So plan your color scheme; if your color scheme's in order, you can do this kind of thing with style.

Taste in Food: Just because we've talked about so many short cuts doesn't mean you still can't be a gourmet if it's in you to be one. In any case, arm yourself with a repertoire (it needn't be a large one) of dishes you make well, trying to make them more nearly perfect each time. Practice *can* make perfect! Good cookbooks are important to the housewife, but there has been such a tremendous number of them published, and the choice of cookbooks is so personal, that it would be of small help for us to suggest a list. However, for the woman who wants to improvise her own variations, there is nothing better than that old stand-by, *The Settlement House Cook Book* (The Settlement Book Company, Milwaukee, Wisconsin).

In the new hospitality, ease, efficiency and work-saving rate higher than conformity to dead, useless forms. We hope we have convinced you that this does *not* mean that our informal entertaining is without its own charm and warmth and grace. It is simply of a different kind than was once considered "proper." Etiquette changes with the times. As it was once geared to our grandparents' way of life, it is now emerging out of our own. So don't look back, but, as exponents of the new etiquette, help to create it!

APPENDIX A

Weekly Living Room and Bedroom Cleaning Routines

1. Bring in "cleaning" basket and two "catchall" baskets or trays (a cart would do for both), and a paper bag.
2. Open windows, turn down heat.
3. With wastebasket or paper bag in hand, and "catchall" basket, do a once-around-the-room pickup job, including rubbish removal and gathering up articles belonging elsewhere in the house; put these articles and wastebasket outside the door of the room.
4. Take to kitchen or bathroom (in basket, cart, or tray) any small articles that need washing or thorough polishing. Include plants for a soaking in the sink, to remove dust. (You can also wipe off leaves with damp tissues.)
5. Return with vacuum-cleaner and all necessary attachments. About the only other tools you need in your basket or cart are treated polishing cloths, a cellulose sponge or two, and a bottle or jar filled with rinseless detergent (see page 134).
6. Then, in a series of once-around-the-room routes, starting with the *dust-brush attachment*, vacuum-clean — as you come to them:
   Window sills (inside and out) and window sash moldings.
   Venetian blinds or shades.
   Radiators (mainly where dust shows).
   Walls where cobwebs and any dust show.
   Exposed areas of bookshelves, including banked front of books.
   Exposed baseboard moldings.
   All furniture (except upholstered portions).
   Books, magazines, larger decorative accessories, lamp bases and shades (lifting each object as it's finished to dust underneath).
   Ashtrays (no need to empty them first —let the vacuum do it).
   Mantel and fireplace fixtures.
7. In a second trip around, with *upholstery-cleaner attachment*, go over:
   Draperies and curtains; then shake them into position and line up.
   Upholstered furniture; then plump pillows and straighten slip covers.
   Hearth, vacuuming ashes from fireplace.
   Small rugs.
8. On a third trip, with cleaning basket, sponge off and dry-polish all furnishings that need it—including dry-polishing mirrors and picture glass. Sponge hearth if necessary. Then remove cleaning basket.
9. Make a fourth trip around, with *floor-brush attachment*, doing all exposed floor areas (including those in closets).
9a. Or if you have a carpeted floor, clean now with *rug-cleaner attachment*—it's easier if your furniture is on rollers, so that large areas can be cleared for fast action.
10. Replace the furniture.
11. Polish or wipe accessories left to soak; bring them back to the room, along with plants, and put all back in place. Remove basket used to carry them.
12. Empty vacuum bag, if necessary, and store tank and attachments.

When-Necessary Tasks

(to be added to weekly routine as needed)

1. Thorough vacuuming of corners, walls, baseboards, doors, and floors. (Heavy furniture should be on rollers, to be easily moved to center of room.)
2. Clean windows (see page 149).
3. Polish metal objects, andirons, lighting fixtures, etc.

4. Vacuum reverse side of rug, rug mat, and floor underneath.
5. Wax floors (see page 147).
6. Clean radiators (using the narrow-space vacuum attachment).
7. Remove cushions from chairs and sofa, and clean crevices with narrow-space vacuum attachment.
8. Dust pictures and light bulbs.

Once-or-Twice-a-Year Cleaning

(not much oftener, we hope)

1. Shampoo rugs (see page 149) and upholstery (or have them done by professionals).
2. Remove draperies and curtains for professional cleaning or laundering; vacuum the wall and ceiling areas they hide.
3. Clean box spring and bed frame, and both sides of mattress (with upholstery-cleaner vacuum attachment).
4. Thoroughly vacuum closets and storage areas, removing the contents first; sort and rearrange the contents.
5. Remove the contents of desk and bureau drawers; vacuum with dust-brushing attachment; sponge clean with hot water and detergent (without rinsing, if possible); sort out the contents, throwing away unnecessary items, and rearrange.
6. Wash walls (see page 148).

Bathroom Cleaning Closet Check List

Plunger
Cellulose sponges, various sizes
Cellulose toilet sponge—long-handled
Cellulose or rubber wet mop—long-handled
Dry mop
Floor brush—long-handled
Dust pan—long-handled
Detergents (washing, cleaning and scouring, see page 134)
Dry-polishing cloths (for mirrors)
Tissues or paper towels
Ammonia, for washing combs and brushes
Rubber gloves

Sample Division of Labor

For a family of four. The father works a five-day week, the son is of high-school age, the daughter in about the eighth grade, the mother a full-time housewife doing all the major housework and the cooking.

Weekdays: A.M.

Each does his share in straightening up bathroom.
Mother gets breakfast.
Daughter packs lunches.
Son puts out garbage, brings in newspaper and milk, feeds dog.
Each carries own breakfast dishes and silver to sink.
If there is time, each makes own bed.

Weekdays: P.M.

Father sometimes does some dinner shopping on the way home.
Daughter sets dinner table, or does some other dinner preparation.
Everyone helps carry dinner to table.
Everyone carries some dishes to sink.
Son finishes clearing table, wipes mats, carpet-sweeps.
Daughter washes dishes.
Father puts away food, pots and pans.
Mother sets breakfast table, does advance breakfast preparation.
Everyone helps straighten up living room and own room before going to bed.

Weekends, Holidays, Vacations

Each makes own bed, cleans room lightly.
Son or daughter thorough-cleans bathroom; the other cleans living room lightly.
Children set, clear, clean up the table.
Mother cooks dinner as on weekdays, with help, except when:
    Children plan and prepare a picnic;
    Father plans and prepares a barbecue;
    Father and children get a cold supper, brunch, or cafeteria lunch.

Special Tasks: To be scheduled for the father's free time, and for after-school time not needed for homework or play.

Children

Take wash from line, fold it.
Wash car, clean the inside.
Take care of pets, household plants, vegetable and flower gardens.
Plan, prepare and clean up in entertaining their friends.
Run errands, keeping a chart of whose turn it is.

Father and Son

Wash and wax floors.
Wash windows.
Bring in wood for the fire.
Take care of fireplace.
Work in the garden.
Do repairs, painting, carpentry.

Father

Takes down and hangs up draperies and curtains.
Takes over refreshments for guests.
Does all outdoor cooking.
Cooks certain dishes for indoor meals.

Son

Mows lawn.
Shovels snow.
Takes care of garbage disposal.
Assists in outdoor cooking.

Daughter

Dusts books.
Polishes silver.
Cuts and arranges flowers for the house.
Shares sewing and mending with mother.
Assists with indoor cooking, baking.

Equipment List for Entertaining

For Seated Meals

Heat Tiles (if table tops need protection, use covered asbestos types).

Paper Service:
Plates (solid color, plastic-surfaced).
Cups (all-white or with solid-color handles; also low dessert cups).
Napkins (solid color; pressed fiber—"Masselin").

Stove-to-table Ware:
Saucepans, fry pans, double boilers, Dutch ovens (good-looking enough to bring to the table—of stainless steel, cast aluminum, or tin-lined copper).
Casseroles, bean pots, *petites marmites*, baking dishes, platters (of pottery lined with salt glaze, or in other "ovenproof" glazes; also pyrex-type glass utensils).
Large platters, with gravy wells; also multipurpose ones without them. Pottery, metal, pyrex, can withstand some oven heat.
Covers, particularly for platters; to be found in housewares departments, silver shops, hotel-supply shops.

Refrigerator-to-table Ware:
Rectangular dishes (for frozen desserts, aspics—mostly in glass, plastic; also attractive pottery bowls in low square shapes).
Covered butter dishes, covered water pitchers—pottery, glass, plastic.
Electric Coffee-makers.
Thermos Bowls, to keep food hot; to keep ice cream cold, to preserve ice cubes.
Disposal Containers for plate scrapings—hinged metal boxes. Oversize "silent butlers" are best.
Trays, molded plywood, plastic, cafeteria-type aluminum.

Side-table Service:
Folding butler tables, small tables and tea carts with lower shelves, Lazy Susans (a good way to get food passed at a large table).

Smoking Equipment:
Covered ashtrays. The smallest you can find, with a concealed chamber for ashes and butts, are especially good for outdoors.
Cigarette boxes, with hinged tops.

Table lighters, to eliminate paper-match clutter.

Coasters, to protect furniture tops if these are not alcohol-proof or waterproof.

For Buffet Service

Heat tiles, paper service (napkins in *large* size); stove-to-table and refrigerator-to-table ware (in *larger* sizes); electric coffee-makers; large thermos bowls, disposal containers, trays, side-table service, coasters. Also:

Large Tablecloths, solid color or self-woven designs—such as plaids; also plastic film by the yard.

Double Boilers, bottom compartment to be filled with either hot water or ice, to keep food hot or cold.

Large Soup Tureens, covered—for the main course.

Electric Equipment: bain-marie, with two or three pots, to keep warm a combination dish, such as chow mein; hot plates, to keep food warm in its own container.

Smoking Equipment: small ash trays, an auxiliary supply; for example, dime-store glass furniture casters.

Silent Butlers (unpainted metal).

For Between-Meal Snacks, Drinks, Teas

Heat tiles, paper service (napkins in *small* sizes), electric coffee-makers, electric hot plates (for hot hors d'œuvres), thermos bowls, trays, side-table service, smoking equipment, coasters. Also:

Glasses, an inexpensive auxiliary supply for large cocktail parties; also a box to store them.

Cups and Saucers, auxiliary supply for large teas; a box to store them.

Large Soup Tureens, for large quantities of ice cubes.

Glass Measuring Pitchers, quart size – for measuring large batches of cocktails.

Glass Demijohns, ½-gallon size – to hold large quantities of cocktail mixture until the ice is added.

Food-storage Jars, refrigerator-to-table ware —to store and serve sandwich spreads.

Bowls of various sizes and shapes, in pottery and wood—for spreads, cocktail tidbits.

Trays: lightweight combination food-and-drink trays, "cheese-and-cracker" trays, "relish rosettes," covered sandwich humidors.

APPENDIX B

List of Manufacturers and Distributors of "Hard-to-Find" Products and Materials; Write Manufacturer for Nearest Retailer

(Reference numbers to be found throughout the book are keyed to this listing.)

1. Dex-O-Tex
   (A custom-type floor covering. Request information from local ceramic tile contractor.)
   Crossfield Products Corp.
   2153 Sacramento Street
   Los Angeles 21, California

2. The Mengel Company
   Cabinet Division
   Louisville, Kentucky

3. Magnesite
   Ask your local floor-laying contractor for Magnesite composition flooring (inexpensive; can be used on wood frame floor—nondenting; available in plain trowelled finish; wood filler sanded finish where wood chips show; sanded finish where marble chips show). If he does not make his own mix, he can obtain it from:
   Allied Products Company
   1125 Forty-fourth Road
   Long Island City, New York

4. *Flor-ever*
   (Vinylite Plastic Floor)
   Sloane-Delaware Floor Products
   Trenton, New Jersey

5. *Rug Anchor*
   E. I. duPont de Nemours & Co.
   Fabrics Division
   350 Fifth Avenue
   New York, New York

6. *Planner Group*
   Winchendon Furniture Company
   Winchendon, Massachusetts

7. Knape & Vogt Mfg. Co.
   Grand Rapids, Michigan

8. Globe-Wernicke Company
   Ross & Carthage Avenues
   Norwood, Cincinnati 12, Ohio

9. Egyptian Lacquer Company
   Jacobus Avenue
   Kearny, New Jersey

10. Knoll Associates, Inc.
    601 Madison Avenue
    New York 22, New York

11. Herman Miller Furniture Co.
    Zeeland, Michigan

12. Edgewood Furniture Co., Inc.
    208 East 27th Street
    New York 16, New York

13. Nessen Studio, Inc.
    40 East 21st Street
    New York, New York

14. Dunbar Furniture Mfg. Company
    Berne, Indiana

15. Kurt Versen Company
    Englewood, New Jersey

16. *Krylon Plastic Spray*
    Foster & Kester Company, Inc.
    Philadelphia 32, Pennsylvania

17. The Wire Mold Company
    Hartford 10, Connecticut

18. Benjamin Reel Products, Inc.
    10700 Broadway Street
    Cleveland, Ohio

19. Jens Risom Design, Inc.
    49 East 53rd Street
    New York, New York

20. E. I. duPont de Nemours & Co.
    Textile Service Division
    40 Worth Street
    New York, New York

21. *Travelon*
    (Saran-Generic name)
    Hafner Associates, Inc.
    350 Fifth Avenue
    New York, New York

22. *Koroseal* (fabrics)
    Comprehensive Fabrics, Inc.
    Empire State Building
    New York 1, New York

    Koroseal (floor covering and
      cove molding)
    Sloane-Delaware Floor Products
    Trenton, New Jersey

23. E. I. duPont de Nemours & Co.
    Wilmington, Delaware

24. *Zelan*
    For list of companies using it, write to:
    E. I. duPont de Nemours & Co.
    Textile Service Division
    40 Worth Street
    New York, New York

25. *Tuf-Flex*
    (Tempered Glass)
    Libbey-Owens-Ford Glass Company
    Toledo 3, Ohio

26. Devoe & Raynolds Company, Inc.
    44th Street & First Avenue
    New York, New York

    Lehman Brothers Corporation
    115 Jackson Avenue
    Jersey City, New Jersey

27. *Formica*
    Formica Insulation Company
    4613 Spring Grove Avenue
    Cincinnati, Ohio

28. *Micarta*
    (U. S. Plywood national distributors)
    Westinghouse Electric & Mfg. Co.
    Micarta Division
    Trafford, Pennsylvania

29. *Mirawal*
    Baltimore Porcelain Steel Corp.
    Baltimore 3, Maryland

30. Brunswick-Balke-Collender Co., Inc.
    623 South Wabash Street
    Chicago, Illinois

31. *Flexscreen*
    Bennett Ireland, Inc.
    1049 Bank Street
    Norwich, New York

32. *Heatilator*
    Heatilator Company
    431 East Brighton Avenue
    Syracuse 5, New York

33. *Bondware*
    Bowes Industries
    5537 North Clark Street
    Chicago 40, Illinois

34. Tyler Refrigerator Corporation
    68 West 58th Street
    New York, New York

35. (on special order)
    General Electric Company
    Major Appliance Division
    310 West Liberty Street
    Louisville 2, Kentucky

    International Harvester Company
    Evansville, Indiana

    Frigidaire
    General Motors Corp.
    300 Taylor Street
    Dayton, Ohio

36. Chambers Range Company
    Shelbyville, Indiana

    Western-Holly
    Western Stove Co., Inc.
    8536 Hays Street, Culver City, California

37. St. Charles Manufacturing Company
    1694 Dean Street
    St. Charles, Illinois

38. *Casco Posture Stool*
    Hamilton Manufacturing Corp.
    Columbus, Indiana

39. Coppes, Inc.
    Nappanee, Indiana

40. *Kencork*
    David E. Kennedy, Inc.
    55 Second Avenue
    Brooklyn 15, New York

41. Firestone Rubber & Latex Products Co.
    Fall River, Massachusetts

42. Westinghouse Electric Corporation
    Appliance Division
    Mansfield, Ohio

43. *Contour Sheets*
    Pacific Mills
    214 Church Street
    New York, New York

44. Steven-Donay Company
    2940 South 38th Street
    Milwaukee, Wisconsin

45. Stor-Aid of Ohio, Inc.
    Sandusky, Ohio

46. The Florell Company
    Department HB-1
    5009 Copley Road
    Philadelphia 44, Pennsylvania

47. Hobar, Inc.
    208 Fifth Avenue
    New York 10, New York
        Children's Closet Rod, Catalog No. 25
        Shoe Rack, Catalog No. 37

48. Protex Products Company
    347 Fifth Avenue
    New York, New York

49. Block Company
    Department HB-2
    200 North Jefferson Street
    Chicago 6, Illinois

50. Princess House Closet Accessories, Inc.
    261 Fifth Avenue
    New York, New York

51. Hammacher, Schlemmer
    147 East 57th Street
    New York 22, New York

52. *Plus-Lite Board*
    Chatfield Clarke Company
    639 Kent Street
    Santa Monica, California

53. C. AeroShade Company
    433 Oakland Avenue
    Waukesha, Wisconsin

54. E. I. duPont de Nemours & Co.
    Tontine Sales Division
    Newburgh, New York

55. *Badgaire*
    Lewis & Conger
    45th Street & Avenue of the Americas
    New York, New York

56. No-Bangs (crib protector)
    Bunny Bear Products
    1350 Broadway
    New York, New York

57. No. 401 Dress'n-Bath
    Storkline Furniture Corporation
    4400 West 26th Street
    Chicago 23, Illinois

58. Creative Playthings
    867 Madison Avenue
    New York 21, New York
        or,
    7730 Forsythe Blvd.
    St. Louis, Missouri

59. Homasote Company
    Fernwood Road—Dept. 16
    Trenton, New Jersey

60. Gould-Mersereau Co., Inc.
    35 West 44th Street
    New York 36, New York

61. Sears & Roebuck
    925 South Homan Avenue
    Chicago, Illinois

62. Ell Bee Manufacturing Company
    Vineland, New Jersey

63. Garden City Plating & Mfg. Co.
    Chicago, Illinois

64. Ace Steel Partition Company
    91-93 Mercer Street
    New York, New York

65. Wooster Products, Inc.
    Wooster, Ohio

66. Roddis Plywood Corporation
    Marshfield, Wisconsin

67. Metal Door & Trim Company
    LaPorte, Indiana

68. Bakelite Corporation
    30 East 42nd Street
    New York, New York

69. Unique Balance Co., Inc.
    296 East 134th Street
    New York, New York

70. Anderson Corporation
    Bayport, Minnesota

71. Chicopee Manufacturing Corporation
    Lumite Division
    47 Worth Street
    New York, New York

72. Ingersoll Steel Division
    Borg-Warner Corporation
    Dept. SD-5
    321 Plymouth Court
    Chicago 4, Illinois

73. Abbey Manufacturing Company
    1036 Third Avenue
    New York, New York

74. *Diana Fyrban*
    (Vinyl-coated)
    Breneman-Hartshorn, Inc.
    2045 Reading Road
    Cincinnati 2, Ohio

75. *Plastishade*
    Breneman-Hartshorn, Inc.
    2045 Reading Road
    Cincinnati 2, Ohio

76. *Bambino*
    (Reed or Matchstick)
    The Holland Shade Company
    999 Third Avenue
    New York 22, New York

    (Bamboo slats, Matchstick, Reed)
    American Windowshade Mfg. Co.
    320 Rockaway Avenue
    Brooklyn, New York

77. *Simpleat*
    Consolidated Trimming Corporation
    27 West 23rd Street
    New York, New York

78. *Cravanette Long Life*
    The Cravanette Company
    729 Madison Avenue
    New York, New York

79. *Aridex*
    E. I. duPont de Nemours & Co.
    Textile Service Division
    40 Worth Street
    New York, New York

80. *Drax*
    S. C. Johnson & Son, Inc.
    33-16 Woodside Avenue
    Woodside, L. I., New York

81. *Eulan*
    General Dyestuff Corporation
    435 Hudson Street
    New York, New York

82. *Larvex*
    Zonite Products
    New Brunswick, New Jersey

83. James Manufacturing Company
    Independence, Kansas

84. *Permaseptic*
    Germicidal Corp. of America
    41 East 42nd Street
    New York, New York

85. *Sanitized*
    U. S. Process Corporation
    369 Lexington Avenue
    New York, New York

86. *Everglaze*
    Banco, Inc.
    40 Worth Street
    New York, New York

87. *Lacet* (Laces)
    Sheerset (Sheer Fabrics)
    American Cyanamid Company
    30 Rockefeller Plaza
    New York, New York

88. Shwayder Bros., Inc.
    (Folding Furniture Division)
    4270 High Street, Ecorse Station
    Detroit 29, Michigan

89. Doehler Metal Furniture Co., Inc.
    192 Lexington Avenue
    New York, New York

90. Lloyd Manufacturing Company
    Menominee, Michigan

91. Old Hickory Furniture Company
    Martinsville, Indiana

92. Littletree Company
    Box 123—Dept. G-5
    Winterpark, Florida

93. California-Asia Rattan Company
    6818 Avalon Blvd.
    Los Angeles 3, California

94. Van Keppel Green, Inc.
    9529 Santa Monica Blvd.
    Beverly Hills, California

95. Troy Sunshade Company
    Troy, Ohio

96. *Neva-Rust*
    John B. Salterini Company
    210 East 72nd Street
    New York, New York

97. Abercrombie & Fitch Co.
    Madison Avenue at 45th Street
    New York 17, New York

98. *Go-Lite Air Beds*
    Abercrombie & Fitch Co.
    Madison Avenue at 45th Street
    New York 17, New York

99. *Kapok Mattress*
    Abercrombie & Fitch Co.
    Madison Avenue at 45th Street
    New York 17, New York

100. *Slat Canoe Chair*
    Abercrombie & Fitch Co.
    Madison Avenue at 45th Street
    New York 17, New York

101. (Collapsible All-purpose Metal Folding Table)
    Greene Manufacturing Company
    1028 Douglas Avenue
    Racine, Wisconsin

102. Ellison's
    Wilmington 11, Delaware

103. Charles H. Swisher
    15 East 26th Street
    New York, New York

    Kelcey Leather Buckle Works
    1687 McDonald Avenue
    Brooklyn 31, New York

104. *Snackoster*
    Jay Thorpe, Inc.
    24 West 57th Street
    New York, New York

105. W. C. Redmond Sons & Company
    Peru, Indiana

106. Union Steel Products Company
    Albion, Michigan

107. *Magnagrip*
    R. E. Phelon Company
    Springfield, Massachusetts

108. Coppes, Inc.
    Nappanee, Indiana

    Bassett Ant Proof Revolving Shelves
    Bob Hipp Welding Works
    1460 El Camino Real
    Menlo Park, California

109. O-Cedar Corporation
    2246 West 49th Street
    Chicago 9, Illinois

110. *Preener*
    A. S. Harrison Company, Inc.
    South Norwalk, Connecticut

111. *Miracloth*
    Miracloth Corporation
    2450 South Ashland Avenue
    Chicago 9, Illinois

112. *Keeps*
    Majikweld Corporation
    1324 Boston Road
    New York 56, New York

113. *Frigidaire*
    General Motors Corp.
    300 Taylor Street
    Dayton, Ohio

114. *Filter-Queen*
    Health-Mor, Inc.
    203 North Wabash Avenue
    Chicago, Illinois

115. General Electric Company
    Major Appliance Division
    310 West Liberty Street
    Louisville 2, Kentucky
    (Many others)

116. George S. Roper Company
     Rockford, Illinois

117. *Soil-Off*
     S.O.S. Company
     6201 West 65th Street
     Chicago 38, Illinois

118. *Hotpoint*
     Hotpoint, Inc.
     5600 W. Taylor Street
     Chicago, Illinois

     Kitchen Aid
     Home Dishwasher Division
     Hobart Manufacturing Company
     Troy, Ohio

     American Kitchens Division
     Arco Manufacturing Corporation
     Connersville, Indiana

119. *Precipitron*
     Westinghouse Electric
     Sturtevant Division
     Hyde Park
     Boston, Massachusetts

120. Apex-Rotarex Corp.
     1070 East 152nd Street
     Cleveland, Ohio

121. *Cornelia Cloth*
     Dow-Corning Corporation
     Midland, Michigan

122. *Pantastic*
     G. N. Coughlin Company
     29 Spring Street
     West Orange, New Jersey

123. *Protect-O-Wall*
     Berke Mfg. Co.
     41 West 24th Street
     New York, New York
     (sold in some 5c & 10c stores)

124. *Quik Suds*
     Osrow Products Company
     95-10—218th Street
     Queens Village, New York

125. Apex-Partridge Company
     501 Fifth Avenue
     New York, New York

126. Sparton Mop Company
     2900 Emerson Avenue South
     Minneapolis, Minnesota

127. *Resistane*
     Resistane Company
     Dept. A
     Madeira, Ohio

128. *Kleenster*
     Garner & Company
     1164 Broadway
     New York, New York

129. *Vina Tred*
     Southbridge Plastics, Inc.
     Southbridge, Massachusetts

130. Cadie Chemical Products, Inc.
     549 West 132nd Street
     New York 27, New York

131. Ami Company, Inc.
     Buffalo 14, New York

132. Zim Manufacturing Co.
     3037-3047 Carroll Avenue
     Chicago 12, Illinois

133. Geneva Modern Kitchens
     Geneva, Illinois

134. Electrolux Corporation
     500 Fifth Avenue
     New York, New York

135. Servel, Inc.
     Evansville, Indiana

136. Admiral Corporation
     3800 Cortland Street
     Chicago, Illinois

137. *Frigidaire*
     General Motors Corp.
     300 Taylor Street
     Dayton, Ohio

     Kelvinator
     Nash-Kelvinator Corp.
     14250 Plymouth Road
     Detroit, Michigan

138. General Electric Company
     Major Appliance Division
     310 West Liberty Street
     Louisville 2, Kentucky

139. Philco Corporation
     Tioga & C Streets
     Philadelphia, Pennsylvania

140. *Rubbermaid Dish Drainer*
     The Wooster Rubber Company
     Wooster, Ohio

141. *Lux Minute Minder*
     Lux Clock Mfg. Company
     Waterbury, Conn.

142. *Easy-Off Oven Cleaner*
     Boyle-Midway, Inc.
     Cranford, New Jersey
     (also, Chicago, Illinois;
         Chamblee, Georgia; and
         Los Angeles, California)

143. Merchandise Presentation, Inc.
     208 East 120th Street
     New York 35, New York

CHART OF CASTERS AND SLIDES FOR FURNITURE

FLOOR MATERIALS	LIGHT CHAIR	LIGHT LOUNGE CHAIR Stationary	LIGHT LOUNGE CHAIR Television	HEAVY LOUNGE CHAIR Stationary	HEAVY LOUNGE CHAIR Television	COFFEE TABLE	DINING TABLE	SPINET OR UPRIGHT PIANO
HARDWOOD (Oak, Maple, Ash, Etc.)	① ①A	①	⑥ 1" Min. dia. ③ Recommended	① 1-1/4" Min. dia.	⑥ 1-1/4" Min. dia. ③ Recommended	① ⑥	① 1"-1-1/4" dia. ③ + ③A ⓧ	③ + ③A ⓧ
MASONRY Piece Laid Floor (Flagstone, Tile)	①	① If smooth laid ③ If rough laid	⑥ If smooth laid ③ If rough laid	① If smooth laid ③ If rough laid	⑥ If smooth laid ③	① If smooth laid ⑥ ③ If rough laid	⑥ If smooth laid ① ③ If rough laid	③ + ③A ⓧ If rough laid ⓧ
MASONRY Poured Floor (Cement, Terrazzo, Magnesite)	① ①A	①	⑥ 1" min. dia. ③	① 1" min. dia.	⑥ 1-1/4" min. dia.	① ⑥	① ③ + ③A If heavy ⓧ	③ + ③A ⓧ
FLOOR COVERINGS								
SOFT SHEET, TILES (Cork, Linoleum, Plastic Tile)	① 3/4" Min. dia. ①A ②	②	②	② 2"-2-1/2" dia. ① 1-1/2" min dia.	② 2"-2-1/2" dia. ③ 1" wide face	① ② If heavy	① 1" min. dia. If light ② ③ + ③A If heavy ⓧ	③ + ③A ⓧ
HARD SHEET, TILES (Asphalt Tile)	① 3/4" Min. dia. ①A ②	① 1" min. dia. ②	② ③ 1" wide face	① 1-1/2" min. dia. ② 2"-2-1/2" min. dia.	② 2"-2-1/2" dia. ③ 1" wide face	① ② If heavy	① 1"-1-1/4" min. dia. if light ② ③ + ③A If heavy ⓧ	③ + ③A ⓧ
THICK PILE CARPET OR RUG (Except Shag Type) See Footnote ⓩ	① 1-1/4" Min. dia. or largest possible ② 1-1/2" dia.	② 2-2-1/2" min. dia.	③ Largest Poss. dia. ② 2" min. dia.	② 2" dia. ③	③ Largest Poss. dia.	②	② 2" min. dia. ③ If heavy	③
SHORT PILE CARPET OR RUG	① 7/8" Min. dia. ②	②	③ Largest Poss. dia. ② 2" min. dia. ⑥	② Largest Poss. dia.	③ Largest Poss. dia.	②	② 2" min. dia. ③ If heavy	③
FLAT WOVEN CARPET OR RUG	② ① 3/4" Min. dia. If close weave	② ① 1" min. dia.	③ ⑥ 1" min. dia. if close weave	② ① 1-1/4" min. dia.	③	② ③ ⑥ If close weave	② 1" min. dia. if light ① ③ If heavy ⑥ If close weave 1" min. dia.	③

ⓧ Some casters are available with side brakes, for furniture such as beds, chests, etc. Only two of four legs need have casters with brakes – but the brakes should be placed on easily accessible legs.

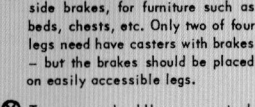

ⓨ Tea wagons should have non-swivelling front wheels. For outdoor use, on lawns, etc., we recommend 5-inch diameter caster wheels.

ⓩ No casters or slides – except possibly automobile tires – have as yet been developed to combat this type of underbrush. All other types tend to catch and tear.

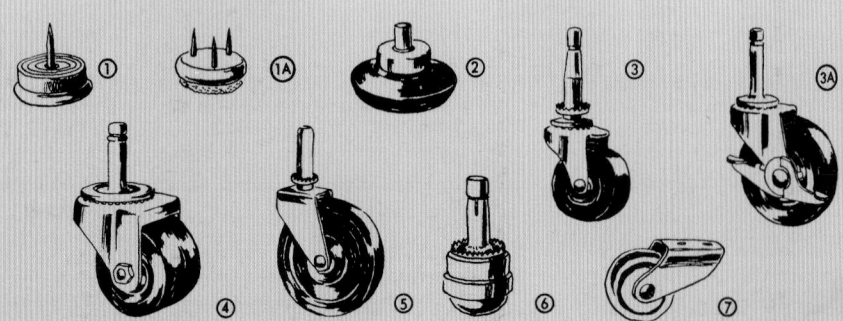

① ①A ② ③ ③A
④ ⑤ ⑥ ⑦

GRAND PIANO	CHEST	NIGHT TABLE	TEA WAGON	REGULAR BED	HOLLYWOOD BED	SOFA	STUDIO COUCH OR SOFA BED Stationary Part / Sliding Part	SECRETARY
④	① ①A ②	① ①A	⑤ 2" dia. Y	② ③ 1-1/2" min. ③A If light ⑥	② ③ If not used as couch ⑥ ③A If as couch ⓧ	① 1-1/4" min. ② ③ + ③A	① 1-1/4" ③A	⑦ ⑥	③ 2" dia. wheel ④ or larger Best Quality
④	① If smooth laid ② laid ③ + ③A If rough laid ⓧ	①	⑤ 3" dia. Y	③ 2" dia. min. ③A If light ⑥	③ If rough ③ If not used as couch ⑥ ③A If as couch ⓧ	① If smooth laid ② If smooth ③ + ③A If rough laid ⓧ	① If smooth laid ③A	⑦	③ 2" dia. wheel ④ or larger Best Quality
④	① ①A ②	① ①A	⑤ 2" dia. Y	③ ③A If light ⑥	① 1" min. ③ If not used as couch ⑥ If as ③A couch ⓧ	① 1" dia.	① 1" min. dia. ③A	⑦ ⑥	③ 2" dia. wheel ④ or larger Best Quality
④	①A 3/4" min. dia. if heavy ②	① 1" min. dia. ①A	⑤ 3" dia. Y	③ ③A If light ⓧ	② ③ If not used as couch ③A If as couch ⓧ	① 1-1/4" min. ②	① 1-1/2" dia. ② ③A	⑦	③ 2" dia. wheel ④ or larger Best Quality
④	①A 3/4" min. dia. if heavy ②	① 1" min. dia. ①A	⑤ 3" dia. Y	③ ③A If light ⓧ	② ③ If not used as couch ③A If as couch ⓧ	① 1-1/4" min. dia. ②	① 1-1/2" dia. ② ③A	⑦	③ 2" dia. wheel ④ or larger Best Quality
④	② ③ If heavy	① 1-1/4" min. dia. ② ③	⑤ 3" dia. Y	③	② 2" min. dia. ③	① 1-1/2" dia. ② ③ + ③A	① 1-1/2" dia. ② ③A	⑦	③ 2" dia. wheel ④ or larger Best Quality
④	② ③ If heavy or ③ + ③A ⓧ	① 1" min. dia. ②	⑤ 3" dia. Y	③	② ③ If not used as couch ③A If as couch ⓧ	②	② ③A	⑦	③ 2" dia. wheel ④ or larger Best Quality
④	② ⑥ ③ If heavy ③ + ③A ⓧ	① 1" min. dia. ②	⑤ 2" dia. "B"	③ ⑥	② ⑥ ③ If not used as couch ③A If as couch ⓧ	① 1-1/4" min. ② ⑥ 1" min. dia.	① 1-1/4" min. dia. ② ⑥ 1" min. dia. ③A	⑦ ⑥	③ 2" dia. wheel ④ or larger Best Quality

All casters and slides tend to catch on the edge of loose rugs, making it necessary to lift the piece; large-wheel casters reduce this problem somewhat.

Caster wheels are available in wood, plastic, metal, and hard or soft rubber. Do not use rubber wheels on light-colored floors or floor coverings, which tend to show marks and streaks.

Wheel casters and ball casters come either with stems or with flat plates. Stems require a drilled hole, into which the socket is inserted; plates require a flat surface and have to be screwed in.

Heavy-duty casters are available for pianos, secretaries, etc. They come with single or double wheels; choose according to the weight of the furniture.

It will pay you in the long run to buy best-quality slides and casters, and to give them proper care. No casters are entirely rust-proof; after rugs or floors have been washed, keep furniture off the surface until it has had time to dry, or place cups under the casters, to protect metal parts. Ball-bearing wheel casters require oiling; fibre-bearing casters and ball casters do not.

For painted floors we recommend *only* soft rubber wheel casters, except that felt-tip domes can be used for light chairs, light tables, chests, stationary light lounge chairs (See Chart).

A note of caution: Wheel and ball casters, if attached to old or well-splayed furniture legs, may hasten their collapse. (To visualize the disaster, just imagine yourself on roller skates, doing a royal split.) Be sure the piece is soundly constructed, and able to 'take' the caster we have recommended for its type.